S0-BDG-563

WAR DOGS

WAR DOGS

Canines in Combat

Michael G. Lemish

BRASSEY'S

Washington / London

Library of Congress Cataloging-in-Publication Data

Lemish, Michael G.
    War dogs: canines in combat/Michael G. Lemish.
        p.   cm.
    Includes bibliographical references and index.
    ISBN 1–57488–031–4
    1. Dogs–United States–War use–History–20th century.
    I. Title.
    UH100.L46   1995
    355.4–dc20   95-379

10 9 8 7 6 5 4 3 2 1

Printed in the United States of America

FOR THOSE WHO SERVED

CONTENTS

CONTENTS

PREFACE

In life the firmest friend,
The first to welcome, foremost to defend,
Whose honest heart is still his master's own
Who labors, fights, lives, breathes for him alone.
                    —NOEL GORDON, LORD BYRON

AN AMERICAN ARMY PATROL MOVED SLOWLY, KNOWING AN ambush could strike at any moment. As their bodies tensed with anticipation, the young infantrymen remained confident; a handler and his German shepherd led the men on a narrow path through the jungle. Suddenly the dog stopped, his ears perked up, and the hair bristled along his back. The handler motioned for everyone to drop. As the soldiers dove for cover, the crack of a single shot rang out, splitting the stillness of the air. A lone bullet tore through muscle and bone as the dog crumpled to the ground. The soldier dropped to his knees and cradled the dog, and he could see the shepherd's eyes were wide with fear, not understanding the reason for this punishment. A moment later the dog stopped breathing and died.

The infantrymen concentrated their firepower toward the direction in which the dog had previously pointed. From a tree, an enemy sniper tumbled into the underbrush. Carefully withdrawing to their own lines, the patrol returned, with the handler carrying the bloodied body of the German shepherd.

This scene and similar ones have repeatedly taken place—on Pacific islands, in Korea, and in Vietnam—hundreds of times since World War I. Over thirty thousand dogs have served in the U.S. military, thrust into harm's way and responsible for saving thousands of American lives. Throughout history, dogs have been employed effectively for sentry and scouting duty, finding booby traps, and locating wounded and lost soldiers. Their only reward was merely praise for doing a good job. Having fought alongside humankind in battle, these dogs are the forgotten veterans.

When I first heard about dogs in combat, I immediately thought of sentry dogs—a stereotypical scene of a handler and dog walking along a fence at some remote backwater military post. It took a while, but I soon realized that the military enlisted the help of dogs for a variety of important roles. The more I tried to learn, the more frustrated I became. Bits and pieces of information lingered about as a scant line or two embedded within a military history book or an occasional magazine article. I wondered why nothing was ever written about the subject. Of course several books had been written years ago, but nothing of merit since 1955.

Throughout my research I've discovered many books about every imaginable military subject, yet the contributions of military canines remain obscure and intangible. There are several reasons why this is so. The macho military establishment will acknowledge, even pontificate on, the weapons of war in both their destructive capacity and how they saved American lives, won a battle, or brought wars to an end. Just look at the recent fawning over the flawed Patriot missile system during Operation Desert Storm. For the upper echelon of the armed forces to attribute such success and sophistication to a *lowly* four-legged animal is a slap in the face to military tradition—except that in reality it is not. Men who enter combat with an animal share a unique experience, and it is not one to be taken lightly. Military working dogs are unlike anything else in America's arsenal, and the armed services make the mistake of associating them with military hardware. Until dogs achieve a unique status and are properly recognized as living, thinking creatures, the U.S. military dog program, although successful, will never reach its full potential.

Animal rights proponents will argue that the use of dogs by the military establishment is nothing more than exploitation. To use dogs in combat is just another form of cruelty inflicted upon animals who do not start the wars that they participate in. Using this argument, a soldier does not create the conflict that he is engaged in—wars are invariably begun by the noncombatants and fought by the young, who retain their youth only as a date on the calendar. When dogs gave up their wild existence ages ago and forged an unparalleled bond with humans, their use as a military instrument was cast, creating a tradition spanning thousands of years.

The United States has not employed, and I do not believe it ever will employ, dogs as an offensive weapon of war. A halfhearted attempt to train assault dogs to attack Japanese positions during World War II failed. This program ended with the determination that dogs could not replace infantrymen, tanks, aircraft, and rockets. Even those charged with developing the program expressed a resentment at the effort. Indirectly this may have contributed to the failure of the experiment.

The Soviet Union, Israel, and perhaps other countries have trained dogs as expendable offensive weapons in the twentieth century, and it is naive to believe that a few military researchers within the United States did not explore this possibility. In 1944, for example, one American concept had dogs carrying explosives into enemy-held caves and bunkers. Another suggestion, which surfaced during the nuclear proliferation of the 1950s, was the idea of dogs carrying small tactical nuclear devices.[1] Today that may seem absurd, but military planners were charged with the defense of our country. And although these ideas were never adopted, they were seriously considered.

During World War II, the Russians exploited an ingenious way to destroy enemy tanks by attaching explosives to dogs to be sent out on suicide missions—a practice carried on to this day.[2] This is not only abhorrent behavior but defies the relationship that bonds dogs and humankind throughout recorded history. Besides, it is doubtful the American people would ever tolerate such behavior (even during times of war) within our own government (assuming, of course, that such information became public). Ironically, throughout my research for this book I found no reference that the Japanese employed dogs as suicide weapons—obviously the Japanese exempted canines from the Bushido warrior code of the Samurai.

Until recently the navy trained dolphins as couriers for explosives and reconnaissance. Once the media got wind of this activity and enlightened the public, animal rights groups quickly denounced the program.[3] Another bizarre effort during World War II involved army technicians attaching incendiary explosives to the bodies of bats. No effort was deemed unworthy if it could shorten the war.[4]

In basic principle, American soldiers often elevated the status of dogs to their lot in times of combat. During World War II, the compilation of casualties after an engagement sometimes listed the dogs as wounded or killed alongside the soldiers—although this was expressly forbidden by army regulations. Many reports used words such as *courage* and *devotion* to explain a dog's behavior and actions in battle. These words are most often expressed among humans and not within the animal world. This elevation of the dog's status in the military ranks showed that the men responsible for handling them treated their dogs with respect and proper care. Some cases of abuse have occurred within the military, and a constant vigil needs to be mounted to ensure that a dog has basic rights and is treated with the same respect as any soldier, male or female, in the performance of his or her duty.

The use of military dogs varies as much as warfare itself, from the muddy, barbed-wire trenches of World War I, with its deadly mustard and phosgene gases, to the steaming triple-canopy jungles of Southeast Asia. Ultimately, it is the character of the conflict that dictates the role of the war dog.

This book does not glorify combat. I hope it creates an awareness of the contribution dogs have made, their sacrifices and devotion, in saving thousands of American soldiers. The book is arranged chronologically. Often the unique capabilities of the war dogs and their handlers within the various branches of service overlap within a given time frame, so each subject is focused on independently when appropriate. For instance, search-and-rescue operations taking place throughout the years of World War II are dealt with under a separate subheading. The military uses its own jargon and acronyms, which can be confusing within its own ranks. For that reason, I've attempted to keep the use of military terminology to a minimum. The unique aspect of dogs in a military environment also means the use of veterinary and medical terms, but most of these words are explained within the text.

Military records can be accurate and expressive, yet frustrating, and more often than not simply pieces of a jigsaw puzzle that need to be assembled by the researcher. This problem surfaces when you attempt to figure out with any accuracy how many Americans owe their lives to dogs. Summaries of confrontations with the enemy, called after-action reports, often contain the phrases "the saving of many lives" or "prevented numerous casualties." These words, or similar ones, appear repeatedly from World War I to Vietnam. If a scout dog locates a cache of enemy weapons, who could possibly estimate how many future deaths or casualties this timely interdiction prevented? No branch of the military has ever reviewed and analyzed the effectiveness of war dogs and their impact in a major engagement in this regard.

There are several reasons why the "modern" military and dog breeders under contract to the government do not want to call attention to the use of dogs in combat, no matter how successful they are. Foremost, military working dogs are considered equipment, no different from a shell casing or a rifle. Once in service to their country, they remain so forever, until they are unable to carry out their job. Unlike aircraft and ships, dogs are no longer sold surplus, nor are they retired; they are terminated as humanely as possible. During their military duty, dogs receive the best of care and treatment, but do not share the longevity of their civilian counterparts. As detailed in later chapters, war dogs have been successfully returned to civilians, achieving a quality of life that they richly deserve. Military working dogs have always been and continue to be an asset to the defense of the United States. Our military dog program needs to be examined and placed into historical perspective, not only for ourselves but also as a tribute to our four-legged companions.

Historians often record conflicts on the large scale: the equipment used, and the machines of conquest. Lost in the statistics, maps, and plans that accompany a battle is the individual. This is one reason why the accomplishments of man and dog, working together, lie scattered in archives or are never even recorded. Even without written records of their deeds we should not forget that, for the common soldier, whether human or canine, war is often simply a matter of survival as each day unfolds on the fields of war.

High-tech wizardry may have changed the look of today's battlefield, but one thing will never change—the need for early detection of the enemy. For thousands of years, dogs have been in front of men engaged in battle. Military tradition dictates and demands that they will always be "Forever Forward."

There are many people who have directly and indirectly helped with this project. Sincere thanks to my good friend SFC Jesse Mendez (ret.), whose experience as a scout dog instructor, ARVN adviser, and staunch champion of military working dogs I found to be invaluable. His continued support helped me immensely.

Among the many handlers I have met, I am grateful to those who shared their unique experiences with me, in particular David Armstrong Jr., Charlie Cargo, John Dupla, Robert Himrod, James Kelley, Randy Kimler, Robert Kollar, John Langley, John Lyon, Paul Morgan, Leroy Marsh, Bobby Railey, John Risse, James L. E. Roy, Daniel Warden, Joseph White, Richard "Zeke" Zika, and all the members of the Vietnam Dog Handler Association.

Many other people helped to contribute information and offered continued support. Colonel William H. H. Clark (ret.), author of *The History of the United States Army Veterinary Corps in Vietnam,* shared a wealth of information. Dr. William W. Putney helped me piece together the World War II Marine war dog story and provided information that just doesn't exist in the official records. Mary Thurston, writer and animal historian, shared information, photographs, her wit, and inspiration. I would be amiss without mentioning Sally Coup, Doris

Flood, James Flurchick, Gordon Greene and his wonderful book, *A Star for Buster,* Dr. Howard Hayes, and Col. Norman Vaughan (ret.). In the course of my research I have encountered many government employees, some of whom deserve special mention, especially Susan Francis at the National Archives in Suitland, Maryland, and Luthor Hanson at United States Army Quartermaster Museum.

Last but not least, a big thank-you to my wife, Susan, who helped make it all possible.

WAR DOGS

1.

Origins of the Modern Military Working Dog

A HISTORICAL PERSPECTIVE

It's only natural that dogs would accompany people into battle. The bonding between humans and canines can be traced to prehistoric times. Exhumed prehistoric fossilized remains include the bones of a dog alongside those of a cave dweller. There is no written record, but pictographs displayed on the walls of caves show the dog as part of the community as primitive people engaged them as a useful tool in the daily quest of food for their survival. No other domesticated animal in history has had the same impact upon humankind as *Canis familiaris*. Throughout recorded history, dogs have shared our triumphs, defeats, starvation, good times, and bad. From the earliest beginnings, the dog is one animal that truly exemplifies the devotion and bond between humans and the animal world. This early interaction and animal domestication led to a canine population exceeding fifty million in the United States today.

At first, the constant quest for food formed this bond. This changed as tribes warred for territory or food. Armies emerged and canines became a standard component of military establishments around the world in both active and passive roles. The earliest known battle dog was a mastiff type from Tibet that was domesticated during the Stone Age. Persians, Greeks, Assyrians, and Babylonians all recognized the tactical advantage of war dogs and deployed them in great numbers as forward attacking elements.

1

As war animals, their use is well recorded during a battle between the Greeks and Corinthians. The Corinthians elevated dogs above the basic tools of war by honoring them as heroes, a practice that continued often and in many different parts of the world to the present day. One engagement during the Peloponnesian War (431–404 B.C.) epitomizes not only their devotion and deployment, but their successes as well.

> The Corinthians also used dogs for purposes of defence, and the citadel of Corinth had a guard of fifty placed in boxes by the seashore. Taking advantage of a dark night, the Greeks with whom they were at war disembarked on the coast. The garrison were asleep after an orgy, the dogs alone kept watch and the fifty pickets fell on the enemy like lions; all but one were casualties. Sorter, sole survivor, retiring from the conflict, fled to town to give warning and roused the drunken soldiers, who came forth to battle. To him alone were the honors of victory, and the grateful town presented to him a collar with the inscription, "Sorter, Defender and Savior of Corinth," and erected a monument engraved with his name and those of the forty-nine heroes who fell.[1]

During the battle of Versella, women led hordes of war dogs against the Romans. This delayed an eventual Roman victory for many hours. After several such encounters, the Romans adopted war dogs for their own use. Military commanders sent complements of attack dogs, encased in body armor and razor-sharp spikes, to harass and disrupt enemy formations. The dogs, bred to ferocity, added another strategic component to an offensive and defensive posture. Plutarch, a Greek biographer, and Pliny the Elder, the Roman naturalist and writer, often recorded the deeds of these fierce dogs in their writings during the first century and stated that the animals would not even cower in front of men armed with swords.

In the fifth century, Attila the Hun understood the advantage of traveling with dogs and journeyed with four-legged sentinels in his conquest of Europe. As with knights and horses during the Middle Ages, canine armor developed, encasing the dogs in battle plates and chains. Indians of North America also employed dogs for both sentry and pack purposes. The Italians and Bulgarians developed their sentry dogs during battles in Tripoli and the Balkans.

The Italian naturalist Aldrovandus, born in 1522, wrote of the development of sentry and war dogs. With minor exceptions, Aldrovandus's writings are similar to an air force manual describing the training of a vicious sentry dog more than four hundred years later. He wrote:

> Those dogs that defend mankind in the course of private, and also public conflicts, are called, in Greek, Symmachi, or allies, and Somatophylakes, or bodyguards. Our authors consider that this kind of dog only differs from the dog which we have just described (the farm and sheep dog) in the matters of training and teaching. The war dog, according to what is laid down by Blondus, would be a terrifying aspect and look as though he was just going to fight, and be an enemy to everybody but his master; so much that he will not allow himself to be stroked even by those he knows best, but threatens everybody alike with the fulminations of his teeth, and always looks at everybody as though he was burning with anger, and glares around in every direction with a hostile glance. This dog ought to be trained up to fight from the earliest years. Accordingly some man or other is fitted out with a coat of thick skin, which the dogs will not be able to bite through, as a sort of dummy; the dog is then spurred upon this man, upon which the man in the skin runs away and then allows himself to be caught and, falling on the ground in front of the dog, to be bitten.[2]

In 1695, the British obtained one hundred savage dogs in Havana, Cuba, and transported them to Jamaica. Here they participated in the Maroon War, a guerrilla action fought by renegade African slaves. During the Spanish Morocco War, dogs surfaced as tactical decoys. The Riffs camouflaged the animals in their garments, sending them to run along the front lines. In the limited visibility of blowing sand and haze, they drew fire from the Spanish, who in turn revealed their gun positions.

Warfare changed with the development of gunpowder and more powerful and mobile weapons. The tactical military use of dogs needed to evolve as well. So dogs, employed as active combatants in the past, had their role shifted to auxiliary support for soldiers in the field. Keen commanders still recognized their value and usefulness for a variety of activities.

In 1798, Napoleon Bonaparte capitalized on the superior senses of dogs by chaining them to the walls surrounding Alexandria, Egypt. These sentinels provided an early warning system not unlike the modern sentry dog. They also proved a delaying tactic for any expected attackers, with their ferocity forcing the enemy to give them with a wide berth. A year later Napoleon wrote to General Marmont before the Battle of Aboukir, stating, "You should have a large quantity of dogs which can be made use of by posting them in front of your fortifications."

Napoleon understood not only how dogs could be employed effectively in battle but the impact they have on the human spirit. During his final years in exile he wrote of an incident that took place during the inspection of a battlefield at the end of an Italian campaign. A dog sat alongside the body of his master, groaning and licking the hand of the corpse. The dog would then spring up and try to bring the emperor to the fallen soldier, either for recognition of his slain master or some pitiful attempt to revive him. The scene emotionally captivated Napoleon so much that he would later write:

> Perhaps it was the spirit of the time and the place that affected me. But I assure you no occurrence of any of my other battlefields impressed me so keenly. I halted on my tour to gaze on the spectacle, and to reflect on its meaning.
>
> This soldier, I realized, must have had friends at home and in his regiment; yet he lay there deserted by all except his dog. . . . I had looked on, unmoved, at battles which decided the future of nations. Tearless, I had given orders which brought death to thousands.
>
> Yet, here I was stirred, profoundly stirred, stirred to tears. And by what? By the grief of one dog. I am certain that at that

instant I felt more ready than at any other time to show mercy toward a suppliant foeman. I could understand just then the tinge of mercy which led Achilles to yield the corpse of his enemy, Hector, to the weeping Priam.[3]

Continued mechanization of warfare did not see any decrease in the use of dogs. Ultimately, man dictated how dogs were to be used in battles, the animal world having no wars to be fought. As man became aware of the dog's intellectual capability and his training techniques improved, the effectiveness of the canine in several different military roles became apparent. By far, the European countries showed a keener interest in developing and expanding upon the dog's role in warfare. This can best be attributed to the great number of working dogs employed within the civilian sector in Europe, most notably as draft animals pulling milk or food carts. The role of the dog in European society is in stark contrast to that in the emerging young country called the United States.

EARLY AMERICAN IDEAS

Well before the arrival of settlers to North America, Native Americans used dogs for both sentry and pack duty. Indians felt comfortable having their larger dogs carry packs that weighed upwards of sixty pounds. Some animals were further trained to stop and howl if an item slipped from their backs during a march. The dogs also provided a rudimentary sentry service during the night, as a perimeter defense for a sleeping encampment. Their versatility did not stop there; larger dogs assumed the role of draft animal, harnessed to a two-pole wooden frame called a *travois*. The travois could carry supplies or, by harnessing two dogs in tandem, could pull someone who was sick or injured. These canines could be considered America's first war dogs, although they never participated in any known offensive roles. That distinction would be left for dogs that came with the white settlers colonizing North America.

Early American colonists also relied on dogs, mostly on farms for herding, and of course for hunting and family protection. The very first law pertaining to dogs, enacted in 1706, was motivated by military reasons.[4] Yet it would be up to one of the Founding Fathers to introduce the concept of using dogs for military work in an active capacity. Benjamin Franklin, diplomat, philosopher, and printer, helped to organize the Pennsylvania militia against Indian raids. Franklin first suggested the use of scout and attack dogs in 1755 in a letter, stating:

> Dogs should be used against the Indians. They should be large, strong and fierce; and every dog led in a slip string, to prevent their tiring themselves by running out and in, and discovering the party by barking at squirrels, etc. Only when the party comes near thick woods and suspicious places they should turn out a dog or two to search them. In case of meeting a party of the enemy, the dogs are all then to be turned loose and set on. They will be fresher and finer for having been previously confined and will confound the enemy a good deal and be very serviceable. This was the Spanish method of guarding their marches.[5]

Franklin, an intellectual and not generally known as a military tactician, probably respected the use of dogs by Cortés in his brutal rout of natives in Mexico. There the Spaniards released large contingents of savage greyhounds to chase the Indians and then attack them as they tired. In any event, no one acted on Franklin's suggestions.

John Penn, the grandson of William Penn, who founded Pennsylvania, and lieutenant governor of the colony from 1763 to 1771, also suggested employing war dogs. On June 28, 1764, Penn wrote a letter to Pay Master and Commissioner of Masters James Young, stating: "You will acquaint the Captains that every Soldier will be allowed three Shillings per month who brings with him a strong Dog that shall be judged proper to be employed in discovering and pursuing the Savages. It is recommended to them to procure as many as they can, not exceeding 10 per company; Each dog is to be kept tied and led by his owner."[6]

Several other proposals surfaced during the American Revolution, but once again with no action taken. William McClay of the Pennsylvania Supreme Executive Council sought to rout the Indians allied with the British and put forth his ideas in a letter in 1779, stating: "I have sustained some Ridicule for a Scheme which I have long recommended, Vis., that of hunting the Scalping Parties with Horseman and Dogs. The imminent Services which Dogs have rendered to our people in some late instances, seems to open People's Eyes to a Method of this kind. We know that Dogs will follow them, that they will discover them, when hunted on by their Masters."[7]

McClay further stated that objections could be raised because they did not possess the "proper" dogs. But like others who followed him, he raised the question: "could not such a Thing be tryed?" There is no doubt that the concept was attempted, unofficially of course. Enlightened soldiers and officers would use their own personal dogs, knowing quite well their limitations and advantages in a given situation.

It is difficult to understand why the American military did not employ dogs, since there was little risk involved and the expenditure would be small to maintain them. Unlike Europe, colonial America had no long-term tradition with military dogs, relying instead on patriotic individuals armed with flintlocks. Also, Americans never really adopted dogs as draft animals, as the Europeans did. In retrospect, the individuality and self-reliance of these early colonists was probably a contributing factor. Throughout American history, success on the battlefield is seldom shared with the animals involved, whether they be dogs, horses, mules, or pigeons.

During the Civil War, some instances of messenger dogs are recorded. These attempts were more an individual effort of soldiers who brought their dogs along with them, trading life on a farm for a battlefield. Still, most dogs appeared only as regimental mascots, but are duly recorded in many honor roles. Supposedly one dog accompanying the Confederate troops at the Battle of Gettysburg was killed and given a military funeral.[8] Several Gettysburg monuments also depict dogs, but these are probably all mascots. General George Armstrong Custer is also noted in literature as maintaining a contingent of dogs, yet the reasons are obscure. Officially at least, there existed no organized military dog program for either side of the war.

However, neither the Union nor the Confederate army was ever dissuaded from having dogs serve in vital military roles. Both sides used sentry dogs to prevent escapes from prison camps and to track down fleeing soldiers. At the infamous Andersonville Prison in Georgia, Captain Henry Wirz maintained thirteen hounds to attack escaping Union prisoners. To be caught fleeing by one of these savage hounds meant severe mutilation or death. One of these dogs, a Cuban bloodhound named Spot, tipped the scales at 159 pounds and stood three feet high. A formidable creature, but then again there was Hero, a sentry dog at Libby Prison and later Castle Thunder. Over seven feet long and thirty-eight inches high, Hero weighed in at a massive 198 pounds. As a comparison, a fully grown Saint Bernard weighs between 140 and 170 pounds. Even the fiercest sentry dogs trained by the air force a hundred years later would pale in comparison to these dogs, referred to as the "Hounds of Hell."[9]

By the late 1800s the military still had not adopted any official war dog program, but the Civil War did plant firm roots for the use of mascots and pets. Trained in basic obedience only, many of these dogs still served a tactical advantage in certain circumstances, as they alerted their masters to enemy movements or provided rudimentary messenger service. Similar occurrences with mascots would also take place during the two world wars of the twentieth century. It was during the Spanish-American War of 1898 when the first true tactical advantage of scout dogs became known and almost prophetic in application. American forces easily overpowered the Spanish on both the land and the sea. Problems arose when the army began to launch patrols on horseback in hostile territory covered with thick vegetation and narrow paths.

Small groups of guerrillas set up ambushes and fired from concealed locations upon the patrols before disengaging and melting back into the landscape.

The commander of one cavalry troop, a man by the name of Captain Steel, made every patrol in Cuba with a dog named Don in the lead. Not once was the patrol ambushed with Don on the point. Steel stated: "Dogs are the only scouts that can secure a small detachment against ambuscade in these tropical jungles."

Years later these words would ring true as American soldiers advanced through the Pacific islands toward Japan in World War II. Decades later, similar situations would occur with patrols in the dense jungles of Vietnam. As with other past successes, Steel's experiences in 1898 did not spur the army to explore the possibility of using dogs. Ironically, Col. E. H. Richardson, in a successful effort to establish a military dog program in Great Britain, recounted the efforts of Captain Steel and Don in a magazine article in 1911. The British would then go on to amass thousands of dogs for use in World War I. During World War II and Vietnam, the U. S. Army requested the expertise of British war dog trainers, bowing to their experience and knowledge in the field.

Americans were becoming more reliant upon technology and mechanization to fight their wars, an effort that seems to parallel the Industrial Revolution. The canine, as an efficient and cost-effective tool for saving lives, simply was swept aside as military commanders focused more on larger guns with more destructive firepower. Military tacticians firmly believed that since this had led to success in the past, inevitably it would lead to success in any future conflicts. History proves without a doubt that this is not always the case. Korea and Vietnam show that overwhelming firepower may win the battle but does not always win the war.

2.

THE WORLD WAR I EXPERIENCE

THE MERCY DOGS 1914–1918

A striking monument resides at the Hartsdale Canine Cemetery in Hartsdale, New York. It is simply dedicated to "The War Dog" for services rendered during "the World War, 1914–1918." The monument was erected in 1922 by contributions from dog lovers. Those who helped establish the memorial had no idea that this was not the "war to end all wars."

Cast in bronze, the German shepherd represented is more an animal of peace than an instrument of war. During World War I, Red Cross institutions of every country used many canines to aid and comfort the wounded men on the front lines. Although the Americans would not join the war until 1917, understanding the use of these dogs, and the others that provided a variety of services for the Europeans, is a key element and a useful comparison for future American endeavors. Dogs employed during the war provided three main services: ambulance assistance, messenger service, and sentry detail. Other dogs were recruited as ammunition and light-gun carriers and scouts, and Jack Russell terriers were enlisted to combat the hordes of rats that often infested the trenches.

The setting for World War I is unique, and it is difficult to comprehend the immense scale of destruction and human suffering endured by millions of people. Most of the time was spent in static positions, with little movement of the battle lines. Soldiers squatted down in trenches, each side facing the other, and furious battles raged to gain just a few scant yards of real estate. Between the combatants lay no-man's-land, and it

The war dog memorial at the Hartsdale Canine Cemetery, Hartsdale, New York, was dedicated to commemorate all the dogs that served during World War I. *(Michael Lemish)*

was here, often under the cloak of darkness, that many dogs worked and achieved their great success.

The Red Cross dogs–or sanitary dogs (*Sanitätshunde*), as the Germans called them–provided wounded men with two essential services. These dogs sought out only wounded men and were trained to ignore the dead soldiers. Medical supplies and small canteens of water and spirits were typically attached across the dog's chest or in a saddlebag arrangement. The wounded man, if conscious, could then avail himself of the supplies at hand. All too often the men simply held on to the dog for a short time, a last moment of companionship before dying.

If the soldier could not move or was unconscious, the dog would then return, inform the handlers that a wounded person had been found, and lead rescuers to the location. These mercy dogs were taught not to bark under any circumstances for fear of attracting enemy fire. At the beginning of the war, the innate sense of retrieval bred into many dogs led to the way they were trained, meaning that the return of a cap or helmet indicated a wounded soldier. In one case a French Red Cross dog named Captain located thirty wounded men in a single day using this method.[1]

If the dog was unable to find a helmet or cap, the animal would pull something from the body of the wounded soldier such as a bandage or a piece of clothing. He might even attempt to yank hair from the soldier's head if unable to find a cap or helmet. This problem increased in frequency until the handlers, the men who trained and worked the dogs, altered the method dogs used to announce the location of wounded men. The quest to retrieve needed to be subdued to a certain degree within the animals. Dog trainers accomplished this by changing their teaching techniques. Now upon their return, the dogs were taught to either lie down, if no wounded were found, or beckon the handler to return to the site.

The Germans, by comparison, devised a short leash called a *Brindel*, sometimes referred to as a *Brinsel*. Upon finding a wounded man, the dog would return with the leash in his mouth. Conversely, if the leash hung loose, no wounded or perhaps only the dead were to be found. It is reported that these dogs were also trained to distinguish the difference between friend and enemy, and disregard the latter. This is probably pure propaganda and more reflective of the time than fact.

The amount of enemy activity in the immediate search area determined whether the Red Cross dogs would be sent out during the day. Most often they worked at night, relying on their sense of smell, called their *olfactory ability*, rather than on sight to find the wounded soldiers. At this time people did not fully comprehend how dogs scented—only that they could. The scientific community did not have the capability to truly understand the olfactory ability of dogs or the extent to which this gift could be developed.

Slit trenches, barbed wire, and chemical gases were among the many obstacles faced by these dogs. Four-footed

A typical British Red Cross collie displays its insignia. Often working at night, Red Cross dogs located thousands of wounded soldiers during the war. *(Library of Congress)*

silhouettes searched no-man's-land quietly and efficiently in the dark for the wounded, with perhaps the flash of an artillery explosion illuminating the landscape. Every country had its own Red Cross organization, and dogs from opposing sides set incredible records. After a single battle, a French dog named Prusco located more than a hundred wounded men. The dog, wolflike in appearence and nearly all white, dragged unconscious and wounded soldiers into protective craters and trenches before alerting his masters.[2] Several dispatches from different regiments mentioned the heroic efforts of Prusco. Hundreds of other canines performed similar services.

The French began using military dogs in 1906, but stopped abruptly in 1914, after the Battle of the Marne. This decision was made by Marshal Joseph Joffre, a lazy and bullheaded commander, and without logical reason. The battle swayed back and forth over a three-hundred-mile front in bloody confusion. Dogs were found to be ineffectual in such combat, probably influencing Joffre in his decision. Some rumors circulated that he just hated dogs. The battle, eventually won by the French, ensured only that the war would continue for a very long time. For the most part, the French maintained few military dogs for the next year, although there were some outstanding exceptions. Coincidental with Joffre's removal, the army reactivated its dog program with vigor in 1915, calling it the Service des Chiens de Guerre. It continued to expand its scope of operations for the remainder of the war.

Many different breeds saw active duty during the war, depending on the job at hand. Bulldogs, retrievers, Airedale terriers, sheepdogs, and German shepherds were used in a variety of roles. Purebreds did not have any advantage over mixed breeds, and this is probably just as true today. The physical parameters preferred were dogs of medium build and grayish or black in color, with good eyesight and a keen sense of smell. Several periodicals of the time noted that if the dog did not display the proper "character" it did not see any wartime service. One passage in a 1918 issue of *Red Cross Magazine* stated that "the aristocrat with the shifty eye goes into the discard." This statement equates the characteristics of dogs with those of humans, and the practice occurs frequently throughout history to this very day. Scientists with a detached clinical viewpoint may argue that this has no basis in fact. But in World War I, as with all conflicts since then, the temperament and disposition of the dog usually came first, and if found physically acceptable, it continued to receive advanced training.

Hundreds of other dogs became useful in the transportation of wounded soldiers. Even though the war became increasingly mechanized, all combatants still relied upon animals in a variety of roles throughout the conflict. The ambulance dogs were larger breeds weighing more than eighty pounds; they pulled two-wheeled carriers especially designed for them. A single dog could pull one prone man or two soldiers in a sitting position. The dogs, often oblivious to the war

A 1918 painting by Alexander Pope portrays a Red Cross dog with a chemical gas attack in the background. The helmet indicates a wounded man has been found. *(Red Cross Museum)*

that raged around them, transported the wounded from the front lines to aid stations located in the more secure rear areas. Once the wounded were removed, the dog alone pulled the ambulance cart back to the battle lines to retrieve more wounded.

Draft dogs offered several advantages over horses—or even motorized ambulances. Horses presented a larger target and needed to be accompanied by a soldier, and they consumed a greater amount of food. Motorized ambulances were subject to mechanical failure, required gasoline that was scarce, and often could not negotiate the rough roads cratered by artillery shells.

The mercy dogs of World War I have been immortalized in a painting that hangs in the Red Cross museum in Washington, D.C. The painting, by Boston artist Alexander Pope, depicts a Red Cross dog sprinting back to friendly lines with a helmet. In the background, creeping along with the draft of a light wind, is the nightmarish chemical gas.

Several thousand mercy dogs participated in World War I. Their accomplishments are often overlooked simply because of the immense scale of the conflict. Thousands of soldiers owe their lives to these devoted animals, yet the dogs could help only a small fraction of the casualties that numbered in the millions during the war, leaving their legacy as just a footnote to history. Trench warfare and stagnant front lines ended with World War I, and with it the necessity ever to employ Red Cross dogs again.

FLEET-FOOTED MESSENGERS

Except for the United States, every country embroiled in the war considered dogs a valuable commodity. When the United States entered the war, few American commanders grasped the advantages of developing the animals to their full potential and needed to borrow them from the French or British. Although ambulance dogs saved countless lives, the messenger dog is also credited with indirectly saving thousands of lives. Much of World War I consisted of trench warfare and battle lines that remained fixed, often for long periods of time. Communication, most often by telephone or soldiers running with messages, remained a vital link to commanders in rear areas. When communications broke down, dogs helped to fill the gap by relaying messages.

In Belgium an entire battalion lost contact with its headquarters after the Germans cut the telephone lines. Yet their messenger dog was able to relay their position and their desperate need for reinforcements. In the midst of an artillery barrage, the dog escaped with a message to headquarters, and the fresh troops that responded kept the battalion from being wiped out.[3] Some of the accomplishments recorded are truly marvels of not only a dog's skill at survival but also the canine's innate sense of completing a mission. An Irish terrier messenger dog named Paddy, although partially blinded by gas, completed a journey of nine miles with a dispatch. Days later, the dog recovered from the effects of the chemical and returned to active service.

Messenger dogs could carry dispatches four to five times faster than the average foot soldier and needed only a small metal canister attached to their collar that could carry several sheets of paper. Besides carrying messages, the same dogs often delivered messenger pigeons in a saddlebag arrangement designed just for them. Dogs also offered a lower profile than men, making them more difficult to locate and a challenge for the enemy to shoot at. In one battle near Verdun seventeen human couriers perished while attempting to deliver messages. A lone dog was able to complete seven message runs before succumbing to enemy fire. If at all possible, however, the enemy tried to capture the dogs rather than just kill them. Unlike their human counterparts, captured dogs were retrained and sent out into the field again—this time providing a service for the enemy in the conflict. Dogs were not considered traitorous, just pragmatic under the circumstances.

The French divided messenger dogs into two groups: *estafettes* and *liaison*. Estafettes carried messages or pigeons, completing one-way journeys to a predesignated point. More danger faced liaison dogs, trained to carry dispatches on round-trips, since their missions doubled their chances of being shot. Perhaps the most famous messenger dog of the war was a mixed breed named Satan, who is credited with saving what later became known as "The Lost Battalion."[4] As the story goes, the French held a small village near Verdun but quickly became encircled by superior German forces. With their telephone lines cut and their messenger pigeons dead, no one knew of their plight. The Germans understood the precarious position of the French soldiers and quickly moved field

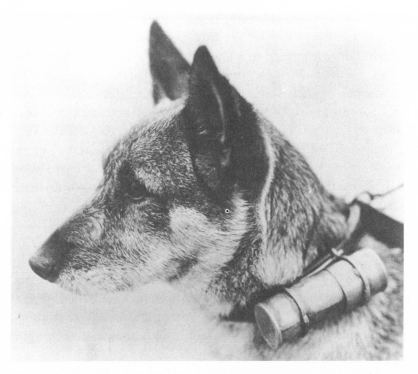

A German messenger dog captured by British soldiers. As in most cases, this one was renamed Kaiser and would be trained again and employed by the Allies. *(Carlisle Barracks)*

artillery pieces to a nearby hill. Artillery shells soon found their mark, and scores of soldiers lay dead.

Amid the turmoil and confusion, a strange apparition appeared from the smoke. It appeared alien because several soldiers recounted that it looked like a winged creature with an unusually large head. In reality it was the messenger dog Satan, with two pigeon carriers on his flanks flapping as he ran, and a bulbous gas mask covering his head. Satan approached in a zigzag pattern, as he had been trained to do to avoid enemy fire. When he was only several hundred yards from the French line, the Germans opened fire. Dozens of Germans began firing until a bullet finally found its mark. Satan fell, recovered, and continued at a slower zigzagging trot. A second bullet shattered his shoulder and the dog stumbled, now just a few scant yards from the French. Satan must have drawn again from the deep well of courage many dogs possess, and he stumbled onward to awaiting arms. He was greeted enthusiastically, and an army doctor tended to his wounds.

Satan had managed to deliver two carrier pigeons from the nearby French forces. The first pigeon flew skyward for only three hundred feet before enemy gunners shot it down. Only one more chance remained. A soldier released the second pigeon, carrying a small message of their predicament. Rifles cracked and the air filled with lead as the pigeon flew high above the soldiers and toward the French lines—only time would tell if the message got through.

Within the hour, long-range guns from the French began a barrage against German positions on the nearby hill. The explosives hit the enemy squarely, and allied forces were able to relieve the village during the same day. The Germans remained confused and regrouped, fearing a counteroffensive from the French. A key battle involving thousands of soldiers was ultimately decided by the determination of a single dog to complete his mission.

Messenger dogs had several advantages during the war that helped them complete their missions. Their biggest asset was their ability to utilize the elaborate trench systems. This, probably more than anything else, accounted for their capability of carrying dispatches for long distances. These dogs could be trained in just six weeks, and Colonel Richardson expounded upon the virtues of the messenger dog, writing:

> The dog has to work entirely on its own initiative and be miles away from its keeper. It has to know what to do, and to think out how it is going to do it. It is easy to understand, therefore, that the messenger dog has to be trained in such a way that it takes the keenest delight and pride in its work. The highest qualities of mind—love and duty—have to be appealed to and cultivated. The whole training is based on appeal. If it makes a mistake, it is never chastised, but is merely shown how to do it over again. Barbed wire entanglements, pailings, fences, water dykes, smoke clouds, etc., intercept its homeward journey and it must be induced at all costs, one way or the other, to surmount these difficulties by going

through, under or over. It is left to the dog to choose, but come he must. Competition with each other is a very strong educator here and is one of the great aids to training.[5]

Richardson always believed the prime motivation for a dog should be positive praise and reinforcement. This would be a key element in developing any type of war dog, and one factor not always adhered to. The development of radio communication eclipsed the future use of these dogs in World War II, although not completely. Events in the Pacific would elevate the importance of the messenger dog once more—if only for a brief moment in time.

FINAL PARTICIPANT

For the three years after 1914, the battle lines of the Western Front were virtually static. In Europe much of the war consisted of lines of trenches and fortifications manned by the Germans on one side and the French, British, and Belgians on the other, with no-man's-land in between. Each side attempted to advance, only to gain a little ground before being pushed back with heavy losses. Many events took place slowly drawing the United States into the conflict. Finally, on April 6, 1917, President Woodrow Wilson declared war against Germany to keep the world "safe for democracy." On June 26, 1917, Americans joined the French, and by the end of the year about 180,000 troops bolstered the Allied effort.

Of all the armies participating in the Great War, only the United States lacked war dogs within its military ranks, with the exception of some sled dogs, kept in Alaska. By this time France and England had amassed twenty thousand war dogs and Germany possessed nearly thirty thousand. One canine contribution by the United States was the delivery of four hundred sled dogs to the French army. Sled dogs helped to haul ammunition and supplies in snowy areas, particularly in the Vosges Mountains. Similar operations involved dogs pulling flatbed railroad cars loaded with ammunition or food to the front lines.

Several American canine associations attempted to per-

In the Vosges Mountains, dogs transport ammunition to the front lines along railroad tracks. *(Carlisle Barracks)*

suade the military to adopt a war dog program, principally the German Shepherd Dog Club of America and the Army and Police Dog Club of the United States. But all requests and demands fell on deaf ears. This was probably due in part to the contention that with America's entry, a speedy end to the war would occur. A letter drafted by Anne Tracy of the American Red Cross in 1917 clearly indicated the position of the government:

> The Red Cross has undertaken to supply dogs trained for sanitary work to the U.S. Medical Corps, but up to now there has been no real work done excepting with a few dogs which went unofficially with one of the California units. Early in May Senator Brady of Idaho received a letter signed by the Secretary of War requesting him to procure the necessary legislation to permit the army to use whatever funds necessary for the purchase, training, and maintenance of dogs for military purposes. Senator Brady introduced a

bill, but the legislation was blocked by individual senators who knew little and cared less about the matter, and although the General Staff and the Medical Corps have recommended it in every possible way, we realize it may be months before they can get the appropriation. The Government, as you know, is not allowed to accept gifts which require continued expenditure, so we now hope for success through the Red Cross, which has accepted the offer of some members of the German Shepherd Dog Club and expects to send over dogs to work with our troops as soon as they are needed.

One tentative plan follows: Dogs will receive their preliminary and trial training on this side at a place designated by the Red Cross. All those dogs proving themselves inapt, shy, stupid, or physically unsound will be returned to the donors or sold. Dogs will be shipped to France in units of twelve in charge of a trained man and will receive their final training on the other side before being assigned to their guides for service with troops. Dogs will be under control of the United States Medical Corps while in service. Dogs must be intelligent, loyal, and fearless. Either sex is acceptable and dark coloring is preferable. Police training is not desirable. Dogs to be trained should be between eight and twelve months old. We hope for donations of dogs suitable for service.[6]

During the spring of 1918, the General Headquarters of the American Expeditionary Forces recommended the use of dogs as messengers, sentries, draft animals, and patrol auxiliaries. The proposal suggested that 500 dogs be obtained from the French military every three months. After training, each American division would be supplied with 288 dogs. The program also specified the establishment of training facilities to be built within the United States and the construction of five kennels that could house 200 dogs each. It promised to give the American army its first official canine unit. The hierarchy of the military, after reviewing the recommendations, dropped the plan entirely for unknown reasons. Many years passed before a similar proposal was finally adopted.[7]

For the balance of the war, Americans relied solely on the British and the French for dogs. Since the American government did not seem interested, many citizen advocates began to approach the Red Cross with the idea of donating trained dogs. Only a handful made the trip overseas, and others bound for the war were found to have a serious flaw in their training. One volunteer trainer in Pasadena, California, explained the problem as follows:

> We have eliminated from the course of training all the police dog work—that is, attacking, refusing food from trainers, etc.—specializing in trailing, forced retrieving, jumping, and other work which might be useful in the Red Cross service. My first and greatest mistake was to train the dogs in the country. When the Ambulance Corps No. 1 was organized in Pasadena, I gave them a pair of the dogs which were letter perfect in their work on the ranch. We made the two boys who had them in charge work right with them every day, and there was practically nothing you could ask them to do that they would not go through with. We failed, however, to take them down into the town, and when they left for the East they were badly frightened, bands, street cars, and the like being too much for them. Since they have been at the training camp in Allentown, they have settled down and I understand are doing quite well. I have four or five others trained, or partially trained, all of which I expect to give to the Red Cross units in this vicinity when they are called out.[8]

Although the dogs eventually adjusted to the noisier urban areas, they would eventually fail in their duties when sent abroad. Since the dogs were trained by civilians, no exposure to machine-gun fire or an artillery barrage could be given. This deficiency in their training regimen made the animals useless at the front, as they understandably cowered under fire. The same problems would plague many war dogs fielded by the United States in the years to come.

STUBBY: AMERICAN MASCOT HERO

Contrary to army regulations, American soldiers adopted many dogs as mascots while fighting in France during World War I. The dogs were not trained for any specific mission, but simply fulfilled their duty as devoted friends, providing comfort under stress in a horrid war. Rin Tin Tin, for example, was a German mascot puppy found alone in a trench after an attack by Americans. The dog would grow up to be a matinee idol and added to the folklore and popularity of the German shepherd breed.[9]

Often canine mascots provided more than simple companionship. Although not formally trained, they still rendered invaluable service and saved many lives by warning a comrade of attacking aircraft or the imminent onslaught of a deadly gas attack. Such is the story of Stubby, a stray pit bull picked up from the streets of Hartford, Connecticut, by Robert Conroy.[10] Europe had its war dog heroes, and although Stubby was not a product of an official military program, he is presented in these pages as an honored warrior, a fascinating example of how soldiers valued their dogs.

During the summer of 1917, Stubby became the mascot of the 102d Infantry, part of the army's 26th "Yankee" Division, while they completed their military training in the Yale Bowl near Hartford. Conroy smuggled him aboard ship at Newport News, Virginia, and the pair landed together at St. Nazaire, France, in January 1918. Stubby joined the fighting with the 102d on February 5, 1918, at Chemin des Dames, just northwest of Soissons. During one night while the troops slept, he warned a sleeping sergeant of an impending gas attack, allowing time for the soldiers to don their masks. Another time, Stubby acted as a sentry, clamping his teeth onto a German infiltrator who was then quickly captured.

The small dog accompanied the men into the Toul sector, where he inadvertently strayed into no-man's-land, receiving a shrapnel wound for the errant walk. After recovery from the injury, Stubby and the 102d participated in battles at Château-Thierry, the Marne, Saint-Mihiel, and the Meuse-Argonne. The men fashioned a Victory Medal with five bars and attached it to his collar to display his participation in each offensive.

As Stubby's popularity grew, several French women fashioned a blanket for him to wear. For unknown reasons, it became popular for people to pin medals on the blanket, and shortly he became known as the "Hero Dog." The actions of Stubby may not be considered heroic, although several messages were carried by the short-tailed dog under enemy fire, but *heroism* is a broadly defined term, and if devotion to duty is included within the attributes of a hero, then Stubby fulfills the definition. Perhaps the medals were presented more as a reward for the companionship the dog offered, as battles raged and the utter destruction and carnage cloaked young men like a shroud. Often the dog sought out the wounded and simply cuddled alongside.

After serving nineteen months overseas and participating in seventeen battles, Stubby returned home with Conroy, and the dog's popularity seemed to grow even more. In 1920 the Eastern Dog Club of Boston awarded him a large silver medal with the inscription "Awarded to the Hero Dog Stubby." A year later, Gen. John Joseph "Black Jack" Pershing, who commanded the American Expeditionary Forces during the war, awarded the little dog a gold medal made by the Humane Society. The American Red Cross, the YMCA, and the American Legion all made the dog a life member of their organizations.

Stubby toured the country by invitation from Legionnaires and probably participated in more parades than any other dog in the world. While the 102d was in France, he was in attendance while President Woodrow Wilson reviewed the troops. President Harding met both Conroy and Stubby in 1921, and in 1925 President Coolidge welcomed the pair during a visit to the White House. What other dog could ever boast of being in the presence of three presidents?

Old age finally caught up with the small warrior in 1926, as he took ill and died in Conroy's arms. Irene Givenwilson Kilner, curator of the Red Cross museum, promptly asked to have the body prepared for permanent display in the museum. Stubby greeted visitors from his glass case for many years, adorned with the French blanket covered with medals. Few people realized how this was achieved. W. L. Brown, a taxider-

Stubby, World War I mascot hero, met three presidents and was decorated after the war by Gen. "Black Jack" Pershing. *(Mary Thurston)*

mist for the Smithsonian Institution, removed the dog's skin and fashioned a plaster mold approximating Stubby's skeleton. With the cremated remains inside, the skin was stretched over the plaster body. Physically he appeared smaller in the display case than when he was alive.

Stubby remained at the museum for about thirty years, though not preserved for immortality–the air and humidity slowly eroded the skin and hair. Eventually, the hero dog of the Great War became just a bizarre curiosity of a long-ago struggle. Stubby outlived his usefulness with the Red Cross, and the curator transferred the decaying memorial to the Smithsonian's Museum of American History. The stray dog, picked up from the streets of Connecticut, now resides in Room 4501 at the Smithsonian, between dusty records and other artifacts long forgotten. The dog who provided unquestionable devotion for many years has his final epitaph scribbled on a shipping crate reading "Stubby the dog–Fragile."[11]

AFTERMATH

The effectiveness and demand for military dogs is affirmed by the numbers placed in service. When the war erupted, Germany immediately sent six thousand dogs to the front and kept four thousand in reserve with their civilian owners. Germany also encouraged its citizens to train their dogs through canine associations like the Verein für Deutsche Schäferhunde (sentry) and the Deutsche Verein für Sanitätshunde (medical).

Italy fielded three thousand dogs for the Allies, and the French quickly surpassed that figure. Belgium had the best draft dogs, developing them throughout the nineteenth century, but lost most of them to the Germans during the invasion. The British began the conflict with just one war dog. It took a dog breeder and civilian, Edwin Hautenvill Richardson, to convince the military establishment of the dog's usefulness. Richardson had previously trained and supplied ambulance dogs for the Russian army during the Russo-Japanese War of 1904. Not only did he start the British War Dog School but immediately became a colonel and commander of the institution.[12]

War losses for soldiers and civilians are only estimates, and it is difficult to comprehend the sheer number of men killed and wounded on the battlefield. In four years of fighting, tens of millions of men were killed or wounded. More than one million Americans marched into war, confident of quick victory and inspired by patriotic songs. Over 53,000 Americans lost their lives in battle, another 63,000 died from disease or accidents, and a staggering 200,000 were wounded. The sobering experience left little to cheer or sing about.

Animals fared little better, and it is not possible to calculate with any degree of accuracy the number of canine losses incurred by all sides during the war. A 1919 issue of *Animals* magazine stated: "About 7,000 dogs were thought to have lost their lives in the war." This figure is probably low, based on the total number of dogs used by both sides. Some reports cited German losses alone at over seven thousand, and a

Lieutenant Milton Monnette and Pvt. D. O. Parks display an enemy messenger dog that was shot dead. If at all possible, messenger dogs were caught and retrained. *(National Archives)*

United States Veterinary Corps history states sixteen thousand battle deaths.[13] Ironically, more losses probably occurred immediately after the cessation of hostilities than during the war. The French military, then possessing fifteen thousand dogs in its employ, destroyed the animals as its great war machine demobilized. The vast quantities of dogs used by the British, Germans, Italians, and Russians faced the same fate. The actual number will never be known since these events were never accurately recorded. Compassion within the military—then and now—is often a precious commodity.

The actions and results of the employment of war dogs in modern warfare left little doubt of their viability and usefulness. The United States did nothing with the knowledge and information gained, concentrating more on peace, demobilization of the American military, and support for the League of Nations. Germany learned its lessons well even in a losing effort. And though the country lay in economic and political turmoil, the German army continued to advance the training of war dogs under the Treaty of Versailles at the end of the Great War. Soon the mold would be cast for a future war. Germany, unlike the United States, would be prepared with its dogs of war.

BETWEEN THE WARS

Although the United States did not embark upon a war dog program of its own after the Great War, it did stay abreast of other countries that did. In the 1928 issue of *Army Ordnance,* captioned photographs depict the training of war dogs by the German army in Berlin. A series of photographs shows dogs equipped for chemical attacks with their gas masks donned and others carrying telephone cable. It also proved that the Germans considered the employment of tracking dogs. One photo shows a device that could make footprint impressions in the ground, but with no human scent attached to them. This is intended to show that dogs could track humans visually and not only by scent.

With the armistice signed, Congress severely cut back annual expenditures for the military. The peacetime military was indeed small, with a limited budget, but could still afford to launch a war dog program had it chosen to. During the 1920s and 1930s no one attempted to adapt dogs for wartime uses, except for maintaining the army sled dogs in Alaska. Some ideas were brought forth by individuals and published in military journals in an attempt to foster some interest. Army Lt. Avery M. Cochran wrote about the need for pack dogs, specifically Alaskan huskies, to supply and support light machine-gun squads.[14] Cochran believed the dogs would give a machine-gun squad a faster rate of march on the battlefield by distributing the equipment to be carried to the animals.

Although a husky could carry upwards of sixty pounds for a short period of time, Cochran's plan limited the dogs to about forty pounds individually—and a pair of huskies could be double-teamed to carry a heavier load. Even with the forty-pound limitation, a single dog could carry one of the following items:

2 ammunition chests (500 rounds)	41.0 pounds
10 rounds 60mm shell	34.8 pounds
12 canteens of water	30.0 pounds
80 clips (640 rounds) M-1 cartridges	40.0 pounds
40 hand grenades, gas, CD-DM, M-6	42.5 pounds
32 hand grenades, fragmentation, MKII	40.0 pounds

Not only could they carry half their weight at up to eight miles per hour, they were also easy to keep, ate just three pounds of food per day, and readily trained for draft purposes. The necessary equipment–and Cochran even provided draw-ings–was cheap and easy to make from common materials. Yet with all the advantages offered, no one nurtured the idea any further. During the 1930s the military had barely enough resources to maintain an adequate standing army without the need to experiment with draft dogs.

By the end of the decade the war drums began to pound again in Europe. In 1938 Adolf Hitler annexed Austria, and then the British and the French delivered the Sudetenland as an appeasement. In 1939 Germany seized most of the rest of Czechoslovakia, and on September 1, 1939, it launched the invasion of Poland. Thus the stage was set for the United States to be eventually drawn into another conflict that was only beginning to rage in Europe.

Still, the idea of developing war dogs, a relatively inexpen-sive proposition, lay dormant. Some overtures continued to appear in several military publications, but all went unheeded. An article in the January 1940 issue of *Infantry Journal* accu-rately stated the war dog's potential in battle. It is interesting to note that the information for the article came from the German and Japanese armies, complete with photographs. The author, reminiscent of Ben Franklin, clearly states the scout dog's potential when he says:

In Panama and the Philippine Islands on jungle trails, where flank security is impossible of achievement because of the dense growth, dogs used as advance guards and scouts could ferret out an ambush before it could take effect. Their ability to work in tangled terrain would be an invaluable security measure in jungle operations.

Considering the many ways in which the dog may benefit the soldier we should begin now to breed and train suitable types of dogs for the various functions of probable employment, to develop the dog's most favorable characteristics, and to expand the number of uses wherever such employment will relieve a man. This program cannot be fully realized after M day [the first day of a war]; it should start at once. Our liaison with dogdom should be much closer than that implied by the common name for the soldier's identification tag.[15]

It would be another two years before the U.S. Army officially recognized the military value of canines. Many of the ideas fostered between the world wars originated with junior-grade officers and therefore received scant attention. No high-ranking officer ever pushed for the enlistment of military dogs. The United States simply had no one in the same capacity as Col. E. H. Richardson, as the British did in World War I, who could advance a similar program. In the mind-set of the time, at least for the Americans, dogs were just an anachronism in modern warfare, like the horse or the mule. The army's short-sightedness revealed itself in due time, but from a highly unexpected source.

3.

STARTING FROM SCRATCH

ANOTHER WAR AND STILL NO DOGS

The United States realized months before the attack on Pearl Harbor that war with Japan was inevitable. Yet, on the morning of December 7, 1941, while people on the island of Oahu quietly slept, Japanese planes began their assault. In just a few hours America's Pacific Fleet was disabled, and many aircraft were destroyed at both Hickam and Wheeler fields. The next day, Pres. Franklin D. Roosevelt and Congress declared war on Japan. Three days later Germany and Italy declared war on the United States–global warfare was at hand.

The only military working dogs to be found within the army at this time were about fifty sled (sometimes called sledge) dogs in Alaska. There were also forty dogs obtained earlier in 1941 upon the return of the Byrd Antarctic Expedition.[1] The army sent these dogs to Greenland, and the Air Corps Ferry Command began using them to locate and rescue crashed pilots. A handful of dogs could also be found at Camp Haan in California, participating in a local sentry program for the Coast Artillery. No official dog program yet existed, and the impetus to begin one would actually come from outside the military establishment.

But within the military came the fear that provided the catalyst to start a canine program. That fear consisted of saboteurs, fifth columnists, and enemy aliens, within the continental United States, who could potentially damage the rapidly expanding industrial plants with strategically placed explosives or incendiary devices. This fear, sometimes bordering on

A sled dog team arrives at a crash site in Greenland. In remote Arctic regions sled dog teams were often the only way in which crashed airmen could be successfully rescued.

paranoia, became an even greater reality as Japanese submarines operated off the Pacific coast and German U-boats increased their activities along the Atlantic seaboard.

Within their own associations and clubs, breeders and fanciers emphasized the important sentry work that dogs could offer the military. They would be of invaluable service to the Coast Guard, which was charged with the defense of the coastline. The proliferation of industrial plants also required nighttime protection. "A single dog could replace eight sentries, freeing them for more important work," was often stated. The idea of dogs' assuming a more tactical and offensive role would still wait. For all the talk of playing up the usefulness of dogs, no one really understood how to approach the military with their ideas.

At this time, the United States census counted horses, cows, and mules, but for some reason not dogs. A casual estimate placed the canine population at between thirteen and fifteen million, with about five hundred thousand purebreds. Several hundred kennel clubs conducted over four hundred dog shows each year, confirming that indeed we are a nation of dog lovers. These numbers revealed a country devoted to dogs, mostly family pets with a minimum of formal training. Few professional dog trainers existed in the country to provide obedience training on the level required by the armed services. Only in 1940 did obedience training schools emerge and become fashionable with pet owners. That year, two women, Mrs. Whithouse Walker and Blanche Saunders, pioneer obedience trainers, launched a famous ten-thousand-mile cross-country trip across the United States giving demonstrations. These exhibitions fired up the public, and by the beginning of 1941, forty-two dog obedience clubs had sprung up across the country. They would ultimately prove to be a training asset for the military.

Unlike foreign countries, America did not use working dogs to any great extent. Police occasionally used bloodhounds, as an offshoot from their hunting regimen, to locate fugitives or escaped prisoners. Even then, American police work with dogs did not extend to the level that the Europeans had developed. The one exception was the use of sled dogs, and here the United States kept on the same footing as and sometimes exceeded the efforts of other countries. If the army decided to adopt a military canine program, it would be from scratch. Logic also dictated that it would begin with people familiar with dogs and their capabilities. This, obviously, meant someone in the civilian sector. For on the day after Pearl Harbor, the entire U.S. Army library contained just one book about dogs: a field manual on the care and transportation of dogs in Arctic regions.[2]

THE VOLUNTEER EFFORT

Shortly after the attack on Pearl Harbor by the Japanese, Alene Erlanger, a nationally recognized dog breeder and exhibitor, placed a telephone call to Arthur Kilbon at the *New York Sun*. Kilbon, a member of the *Sun*'s editorial staff and a columnist, wrote under several pseudonyms for other prominent newspapers across the country. "I must see you," Erlanger said. "It's about what the war means to dogs and fanciers. I have an idea and need your help. The dog world must play its part in this *thing*. Other countries have used dogs for years and ours have not. They've got to do it!"[3]

The two dog fanciers placed several telephone calls and enlisted the help of other people to discuss the situation. These meetings included Leonard Brumby, president of the Professional Handlers Association; Dorothy J. Long, an authority on obedience training; and Harry I. Caesar, an influential banker and a director of the American Kennel Club. Henry Stoecker, a trainer employed by Erlanger, attended these early formulative discussions, along with Felicien Philippe, ex-chief of the Italian State Game Preserve and very knowledgeable about the ongoing war dog programs in Europe.

These meetings resulted in the establishment of Dogs for Defense (DFD) in January 1942.[4] Brumby suggested the name—the United States being in no position to adopt an offensive stance at the time. Also, the volunteers contemplated dogs as sentries along the coast of the United States and around key installations. Little consideration was given at the time to more offensive and tactical roles for these dogs. The new organization banded together both amateur and professional dog breeders and trainers across the country. The American Kennel Club heartily endorsed the project but soon stated, "We cannot participate officially since there are no provisions within our charter to do so."[5]

The DFD began to develop a nationwide network of volunteers, trainers, and kennel clubs on the assumption that the army would jump at the opportunity to use dogs—they didn't. Both Brumby and Erlanger continued to knock on doors in an attempt to reach a receptive audience. They found selling a dog program to the military a frustrating experience. There was no American military tradition involving dogs—but there was a military tradition that civilians do not tell the army how to conduct its affairs, especially female civilians.

While the DFD attempted to approach the government for a large-scale program, the American Theater Wing held a meeting at the Hudson Theater in New York, looking for a volunteer project to support the war effort. Comprised of radio, movie, and stage personalities, the wing sought volunteer opportunities for their entertainers to assist as part of the war effort on the homefront. Actress Helen Menken and the wing's public relations director, Sydney Wain, met with the quartermaster general, Maj. Gen. Edmund B. Gregory, to offer their services. Gregory lacked immediate need for their expertise, offered his thanks, and promised to inform the wing when an appropriate project arose.

Within a few days of that meeting in Washington, Lt. Col. Clifford C. Smith, chief of the Plant Protection Branch, Inspection Division, Quartermaster Corps, met with Gregory to discuss army supply depot security. With an increased awareness of the possibility of sabotage now that the United States was at war, Smith suggested the use of sentry dogs to support the depot guards. Gregory approved an experimental program, with an initial allotment of two hundred dogs.

Gregory then contacted Menken at the American Theater Wing and suggested that this might be the program her group could support. Menken, raised with dogs and familiar with war dogs in Europe, embraced the proposal and offered the wing's services. Within a short time she realized that they did not have the resources or the trained personnel to carry out a volunteer mission of this nature. Fortunately, she had just recently heard of the formation of Dogs for Defense and promptly notified Erlanger and Caesar of the experimental program. It was decided that DFD would accept responsibility for the recruitment and training of the dogs, and the wing became more comfortable with its job of publicizing the program via radio. The wing volunteer group also aided in more suitable projects–like the Stage Door Canteen, offering entertainment for military personnel.

On March 13, 1942, Colonel Smith notified Caesar of the quartermaster's requirements and informed him that the DFD would be the appointed agency for canine recruitment and training. This was the first time in the history of the United States that marked the official recognition of war dogs. It also showed that at least some segment of the military displayed a willingness to work with a civilian organization.

The DFD found someone willing to give sentry dogs a try immediately before supplying the Plant Protection Branch with two hundred dogs. On April 13, 1942, the Munitions Manufacturing Company in Poughkeepsie, New York, accepted the offer to try some sentry dogs. The DFD had several dogs trained as sentries by this time and sent three to the factory immediately. Major General Philip S. Gage, commanding Fort Hancock, on the New York waterfront, also liked the idea of security dogs. Another nine dogs went to him on a trial basis, and seventeen more went to Mitchell Field, Long Island, and to an oil plant on Staten Island. All the dogs worked well, and Gage issued an enthusiastic report on their performance in July. This one small step by the DFD helped secure a foothold for the launch of a more widespread canine program.

Caesar promptly enlisted 402 kennel clubs across the

Dogs for Defense representative Alene Erlanger meets with Quartermaster General Maj. Gen. E. B. Gregory to discuss sentry dogs for industrial plant security. At the beginning of the war Erlanger was a key figure in the effort to have the army employ military working dogs. *(National Archives)*

United States for dog recruitment. The first problem was that no single facility existed to handle the two hundred dogs requested by the Plant Protection Branch. Consequently, the training was spread out to a dozen private kennels across the country, each staffed by volunteer handlers and trainers. Although this solved the difficulty of kenneling dogs and having a sufficient number of trainers on hand, it sprouted several other problems. No standardized training syllabus existed, and most trainers were not familiar with the requirements of a sentry dog or with what the army expected from one. An army inspection in June 1942 showed few dogs making progress. Another problem surfaced with the dogs that were properly trained; often they were given to civilians, who had little or no experience or training as dog handlers themselves. The novel and innovative idea became a discouraging start for an all-volunteer group intent on supporting the military and their country the best way they knew how.

THE EARLY DISAPPOINTING RESULTS with training sentry dogs did not dissuade the army from expanding the war dog program. After all, there were many other key successes to bolster these early efforts. The dogs also netted another side benefit as morale boosters. Companionship, either to relieve the boredom associated with sentry duty or to soothe the stresses of soldiers in frontline combat, is a tangible asset. This would be clearly shown at later stages of the war, particularly in the Pacific, as dogs took a more active tactical role with substantial results. Besides trained dogs, the companionship fostered could be seen in the hundreds of local dogs adopted as mascots by various units in every branch of the military and in every theater of operation.[6] They provided a subtle impact on the war effort, as they comforted the human spirit in the highly charged atmosphere of combat.

The expansion of the program and the potential military value dogs offered became officially recognized on July 16, 1942. Secretary of War Harold Stimson directed the quartermaster general to train dogs for functions other than simple sentry duty. The tactical activities envisioned included search-and-rescue sled dogs, roving patrols, and messenger services. The directive, sent to all service branches, stated the secretary's wish "to explore the possibilities of using dogs advantageously in the various activities under their control." This effectively gave each service branch carte blanche in deciding the number of dogs to be recruited and how they would be deployed.

This first step also relieved the Plant Protection Branch of training and procurement, transferring these responsibilities to the Remount Branch of the Army Quartermaster Corps (QMC). The Remount Branch, aided by a long history of dealing with animals, although mostly horses and mules, was eminently more suited for this role. Meanwhile, the Plant Protection Branch would still issue sentry dogs, if only for the next couple of months, with the Remount Branch assuming all control during September 1942. This realignment meant that Dogs for Defense could concentrate solely on the procurement of dogs, being released from any training endeavors. The new orders from the War Department also dictated that instruction for handlers and the establishment of training facilities be assumed by the Remount Branch. These orders expanded even more during the fall of 1942 as the QMC obtained and trained dogs for both the Coast Guard and the navy.

By now the canine program had become commonly called—unofficially, of course—the K-9 Corps, and the army officially designated the dogs as the K-9 (Canine) Section.[7] Obviously, somewhere in the army either a sense of humor prevailed (probably not) or the military just needed to state the obvious, as someone added "Canine" in parentheses. A few people wanted the war dog section designated as WAGS or WAAGS. Thankfully, only the *New York Times* had the audacity to use this wimpy term. The Marines stayed with the basics and referred to military canines simply as "war dogs." Erlanger remained in the picture as a civilian consultant to the quartermaster general in establishing the war dog program. Working directly under Col. E. M. Daniels, chief of the Remount Branch, she is credited with authoring the first technical manual, "TM 10–396–War Dogs," along with several training films. Erlanger's enthusiasm and experience helped propel the program forward, a feat never truly recognized by the public at large.

The number of dogs supplied to the QMC escalated accordingly as the public was made more aware of the need for dogs for the war effort. An announcement by the quartermaster general on December 30, 1942, sent shock waves that reverberated throughout the DFD organization. General Gregory notified Caesar, saying, "Our present estimate is that the Army, Navy, Marines, and Coast Guard will require approximately 125,000 dogs." The news inflated the esteem of the volunteers, but it also meant that a daunting task lay ahead. Several DFD officials quietly wondered among themselves if the organization could secure such a vast number of canines. Even within the present program, shortages of canine recruits were becoming acute.

ESTABLISHMENT OF WAR DOG CENTERS

During August 1942, the QMC began to establish several war dog reception and training centers across the country. Here all dogs obtained by DFD were examined by the veterinary staff, classified as to their suitability for work, and finally trained for those duties. Front Royal, Virginia, established itself as the first training and reception center for K-9 recruits. By the end of the year, three other centers were established: Camp Rimini, Montana; Fort Robinson, Nebraska; and San Carlos, California. In April 1943, the Cat Island (off the coast of Mississippi) facility opened. This base was originally started by the Army Ground Forces (September 1942 to April 1943) but was subsequently operated by the Quartermaster Remount Service.

The army did not bear sole responsibility for training and procurement, and in the early stages of the war other services maintained their own camps. The Marines maintained a training and reception center at Camp Lejeune in North Carolina, and the Coast Guard, requiring only sentry dogs, had three facilities on the east coast. Although the War Department au-

A variety of dogs are shown at their kennels at Front Royal, Virginia. At the beginning of the war the army accepted thirty-two different breeds but soon whittled it down to eighteen. The most prominent breeds during the war were the German shepherd and the Doberman pinscher. *(National Archives)*

thorized Dogs for Defense to be the only recruitment agency for the army, for a short time the navy and the Marines procured some of their own dogs directly from private citizens. Eventually the navy appointed the DFD as procurer, as did the Coast Guard and Marines, the latter in conjunction with the Doberman Pinscher Club of America. For unknown reasons, the Marines preferred male Dobermans and the Coast Guard recruited mostly females.

Training for sled and pack dogs took place at Camp Rimini under civilian contract with Chinook Kennels in Wonalancet, New Hampshire. These sled dogs were destined for Newfoundland, Greenland, and Iceland. Simulated jungle training took place at Cat Island, a primitive location with no electricity or fresh water. Several other temporary facilities were also secured at Beltsville, Maryland, and Fort Belvoir, Virginia. Beltsville was part of the Agricultural Research Center, providing research on canine nutrition and developing an army dog ration. By the middle of 1944, all centers would close with the exception of Fort Robinson. Each center maintained a veterinary detachment and a hospital. The hospitals were built outside the training areas and near the existing hospitals established for horses and mules in an effort to economize resources. The hospital kennels could house 6 percent of the center's total dog population, and this equated to about four hundred hospital kennels nationwide.

The Territory of Hawaii poised a special problem. Under local laws and regulations, army dogs could enter from the continental United States but needed a four-month quarantine period. This would delay deployment and adversely affect the training of army dogs that had already been received. A plan originated on May 24, 1942, and was approved by the headquarters of the Hawaiian Department, to establish a dog training center at the provisional Veterinary General Hospital at Fort Armstrong, Oahu. Acting as a quarantined environment, the army center could provide dog training with no delay for deployment. The facility opened on August 5, and a smaller subcenter was established five months later on Maui. These operations came under direct civilian authority of Harold Castle, a local authority on dogs who was well-known to many islanders. The Oahu facility allowed enough space to continue training while the dogs remained in quarantine or until they shipped out. The QMC also obtained the services of Elliot Humphreys, whose experience stemmed from his training programs at Seeing Eye Dogs, Inc., located in Morristown, New Jersey. Humphreys coordinated the training activities and worked with the chief trainer, M.Sgt. Emile Prigge.

At the time, approximately 17,000 dogs resided on the Hawaiian Islands. Veterinarians conducted examinations on 3,259 dogs donated by the islanders. From this pool of dogs, 815 were accepted and 344 completed their training. Most rejections ran the gamut of canine diseases. Filariasis, indigenous to the islands, was found in about 12 percent of the dogs, but veterinarians rejected the animals only if visible signs were present. Dogs were inoculated against canine distemper but not rabies, since this disease did not yet exist in the Hawaiian Islands.

THE DFD REGIONAL CENTERS, each supported by large numbers of enthusiastic volunteers, ensured that a suitable number of dogs would be available for enlistment. Widespread publicity of the dog recruitment campaign meant that practically every dog owner in the United States had at least some knowledge of the civilian agency and what it was doing. The DFD considered all dog acquisitions as gifts, and there was no guarantee that the dogs would be returned to their owners at the conclusion of hostilities.

The dogs were returned only if found unsuitable for training. Volunteers conducted preliminary physicals and checked that the dogs met the initial military specifications. Prospective donors filled out a basic questionnaire, giving physical characteristics, health record, and whether the dog displayed any gun or storm shyness. Just about any dog was accepted during the early days, despite breed. Physically, they needed to weigh between fifty-five and eighty-five pounds, with a shoulder height of twenty-three to twenty-eight inches. At first, dogs one to five years in age were accepted; this was later amended to fourteen months to three and one half years.

Army veterinarians processed the dogs on arrival: blood and fecal tests, rabies and distemper inoculations, and worming if required. Dogs found to be infected with leptospirosis (a highly contagious disease) were destroyed immediately. Parasitic infections—or even contagious diseases, such as canine distemper—were treated and the dog was held until recovery. Dogs received a rabies vaccination and were dipped to control external parasites. All dogs that passed the examination were placed in a quarantine kennel for twenty-one days.

The dogs that were deemed acceptable were tattooed on the left ear with a serial number for identification instead of being given dog tags, as their human counterparts were. This tattooing process is known as the Preston brand system and is also used with horses and mules. This system makes it possible to tattoo 4,000 dogs with a single letter and a combination of numbers.[8] Since the quartermaster general estimated the possible procurement of 125,000 dogs for the war effort, this would be the only suitable system for tracking the animals. Upon a dog's final acceptance, the War Department issued a certificate to the donor signed by the quartermaster general that read: "Appreciation is expressed for your patriotic action donating your dog ___ for use in connection with the Armed Forces of the United States."

With the many breeds first accepted, a large number of dogs failed physicals conducted by army veterinarians, even after the preliminary examination by the DFD. About fifteen hundred dogs died or were destroyed due to physical impairments or disease, and another thousand were destroyed because of temperament. This was all done with the owners' consent. But in retrospect, not every donation could be deemed patriotic. It is not known how many dogs were given up by their owners simply because the owners could not afford to keep them or because their behavior at home made them undesirable pets.

Still, spirited Americans who wholeheartedly felt that a member of their family was joining the army donated thousands of dogs. This caused a problem that the QMC had not anticipated as letters began pouring in to each center asking about a donated pet. In an effort to stem the flood of mail, the war dog reception and training centers issued a form letter to each owner. The letter did little to stop the flow of mail and Christmas cards to the new recruits. Officially, the QMC issued no further statements, but handlers stationed overseas often wrote to the former owners, keeping them appraised of their dogs' actions within the limits of the censors. The QMC form letter read:

Clyde Porter Jr., of Texas, hands over his dog to Sgt. Bill Bryant in this publicity shot for Dogs for Defense. Thousands of patriotic citizens donated their dogs during the war. *(National Archives)*

We are happy to advise you that your dog, with name, brand number, and breed as follows, has arrived at this Depot in good condition:

At this time, we are not able to predict your dog's adaptability to the rigors of Army training.

You will, of course, understand why the interests of military secrecy will best be served if further information is withheld from this point forward.

Thanking you for your generous donation at the time of this national emergency, I am,

(Signature of Commanding Officer)

According to the Army Technical Manual 10–396 (July 1, 1943) thirty-two breeds and crosses were accepted.[9] In a few months the army realized that particular breeds were more suited to specific jobs, but no consideration seems to be attributed to purebreds. Within a few months the army shortened the preferred list to eighteen breeds. Late in 1944 the army began to prefer seven breeds: German shepherd, Doberman pinscher, Belgian sheepdog, collie, Siberian husky, malamute, and Eskimo dog. Several crossbreeds could also be taken from within this group. The army also understood the problem that arose from unspayed bitches, and it finally issued the following taciturn order: "It has been determined that the spaying of bitches is a military necessity and to be in the best interest of the military service."

Dogs for Defense eventually accepted the voluntary contribution of approximately 40,000 dogs in a two-year period. After the preliminary examination by DFD volunteers, about 18,000 of these dogs arrived at the training and reception centers. Of these, nearly 8,000 failed initial examinations due to improper size, health, or temperament. The dedication of these civilian volunteers truly exemplified the patriotic spirit of Americans during World War II. Without the efforts of DFD volunteers, it is doubtful that the Quartermaster Corps alone could have launched a military dog program on the same scale from scratch. Obviously dogs were just a small component within the arsenal of democracy. The payoff for these labors would surface as the United States began to take an offensive posture in the war.

GUARDING THE HOME FRONT

Military commanders viewed the potential invasion of the continental United States by either the Germans or Japanese as a remote possibility. Germany was already fighting a war on two fronts, and the Japanese were overextended in the Pacific and China. Still, there remained a large amount of Axis submarine activity on both coasts, and the sinking of some merchant ships could be spotted from land, making civilians living along both coasts a jittery bunch.

A possible threat emerged that saboteurs could easily be dropped off by submarine in remote coastal areas. The threat became fact on June 13, 1942, as four Nazi saboteurs landed on Long Island. A few days later a U-boat dropped off four more agents on Florida's east coast.[10] Many people also recalled that back in 1916 German agents had destroyed ammunition supplies stockpiled on Black Tom Island in New York Harbor. All these events helped to establish the need for proper beach security.

The protection of the nation's coastline came under the joint jurisdiction of the Coast Guard, the army, the navy, and the Federal Bureau of Investigation. Even though some foot patrols were already in place, they were soon augmented by additional men, horses, boats—and, of course, dogs. The army conceded early on that it would be impossible to place sentry guards at a respectable distance across the thousands of miles of shoreline. The first suggestion for the possible employment of dogs occurred just seventeen days after the first Nazi landing. Writing in the *New York Times*, Lt. Comdr. McClelland Barclay, United States Naval Reserve, and a Long Island resident, stated:

> The Amagansett section of Long Island is marked by a great number of foggy nights, fogs so thick that it is impossible to see more than six feet. It is a well-known fact that in this type of weather the sense of smell and hearing become much more acute and dogs are the type of animal that can take advantage of this to the greatest degree.
>
> If dogs were placed in shelters along the beaches every one-fourth of a mile they could hear any sound whatever within that range. One Coast Guardsman could easily cover three miles of beach by this method and his chief duty would be feeding and caring for the dogs.

Unless we adopt something of this sort for our defense it will be very difficult to prevent the landings of enemy agents at all points of our coastline. Our coastline is so long that we would have to erect a solid line of men to guard it. This is, of course, impossible.[11]

Barclay's reasoning, although flawed and simplistic, was based in sound reasoning: Dogs could displace an inordinate amount of human sentries, freeing them for other jobs. Less than a month later, on July 25, 1942, a Coast Guard directive announced: "These beach patrols are not intended as a military protection of our coastline, as this is the function of the Army. The beach patrols are more in the nature of outposts to report activities along the coastline and not to repel hostile armed units."[12]

The first beach patrols using dogs took place at the end of August 1942. In the beginning, coastguardsmen received their training directly from the army at the Front Royal War Dog Training and Reception Center. The Coast Guard soon established three training centers along the East Coast: Widener Kennels at Elkins Park, Pennsylvania; Hilton Head, South Carolina; and Curtis Bay, Maryland. Other smaller kennels and training facilities sprouted up on both the east and west coasts to fill local demand.

The Coast Guard worked directly with the army and Dogs for Defense to procure a sufficient number of dogs for patrol duties. Within a year, over 1,800 dogs patrolled beaches throughout the United States. Almost all of the eighteen approved breeds, and then some, participated on patrols, with the German shepherd regarded as the best suitable breed. In a short time, the Coast Guard had more trained handlers than the army for sentry duty. By the end of the war, 2,662 coastguardsmen, known as "coasties," had received training as handlers by both the army and within their own training camps.[13] Ten coastal districts were established, and beach patrols covered nearly fifty thousand miles of shoreline. Depending on the terrain, patrols were comprised of sailors on horses or accompanied by dogs in jeeps or on boats. Since each district or-

A coastguardsman and his German shepherd on shore patrol during the war. The Coast Guard employed over two thousand dogs to secure our nation's coastline. *(National Archives)*

ganized its patrols according to its own needs based on the local climate and topography, the activity of sentry and attack dogs varied accordingly.

At first glance, beach patrols appeared to be easy duty– walking along a deserted beach on a warm summer night framed by the light of the moon. But the Coast Guard had to provide patrols around-the-clock, year-round, in every type of weather. This could mean subzero temperatures along the rocky Maine coast or a hot sweaty walk along a mosquito-infested marsh in Louisiana. Regardless of the inhospitality of the terrain or weather, patrols needed to be made.

There was no formal standardized procedure for the use of dogs by the Coast Guard. Most of the training involved two handlers for each dog, beginning with the basic commands such as "Sit," "Down," "Heel," and "Get him." During the attack phase of the training, well-padded Coast Guard personnel acted as "aggravators," shouting and waving sticks as handlers

Many dogs were provided with canvas boots to protect the pads of their feet from coral and seashells. *(National Archives)*

taught their dogs to go after them unleashed. If the aggravator carried a pistol, the dog was taught to seize the arm holding the weapon. The dog always "won" these battles—of course they were also taught to disengage from the enemy and guard the "prisoner" after being called off.

During training, both handlers walked side-by-side with the dogs, but on actual patrols this was seldom done. Sometimes a single handler worked the dog, and in other cases a second man, armed with an M-1 carbine or perhaps a Thompson submachine gun accompanied the pair. District commanders, responsible for organizing local patrols, soon found out that this combination often reduced the effectiveness of the dog while on patrol. As the rifleman followed the pair, the dog naturally turned to alert to him. If the handler kept correcting the dog, who was obviously doing his job, the animal naturally became confused when suspicious persons were in the area. On crowded beaches many aggressive dogs soon became quite docile. Although it was not permitted for anyone to pat or touch the dog, the patrol teams usually relented over a period of time. The snarling attack dog wound up being detrained in only a couple of weeks.

No planned enemy invasion ever took place, of course, and there were no further known cases of saboteurs being landed by submarine. Dogs did alert to several fires in beachside warehouses, and there were some reports that potential arsonists were captured, many of them characterized as German or Japanese and no doubt part of the wartime propaganda program. In several cases, dogs went for help when their handlers became ill or were injured while on duty. And a curly-coated retriever named Dipsy-Doodle helped to recover several bodies after a merchant vessel was sunk off Long Island.[14] Thousands of dog patrols were conducted during the war, punctuated only occasionally by an exciting event to break the boredom.

The threat to the nation's coastline decreased proportionately as the country achieved more victories in the Pacific and in Europe. By the beginning of 1944, no thought at all was given to any invasion, and even the idea that spies and saboteurs would come ashore soon disappeared. Orders were issued on May 10, 1944, to begin the official demobilization of all dog and horse patrols. Several districts had already begun to cut back significantly on dogs a few months earlier. The Coast Guard ultimately became the largest procurer of dogs from the army, with a peak population of 3,649. Most dogs were returned to Fort Robinson, Nebraska, and then processed into the army or demilitarized and returned to civilians. The Coast Guard also closed each of its dog training centers. Captain A. M. Martinson, chief of the Coast Guard Beach Patrol Division, stated:

> . . . the change of policy does not, as some have surmised, reflect any lessening of the demand for strong, aggressive dogs. It simply reflects changed conditions in this global war. The danger to our coasts has been lessened. Fewer dogs are needed for beach patrol. With the emphasis now on offensive rather than defensive tactics, more dogs are needed for scouting and other work, and training

for this can best be done by the rapidly expanding K-9 Corps centers of the Army.[15]

The disbanding of the home front dog patrols meant that personnel were now available for other duties. In mid-1944, the War Department directed the Coast Guard to make available eight trainers to help establish a sentry dog program in China. The detachment left for Chungking along with twenty-three dogs and several specialists in horsemanship. Not only did they have to deal with the language barrier, they also soon realized that few Chinese were interested in using the dogs. The detachment was specifically delegated to train about five hundred members of the Nationalist Chinese Army, obviously for the impending fight with Mao's Communists. The Chinese Nationalists never adopted a formal war dog program, and their lack of enthusiasm during the training, and the rout of Chiang Kai-shek's forces in the next few years, doomed the entire project. It is interesting to note that the sending of coastguardsmen to China to furnish sentry dog training is just another important indicator of how valuable the military considered a properly trained dog.

CAT ISLAND

Cat Island was a natural environment for training military dogs involved with scouting, casualty location, and communications. Putting the name aside, the island provided a jungle-type setting similar to the Pacific islands then held by the Japanese. The island also provided enough isolation and security for the army to embark on a new experiment: assault dogs.

Only eight miles south of Gulfport, Mississippi, the small island is about seven miles long and six miles wide, dotted with scrub oak, palmetto palm trees, and marsh grass. Fine white sand covers the beaches, which are separated in places by swamps that extend inland. Unlike other training facilities, Cat Island was to operate under the aegis of the Army Ground

Forces (AGF) and not the Quartermaster Corps Remount Division. But because the island was privately owned, the AGF first needed to secure a lease on the property.

The idea of using dogs to attack and kill the enemy actually began with a civilian Swiss national named Walter B. Pandre,* a resident of Santa Fe, New Mexico. A former Swiss army officer, Pandre wrote to the War Department in June 1942 proposing that the army train dogs to attack Japanese positions. His idea was that packs of dogs could rout the enemy or at least cause so much disruption in his ranks that his position could easily be taken by normal means. The army considered the idea sound enough to investigate and brought Pandre from Santa Fe to Washington, D.C., for a consultation meeting with staff officers from the Operations Division.[16]

An eccentric and consummate salesman, Pandre outlined his ambitious plan. After initial training, he proposed that the army secure twenty thousand to thirty thousand dogs. Besides assault training, he would also help to oversee the establishment of scout and trailing dogs, stretcher bearers, and casualty locators. These services were not donated, since Pandre insisted on a captain's rate of pay during his employment. Overseeing the project on Cat Island was Lt. Col. A. R. Nichols from the AGF. Nichols, impressed at first with Pandre based on their conversations and Pandre's qualifications and background, came to feel that the man was too optimistic about what could be accomplished in a short period of time. This relationship deteriorated throughout their time together on the island and culminated with serious allegations being raised by Pandre against the officer.

The first order of business sent Pandre to the war dog center at Front Royal, Virginia, in September to view the QMC approach to training sentry and scout dogs. Upon arrival he checked on the quantity, quality, and breed of dogs to launch the experiment. The AGF supplied him with a list of available handlers, but the civilian trainer immediately dismissed most

---

*Name changed.

of them as unsuitable.[17] Shortly thereafter, things went even sourer. Pandre arrived at Cat Island totally unprepared for the primitive conditions and immediately began to badger Lieutenant Colonel Nichols. Nichols wanted the program to start by October 15, and finish ninety days later. Pandre began spouting his requirements for kennels, horses, food rations, and a long list of strange-sounding training equipment.

Pandre then returned to Front Royal along with Nichols to inspect the available dogs and men for the experiment. Pandre's requirements, which differed slightly from those of the QMC, allowed only dogs between one and a half and two years of age. Ideally there would be ten dogs from each of the following breeds: greyhound, Irish or Russian wolfhound, staghound, Airedale, German police dog [German shepherd], mastiff, giant schnauzer, and foxhound. He preferred that the foxhounds not be trained on wild game and be of the American black-and-tan strain. Nichols also pushed for bloodhounds, as he believed them to be the best dogs for tracking purposes.

After reviewing almost four hundred dogs, Pandre considered only a dozen suitable for training, none of them as assault weapons. On this point, Nichols questioned him further, and Pandre said that perhaps nine (five Great Danes and four German shepherds) might be suitable for assault dogs. Pandre then stated (the first of his many excuses) that to successfully complete the mission, perhaps the army should consider a breeding program. Nichols immediately told him that it would take too long and if that were the only option then the entire experiment would have to be abandoned.

Sensing that he might have overstepped his bounds, Pandre said he would make do with what he had at Front Royal. But to properly carry out the experiment, "live bait" would be needed. In other words, the experiment required people whom the dogs could be trained to attack and "kill." Nichols was particularly concerned with this aspect of the program and sent a secret telegram to Major Kimmel at the Army War College in Washington, D.C., stating:

WHAT KIND OF LIVE BAIT ARE WE GOING TO GET LET ME KNOW AS EARLY AS POSSIBLE AS THE TYPE WILL ALTER THE KIND OF FACILITIES REQUIRED FOR THAT. PLEASE VOID ANY ARAB SOLDIERS IF IT IS HUMANLY POSSIBLE TO DO SO. SECONDLY THEY ARE HIGHLY UNDESIRABLE BECAUSE WE HAVE TO HOUSE THEM AND TREAT THEM THE SAME AS OUR TRAINERS AND WHITE SOLDIERS AND PRIMARILY THERE'S THE CHANCE OF AN ACCIDENT WHICH WOULD BE DAMN HARD TO COVER UP AND KEEP A SECRET IF ONE OF THEM HAS TO BE HOSIPATALIZED [*sic*]. (YOU BETTER TEAR THIS LETTER UP AND EAT IT). THE FIRST CHOICE IS PRISONERS AND THE SECOND CHOICE IS ALLIENS [*sic*] *PREFERABLY WITHOUT FAMILIES IN THIS COUNTRY.*[18]

Pandre leaned harder on Nichols and asked for twenty-four Japanese-American soldiers, since the dogs would no doubt be deployed to the Pacific. This request posed serious difficulties, and Nichols, Kimmel, and everyone else involved in the project felt that American prisoners of war could face severe repercussions if word leaked out. The army relented and twelve Japanese-American volunteers were flown from Camp McCoy in Wisconsin to New Orleans under conditions of extreme secrecy on November 3.[19]

Other altercations between Pandre and Nichols soon surfaced on the island. Pandre, as part of the training, used electric shocks and bullwhips and even tied some dogs behind horses and dragged them along the beach or had them fight for food in the sand along the beaches. Nichols thought these methods were not only disgusting but brutal and forbade many of them. Pandre complained that this interference was jeopardizing the entire project. The assault dog project was beginning to bog down, and new "competition" also arrived on the island.

Master Sergeant John Pierce, an army dog trainer from California, arrived to help Nichols with the project. Pierce brought his own dog, a grandson of Rin Tin Tin, and also purchased two mixed-breed dogs locally. Two Japanese-American soldiers worked with Pierce and trained all three dogs for assault work. Pierce's dogs would scout the enemy's location and then attack only on command and with a ferocity that Pandre could not achieve with his dogs, working in packs. Pierce's position was that a man could control no more than two dogs at a time.

The friction between Pandre and Pierce was intense. Pierce, the newcomer, managed to accomplish in just a couple of weeks what the entire project had been trying to do for several months.

Pandre pushed on with an assault dog program that was disintegrating around him. Training continued and a demonstration was held on January 12, 1943, for officers from the AGF. Attending was Colonel Ridgely Gaither, who characterized the event as "somewhat of a vaudeville animal act." Pandre even led the dogs to the heavily padded Japanese-American volunteers, prompting Gaither to remark, "There was no apparent ferocity or intent on the part of the dog to do any bodily harm. It was simply part of a routine."[20]

Based on the demonstration and Nichols's observations, it was decided that the idea of assault dogs working in packs was not practical. Nichols verbally informed Pandre, and Kimmel shot off a telegram stating that his services were no longer required as of February 1. He pleaded for another "show," and Nichols reluctantly complied.

This demonstration, similar to the earlier one, did not impress anyone. Nichols stated, "In my opinion it [the demonstration] would be convincing to a person without knowledge of both tactics and dogs. To me the performances of the animals with one exception appeared artificial and forced and with one exception I do not believe I saw anything that could be developed in something of military value." Nichols's exception was the trailing hounds, called scout dogs by the QMC, and that program was already well under way.

Pandre flew into a rage and left the island with the intention of going to Washington, D. C. There he made allegations to Nichols's superiors that the experiment had been sabotaged and threatened to take his case to the American people, the War Department, and even the president of the United States. After questioning Nichols about the allegations and dismissing them, Major Kimmel wrote in his report, "It is believed that Mr. Pandre is extremely eccentric and potentially dangerous subversively. It is believed advisable to acquaint the FBI with his actions and attitude and request that he be placed under surveillance if deemed necessary."[21]

Had the AGF recognized the character of the man months earlier, it would have saved labor and supplies and improved the health and well-being of many dogs. The AGF must also share the blame since they allowed this experiment to continue. The army had no business attempting to train dogs to attack fortified enemy positions, something that had not been done for hundreds of years. Fortunately this would be the first and last dog-training program the Army Ground Forces would launch during World War II.

SEVERAL MONTHS LATER, after the departure of the assault dogs, a detachment of the 828th Signal Pigeon Replacement Company began its own exercises. An experimental program attempted to team messenger dogs with carrier pigeons. The pigeons provided communication between the main camp, on the western part of the island, and the advanced training bivouac, four miles away to the east. Simulating actual battle conditions, the training program had dogs carry pigeons to isolated positions that could not be reached by vehicle or on foot. Signal Corps personnel designed a special carrier so that a messenger dog could easily transport two pigeons with relative ease. In an emergency, individual birds could be carried over short distances in cardboard shell casing covers.

The dog and pigeon combination proved successful and feasible, offering another communication alternative for troops in battle. The toughest problem to overcome was not the severe summer heat and humidity but the mosquitoes. Army personnel, pigeons, and dogs all suffered from the annoying insects. Mosquitoes attacked the pigeons around their eyes and legs. A tightly woven screen mesh was incorporated into their cages to prevent the birds from being bitten. Little could be done for the men or the dogs.

Training for dogs at this specialized location leveled off early in 1944. Most of the exercises conducted on the island were experimental in nature, and because of the poor conditions prevalent on the island and its lack of facilities, the army did not attempt to train dogs there in any large numbers. To consolidate the training centers across the country, the camp officially closed on July 15, 1944.

MARINE DEVILDOGS

In one way, the Marines had a slight edge over the army in the tactical use of war dogs. In chapter 24 of the 1935 publication *Small Wars Operations*, author Col. Victor F. Bleasdale states, "Dogs on Reconnaissance: Dogs have been employed to indicate the presence of a hidden enemy, particularly ambushes."

The author later stated that this passage was inserted because it was believed that dogs could participate in jungle warfare and this would help to promote the idea. The concept first developed in the 1920s, when a Marine Corps officer serving in Garde d'Haiti trained a dog to work point. By leading patrols through the jungle, the dog could alert the men to any possible ambushes by bandits. Besides this one venture, the Marines would not adopt any war dog program, albeit an experimental one, officially until November 26, 1942.

This followed the offensive operations of landings on Guadalcanal, which began on August 7, 1942. Dense jungle and vegetation made it particularly difficult to clear out pockets of hidden enemy positions. Even though Marines are experienced in jungle warfare, their losses due to ambushes and snipers were particularly high. Ranking officers also realized that Guadalcanal comprised just one island operation in a chain that extended all the way to Japan. The "experiment" began with a letter by the commandant of the Marine Corps to the commanding general of the training center at New River, North Carolina (designated Camp Lejeune on December 20, 1942). It stated in part the commandant's wish to "inaugurate a training program for dogs for military employment when personnel and material become available."[22]

During the fall of that year, one officer and nineteen enlisted men were undergoing cross-service training with the army at Fort Robinson. They were expected back in North Carolina by the end of December accompanied by thirty-eight dogs. At Fort Washington, Maryland, four enlisted men began training with two messenger dogs and were expected to be finished by the middle of January 1943.[23] An additional twenty dogs were acquired from Roslyn Terhune of the Doberman Pinscher Club of America. They received basic obedience training in Baltimore and then proceeded to Camp Lejeune at the end of January.

A key aid in the recruitment of war dogs would be the Doberman Pinscher Club of America, which supplied dogs along with other breeds from the Dogs for Defense organization. An equal number of German shepherds were also used, but the Doberman is the breed most often associated with the Marines. The term *Devildogs* actually originated with the German army that opposed the Marines in the 2nd Division in 1918 during World War I. The fighting tenacity of the American Marines prompted the Germans to regard them as "devil dogs." This term eventually migrated to the Dobermans that the Marines used during World War II.

The Marine Corps dictated to civilians donating dogs that "the owner must relinquish title of the dog as an outright gift without any restricting clauses." Even though there was no guarantee as to the disposition of the dog after its service was terminated, the Corps did ask prospective donors if they desired the return of their animals once their services were no longer required. The Corps then followed standard indoctrination procedures similar to those of the army regarding isolation, identification, and record keeping. Dogs acquired from the army retained their Preston brand number. Those dogs that the Marines obtained directly from civilians were tattooed with a serial number begining with 1.[24]

The Devildogs received promotions based on their length of service. The ranking system promoted a dog after three months to private first class. Thereafter ranks were issued on an annual basis; one year, corporal; two years, sergeant; three years, platoon sergeant; four years, gunner sergeant; five years, master gunner sergeant. Marines also provided a discharge certificate detailing the dog's separation due to expiration of enlistment, medical reasons, killed in action, died, destroyed, or simply unsuitable for the work at hand. Taking the process one step further, an honorable discharge regarded character as outstanding, excellent, or very good. Dogs that posed continual behavior problems faced a dishonorable discharge. These provisions were not simply public relation devices but were part of a greater plan of instilling an esprit de corps within the war dog platoons.

Captain Jackson H. Boyd commanded the initial training group at Camp Lejeune, occupying a former Civilian Conservation Corps camp composed of about two square miles of varied terrain. The first group of dogs, thirteen Dobermans, was formed in January 1943. Contrary to popular belief, the Doberman pinscher did not become the official dog of the Marines.[25] Since the Doberman Pinscher Club of America secured a large number of dogs for the Marines, the initial emphasis was placed on that breed. Also, the Marines thought the Dobermans could handle the heat of the tropics much better than the long haired breeds. But the Corps made it a policy not to endorse any breed and even declined to participate in dog shows, much to the chagrin of the Doberman Pinscher Club officers.

Some of the first dogs trained were sentry dogs, but because the Marine Corps is strictly a combat organization, it was felt that time should not be wasted on training dogs unless that training contributed to directly killing the enemy or to reducing Marine casualties. In the early part of 1943, with the 1st Marine Division still fighting on Guadalcanal, it was determined to train scout and messenger dogs only as part of a fourteen-week course.

As with the army earlier, the Corps had its share of problems with the first batch of trainers. Typically, these personnel had trained dogs in civilian life or in police work and had little appreciation for combat operations. It was quickly determined that the most useful dog required a good, capable, combat Marine handler. The best person was one who could scout and patrol on his own and simply used the dog as an extension of his own talents. Captain Boyd understood the value dogs offered when he said:

> The dogs are not to be considered as a new weapon; they have not replaced anyone or anything. They have simply added to security by their keen perception, and their use should be limited to situations where that increased perception is of service. Where a man can function satisfactorily by his own intelligence and perception, the dog is superfluous.
>
> On the other hand, it has been found that the dog's care and feeding present a very minor problem and add little to the burden which already exists for an outfit in the field. The dog can thrive on the biscuits and canned meat in the field ration. He needs no shelter beyond that provided for a man, and a dog can safely drink any water not deliberately poisoned. His medical care parallels a man's.[26]

Boyd made a key statement when he introduced the doctrine that dogs were not a new weapon. Unfortunately this was not always heeded, and all too often handlers and dogs were thrust into positions beyond their capabilities. Boyd would also find that keeping and maintaining dogs engaged in combat within a jungle environment would be a bit more difficult than tossing down a biscuit or opening up a can of C rations.[27]

Both scout and messenger dogs received fourteen weeks of intensive training, during which either the handler or the dog could be rejected if considered subpar in performance. The dogs could not spend too many hours of each day training, because it was found that this actually inhibited their development. Dogs, like people, needed rest and relaxation on a daily basis; too much training had a negative impact. Therefore, the handlers spent half their training period with the dogs and the balance learning the duties and rigors of being a scout-sniper.

Upon the completion of training at Camp Lejeune, both men and dogs were formed into squads consisting of six men, three scout dogs, and one messenger dog. Three squads comprised a war dog platoon consisting of one officer, sixty-five

A messenger dog goes beneath barbed wire during a demonstration. With proper training, these versatile canines were rarely prevented from delivering their dispatches. *(National Archives)*

men, and eighteen scout and eighteen messenger dogs. An additional six men provided relief for handlers who were wounded or became sick, and a single platoon sergeant managed the platoon on a day-to-day basis. The platoon was assigned to a Marine infantry regiment, and the officer both commanded the platoon and served the regimental staff as an adviser. The platoon could be used whole, but usually it was divided into squads and sent to forward positions that offered the best tactical advantage for the employment of dogs.

The 1st Marine War Dog Platoon left San Diego, California, on June 23, 1943, to enter the ongoing battle in the Pacific as an attachment to the 2nd Marine Raider Regiment (Provisional). Their baptism of fire was near at hand, and within four months they would join their fellow Marines for the invasion of Bougainville, in the Solomon Island chain.

SEARCH AND RESCUE

At the onset of World War II, the United States possessed only fifty sled dogs that were stationed in Alaska. The Quartermaster Corps then recruited another forty dogs that had participated in Admiral Byrd's Antarctic exploration in 1939, dispersing them to Baffin Island and Greenland immediately following the attack on Pearl Harbor. The determination by the army to use sled dogs was a simple decision, unlike making a case for sentry and scout dogs. They could often travel where aircraft, horses, or vehicles could not, and the army had years of experience with them. Ferrying aircraft to Russia and Great Britain dictated that northerly Arctic routes would be developed. Aircraft would cross long stretches of desolate and snow-covered land masses, and losses due to weather or mechanical failure were to be expected. Sled dog teams would be

David Armstrong with sled dogs, nicknamed the "Cream Team," after making a training film for the Signal Corps. The army believed that all-white sled dog teams provided suitable camouflage for possible commando operations. *(David Armstrong)*

the only practical method for retrieving crashed aircraft crew members.

In the fall of 1942, the Quartermaster Corps began an aggressive training program to provide sled and pack dogs for search and rescue under the aegis of the North Atlantic Transport Command. The sled dogs would also support the 10th Mountain Infantry during cold-weather operations. A War Dog Reception and Training Center was established at Camp Rimini, near Helena, Montana. This facility was situated at the site of a closed Civilian Conservation Corps camp and was ideally suited for specialized cold-weather training.

According to David Armstrong, a sled driver and trainer, the camp was small and the dogs outnumbered the men. "We had about 150 personnel under the command of Major E. J. Purfield and about 750 sled and 150 pack dogs," he stated. "Most sled dogs were Siberians, Malamutes, and Athabasca landing huskies. The pack dogs were St. Bernards, Newfoundlands, Great Pyrenees, and a few mixes, mostly donated to the army."[28] Besides Camp Rimini, sled dog training also took place at Presque Isle, Maine, and at small army camps in Alaska and Newfoundland. Civilian-owned Chinook Kennels in Wonalancet, New Hampshire, also provided sled and pack dogs under contract with the army and supported limited training facilities.[29]

The army opted to purchase most of its sled and pack dogs rather than rely on civilian donations. They would be dispersed to several specific theaters of operation: Alaska and the Aleutians, the Northwest Service Command (Canada), Newfoundland, and Greenland. Each location provided peculiar problems for the dogs involved, many of them diet related. Wartime shortages presented challenges in the development of dog food that was nutritionally balanced and palatable. Often, each location around the globe used various foods and supplements simply based upon whatever was available locally.

Alaskan dogs were probably the best fed, as the veterinary service there developed a canned dog food comprised of ground horsemeat and herring. A relatively short distance away, at Camp Prairie in Alberta, Canada, a major problem

Two huskies are lowered down the side of Mount Washington in New Hampshire and across a ravine during a training exercise. *(National Archives)*

developed with the dogs' diet. A serious outbreak of taeniasis, a potentially deadly intestinal parasite, occurred in a group of thirty army dogs. This problem was soon traced to the raw rabbit meat fed to the dogs. Once this practice was terminated, the problem disappeared.[30]

The dispersing of sled and pack dogs began in 1942, with Stephensville, Newfoundland, receiving 35 dogs and the 3rd Infantry Division, based at Harmon Field, Newfoundland, picking up four. Distemper was quite rampant among the civilian dogs at this base, and the veterinary service took the added precaution of vaccinating all animals on an annual basis. In December 1943, 125 dogs were stationed at Sondre Sjrom Fjord in Greenland as part of the Army Air Forces Arctic Search and Rescue Squadron. It is interesting to note that, prior to the fall of 1944, canine distemper and rabies were reportedly nonexistent in Greenland. Unfortunately, once the American dogs arrived, the local canine population acquired the diseases. This information would help to provide minimum guidelines in the future for importing and transporting animals, including their quarantine periods, all around the globe.

By December 1943, all sled dog teams and drivers were shifted to the North Atlantic Wing, Air Transport Command, of the Army Air Corps. Under the command of Col. Norman Vaughan, the teams were assigned the job of organizing search-and-rescue groups to recover downed pilots and cargo. Vaughan had quite a bit of experience working with sled dogs and had participated in Admiral Byrd's expeditions to the South Pole.[31]

Camp Rimini closed in the middle of 1944, and the men and dogs were transferred to the Western Remount Division, Fort Robinson, Nebraska. After the camp's closure, several drivers shipped out to Newfoundland and immediately began the freighting of radio station equipment to the top of Table Mountain at Cape Ray for the Army Signal Corps, to be oper-

Siberian huskies could carry a tremendous amount of weight. This dog is being trained to carry a .30-caliber machine gun. *(National Archives)*

ated by the Royal Canadian Air Force. With steep terrain and no roads, sled dog teams provided the only transportation.

But the bread and butter of the sled drivers remained search and rescue. "Unfortunately," says Armstrong, "all too often, our job was simply to recover bodies from crashed aircraft." By March 1944, the Newfoundland team consisted of five men, eighteen sled dogs, and five pack dogs. That same month, a C-54 transport plane inbound for Harmon Field crashed. Search-and-rescue teams brought out the entire crew safely, along with the cargo. Later, the sled dog teams returned to salvage parts of the aircraft. By the end of the war about one hundred aircrew members had been recovered by sled dog teams.[32]

The army also envisioned other uses for the dogs and their drivers. Some commando operations were planned for Norway, and military commanders, unfamiliar with dogs, believed dogs could offer silent transportation and remain undetected during these operations. The sled drivers were quick to point out that the dogs left tracks, made a lot of noise, and ate a tremendous amount of food—some of which would later be deposited on the snow. The idea was never brought up again.

However, in February 1945, the largest recorded movement of dogs into a war zone took place. For over a month, Colonel Vaughan argued for the use of sled dogs in the Battle of the Bulge. Heavy winter snows blanketed the Western Front and Vaughan believed the dog teams would be useful for picking up and returning wounded soldiers to the rear. The idea lingered in Washington for a month before it was finally forwarded to Third Army operations in Europe. That same day a reply came back—"Send the dogs"—signed by Gen. George Patton.[33]

Vaughan assembled 209 dogs and 17 men at Presque Isle, Maine. The men and dogs came from six different northern rescue stations and boarded four C-54 cargo planes for the trip over the Atlantic. Weight was a prime factor as each team, comprised of a driver, nine dogs, two sleds, and a toboggan, checked in at roughly twelve hundred pounds. The planes climbed to twelve thousand feet, where the thinner air made

Because of administrative delays, sled dogs did not arrive in time to participate in the Battle of the Bulge. These dogs, stationed at an airfield in France, await a possible late-winter storm. *(National Archives)*

the dogs sleepy and less likely to fight with each other. The four planes rendezvoused in Greenland and then continued on as one flight to Prestwick, Scotland, bypassing Iceland due to weather. All planes arrived at Orly Field, France, on February 4 and were then assigned to the Twelfth Army Group. The men and dogs were further divided up, with nine dog teams traveling to Spa, Belgium, and thirteen to Hayange, France.

Unfortunately the weather continued mild, and soaking rains began eroding what little snow remained. The dogs were worked at least two hours a day by pulling a sled over the wet grass or hauling coal and wood. The men and dogs were retained until the threat of snow disappeared and were reassembled on March 11 to return home. The sled teams boarded the S.S. *Robin Locksley* and became part of a convoy that would survive five submarine attacks. The ship finally reached Staten Island on March 9, and within a few days all personnel and dogs returned to Presque Isle. Because of delays, the teams never had any opportunity to perform medical evacuations on the Western Front. But the operation had proved that sled teams could be assembled and dispersed quickly when required.[34]

Two huskies and their handler prepare for parachute training in Alaska. *(National Archives)*

The huskies deploy under the same chute. The dogs could be dropped singly or in pairs, depending on the chute's size and on the requirements of the specific search-and-rescue operations. *(National Archives)*

The army would maintain a contingent of sled drivers and dogs based in Alaska after the war. This continued until the mid-1950s, when helicopters began to realize their full potential in search-and-rescue situations. Quietly and with no fanfare, sled drivers and dog teams faced the end of the road for their services.

4.

READY FOR COMBAT

CHIPS

Many army officers questioned the usefulness of the K-9 Corps, acquiescing that dogs might be appropriate for guarding installations in rear areas or at home but believing that they did not belong on the front lines of the modern battlefield. Dogs for Defense argued the case for the use of dogs based on history, but a baptism of fire for the war dogs had yet to prove their worth. Fortunately, success came early and helped to bolster the general concept of the canine program. Had fortunes been reversed, the program might have been derailed or at least stalled. The first major success was directly attributed to Chips, brand number 11A, a member of the first War Dog Detachment sent overseas.[1]

Chips was a mixed-breed German shepherd, husky, and collie, and was donated to the army by Edward J. Wren of Pleasantville, New York. He arrived at the Front Royal War Dog Center in the early part of 1942. Upon completion of the sentry training class he was attached to the 30th Infantry, Third Infantry Division, based at Camp Pickett, Virginia, and was paired with Pvt. John P. Rowell as his handler. Three other dogs—Watch, Pal, and Mena, a bitch that the press dubbed a "K-9 WAC"—comprised the casual detachment.[2]

In October 1942 they departed Newport News, Virginia, as part of the North African invasion fleet and soon landed at the Vichy-held beaches of Fedallah in French Morocco. As the shore batteries opened fire, Mena succumbed quickly to fear from the intense artillery fire, rendering her useless as a war dog. This would be a major complaint of many infantry commanders as dogs first entered service and were not accustomed to the harsh aural environment.

The dogs, trained as sentries and not scouts, accompanied their handlers during the day yet provided basic perimeter defense at night. Although some deaths occurred at the hands of Senegalese and French Colonial troops from nightly infiltrations, no such occurrences were recorded in the areas where canine sentries were posted.

As the French resistance crumbled under continuous assault, the Third Division retired to the coast for a well-deserved rest. The 30th then received orders to provide guard and sentry duty for the Roosevelt-Churchill conference, to be held from January 14 to 24, 1943. Along with the honor guard, the three sentry dogs of the 30th Infantry accompanied their handlers as part of the security contingent. Mena had by this time produced a litter of nine pups, attributed to a dog within the detachment. Some credited Chips, others Watch. This incident was typically cited as the reason behind the decision not to send unspayed bitches overseas. Several of the pups were sent back to the States, and the others were kept as mascots.

Refresher training in amphibious maneuvers continued, not only for the dogs but for the 30th Infantry as a whole. On July 10, 1943, the Third Division landed in Sicily as part of Brig. Gen. George S. Patton's Seventh Army. The landing, the largest amphibious operation up to that time, took place near Licata, on Sicily's southern coast, and was code-named "Beach Blue."

At about 0420, in the early morning light, Rowell and Chips worked inland about three hundred yards toward what appeared to be a small grass-covered hut but was in reality a camouflaged pillbox. A machine gun opened fire and immediately Chips broke loose from Rowell, trailing his leash and running full-steam toward the hut. Moments later, the machine-gun fire stopped and an Italian soldier appeared with Chips slashing and biting at his arms and throat. Three soldiers followed with their arms raised in surrender. Rowell called Chips off and took the four Italians prisoner. What actually occurred in the pillbox is known only by the Italians and, of course, the dog. Chips received a minor scalp wound and displayed powder burns, showing that a vicious fight had taken place inside the hut and that the soldiers had attempted to shoot the dog with a revolver. But the surrender came abruptly, indicating that Chips was solely responsible.

Chips stayed on duty after receiving treatment for his wounds, and later that night he alerted to ten Italian soldiers approaching on a road. Rowell, showing his rifle, took all ten prisoner. The exploits of the war dog soon became well-known throughout the division, and the press seized the opportunity to promote the "hero dog."

On September 9, 1943, Capt. Edward G. Parr recommended that Chips be issued the Distinguished Service Cross. Major General Lucian K. Truscott Jr., 3rd Division commander, decided to waive the regulation prohibiting the issuance of medals to animals. On October 24, 1943, General Order No. 79, issued by Headquarters, 3rd Infantry Division, Reinforced, APO 3, carried the citation for award of the Silver Star for "Chips, 11-A, U.S. Army Dog, Company I, *** Infantry." (For security reasons censors deleted the infantry detachment.) Several weeks later his award for the Purple Heart took place.[3]

The newspapers in the United States, always eager for good news in times of war, related the dog's exploits across the country. They had a field day with the story, detailing the awards, and Dogs for Defense quickly seized the opportunity as a publicity coup, urging more Americans to donate dogs. Chips became the subject of two speeches given in Congress, as even politicians lauded the hero dog.

All this did not go unnoticed by William Thomas, the 1943 national commander of the Military Order of the Purple Heart. Thomas protested in writing to President Roosevelt and the War Department, insinuating that giving an award to a beast denigrated our first president and every American who had received the Purple Heart. Thomas wrote in part, "It decries the high and lofty purpose for which the medal was created." A high school principal in New Rochelle, New York,

Thomas ended on a conciliatory note, stating, "Lest there be the slightest misunderstanding regarding my appreciation for the contribution that our four-footed friends have made and are making to the successful prosecution of the war on the field of battle, it is humbly suggested that a distinct medal be created for the specific purpose of rendering tribute to man's most faithful friend."[4]

Major General J. A. Ulio, adjutant general of the U.S. Army, replied to Thomas on February 4, 1944, with the following:

1. The award of War Department decorations to other than persons, that is, human beings, is prohibited.

2. If it is desired to recognize the outstanding services of an animal or fowl [Ulio is obviously referring to carrier pigeons employed by the Signal Corps], appropriate citation may be published in unit general orders.

Ulio's letter obviously meant he did not want another embarrassing situation to surface in the future and rescinded Chips's decoration awards, ordering that the medals be returned. The idea of creating a specific award or medal for war dogs did not occur, and Dogs for Defense did not pursue the issue of Chips's medal revocation, fearing a publicity backlash. Chips would be the first and last dog decorated (officially) during World War II.[5]

But politics on the home front meant little to the men fighting in Italy. Rowell and a few others fashioned their own medals for the dog and held a private ceremony. As was often the case, no one who ever worked with a dog felt it demeaning to have a medal bestowed upon the animal.

Chips arrived in Italy on September 18, 1943, and participated in both the Naples-Foggia and the Rome-Arno campaigns. While in Italy, General Eisenhower met the dog in person and innocently tried to pet him—Chips promptly nipped the general's hand. By December 1943, the dog began to grow weary and skittish from constant artillery shellfire. A letter to the former owner told him that the dog was being transferred from the front lines to divisional headquarters in the rear for easy sentry duty. On August 15, 1944, Chips arrived in southern France, serving in the French, Rhineland, and Central European campaigns. Eventually, the dog was again transferred to a rear area as a POW sentry for the Military Police. Months would pass, the stress and diet having an accumulating effect on the canine. By October of the following year, with the war now over, it was finally time to go home.

Chips arrived back where he started from, Front Royal, on October 20, 1945. Here the demilitarizing process took place, and with the original owners requesting his return, he

Chips the hero dog, as he appeared in Italy. Chips was the only dog to have been awarded a Purple Heart and a Silver Star (both were later revoked). *(National Archives)*

was discharged on December 10, 1945, after serving nearly three years in the army. The dog was not alone on the railroad trip; he was accompanied by six reporters and photographers.

His home life was a short one. The toll of the war wore heavily on the dog, and with his kidneys already failing, his heart stopped beating on April 12, 1946. Unofficially, he was awarded the Theater Ribbon with the arrowhead (to show an assault landing) and eight battle stars.

Other dogs within Chips's casual detachment and with other units in Europe had similar valiant accomplishments. Silver (A595) alerted to a German attack and then was killed by a hand grenade on February 17, 1945. On March 20, 1945, Peefke (T133) was killed by an enemy hand grenade after alerting to a trip wire attached to three mines. Pal (8M2), who had accompanied Chips for a while, was killed in enemy action on April 23, 1945, in Italy after blocking a shrapnel charge while leading a patrol. In all cases, the men who worked with the dogs honored them, but few other people ever heard of these incidents. This does not diminish Chips's accomplishments at all—being first carries its own special recognition. Ultimately most war dogs are faithful unto death, and this is something that needs to be duly recognized.

FOCUS ON TACTICAL DOGS

Like the war dog program in general, the training of tactical dogs, those who work as scouts and messengers, started as an experiment, with combinations of successes and failures. Qualified trainers were in short supply, the military establishment generally did not understand the value or nature of the dogs, and the AGF had no definite policy for their use. For instance, most people believed that dogs could not be used in the Pacific theater because of the wide range of diseases and parasites prevalent in tropical climates. Also, reports received from the British, with an established tradition of utilizing war dogs, indicated that they had proved unsatisfactory in operations conducted in North Africa during 1942.

The British reported that loud artillery fire scared and

A handler and his German shepherd during cold-weather training during Operation Hailstorm at Camp Hale, Colorado, reaffirm that German shepherds could tolerate both cold and heat extremely well. *(National Archives)*

confused the animals. Messenger dogs in service would fail to complete their missions with the commencement of an artillery barrage. The same held true for scout dogs. But even the British forgot the lessons learned from World War I–that for the dogs to be effective they needed the proper training. Yet, when tactical training began in the United States, dogs were trained only around small-arms fire and were not exposed to the thunderous artillery barrages present at the front.

Still, the British were the best among the Allies in the training of war dogs. The Quartermaster Corps had zero experience with scout and messenger dogs and sought assistance in developing a formal program for the United States. On February 1, 1943, this help came in the form of Capt. John B. Garle, director of the War Dog Training School in Great Britain. Two noncommissioned officers and trained handlers accompanied Garle, along with two messenger dogs and two scout dogs, for their first stop at the war dog training center at Beltsville. Garle's demonstrations proved so successful that the group toured all the training centers in the United States, demonstrating tactical advantages and indoctrinating new trainers in the British techniques.[6] The first group of tactical dogs would be ready for combat within six months.

The army started with the basic instruction for scout dogs, pretty much the same as that for sentries but with more emphasis on getting them used to gunfire. Further training developed the dogs' responses to scenting and hearing the enemy and, of course, not to bark at any time. It must be remembered that the casual detachments already sent out, dogs like Chips and Pal, were sentry dogs, and handlers often experimented and began working patrols with them on point. The QMC was beginning a scout dog program from scratch and, as such, needed to get the dogs into combat, see the results, and then alter the training back home as required.

The first tactical unit trained at Beltsville consisted of six scouts and two messenger dogs, all German and Belgian shepherds.[7] On June 14, 1943, a detachment of six men from the Quartermaster Corps and the dogs departed a freighter from Fort Mason in San Francisco. After arriving in Brisbane, Australia, the detachment transferred to another ship and landed at Port Moresby, New Guinea, on July 29. This would be the first actual test of the efficiency of both scout and messenger dogs for the United States in the war. Since this small complement of men and dogs did not meet the requirements of a full platoon, the army considered them a casual detachment. Several more casual detachments were to follow in both the Pacific and European campaigns before the QMC would constitute more formally organized platoons.

The small detachment first met with the Australian Corps of the Allied New Guinea force, stationed near Nadzab. From there they were air-transported over the Owen Stanley mountains to a small airstrip in Kaiapit. It was here that the Australians began making an advance up the Ramu River Valley to Madang. The reconnaissance patrols using scout and messenger dogs worked continuously and with success, but several problems did surface. The heat and the humidity caused the dogs' feet to swell, and an army veterinarian, located nearby, helped to alleviate the problem. The leather pouches used by the messenger dogs were found to rot rapidly in the humid air, and these were replaced with metal canisters. It was during this time period that the dogs were first subjected to heavy artillery fire, principally Australian twenty-five-pounders, and it was noted that it bothered the dogs for a while. In October the detachment was reassigned to a U.S. Marine Raider regiment operating near Milne Bay. From this staging area, they would eventually move to Finschafen in December and then regroup for the assault on New Britain Island.

Second Lieutenant Robert Johnson, the detachment's senior officer, issued a report on December 6, 1943, of the dogs' performance in New Guinea between July and December. Used in forward areas, Johnson stated, they "had given consistently excellent performance. Japanese personnel could be detected at one thousand yards depending on terrain and wind condition, and were very effective during amphibious landings detecting the enemy on the beach and in undergrowth."[8]

Johnson also reported that the messenger dogs effectively covered distances of sixty to one thousand yards with great speed despite rough terrain. Their chances of getting through were good because of their inherent speed and the fact that dogs naturally presented such a small target. Marines conducted a separate test that involved a race between a man and a dog through the heavy jungle. The dog emerged in four and a half minutes while the soldier followed eleven minutes later.

Like the British before him, Johnson reported that the performance of scout and messenger dogs deteriorated under artillery fire. Another observation was that the dogs and handlers worked at peak efficiency when they were thoroughly familiar with each other. This bonding between handler and dog, once recognized, resulted in a change of army policy. Handlers and dogs were kept together from the early training process throughout their deployment whenever possible. One other critical factor would be the tendency of some dogs to

In Philippine operations, scout dogs worked well in the thick undergrowth but could not be deployed fast enough when needed. *(National Archives)*

bark during the night. Johnson figured better training would eliminate this problem in future combat situations.

The U.S. Sixth Army landed at the Arawe Peninsula, on New Britain's south coast, on December 15, 1943. They were followed by the Marines, who landed at Cape Gloucester, on the northwestern end of New Britain, on December 26, along with the dogs and handlers in the first wave ashore. For the first week, the dogs kept sentry duty as the Marines established a beachhead and seized two landing fields en route to meeting the Sixth Army near Gilnit.

Once again, the handlers and dogs proved themselves by conducting forty-eight patrols in fifty-three days while fighting on New Britain. The patrols accounted for 180 Japanese soldiers killed and 20 captured. All maneuvers were conducted during the day, and the dogs did double duty as sentries at night. These reconnaissance patrols lasted from one to seven days, and a patrol could be as small as four men or as large as a reinforced platoon of two hundred men. The messenger dogs proved to be an added benefit as communications gear proved unreliable in the searing heat and high humidity, with frequent failures caused by tropical downpours.

The success of this first casual detachment should not be overlooked. Had the men and dogs failed, any future use of scout dogs might have been jeopardized. In the record of military K-9 history this detachment sowed the seed for all future operations. Failures can be expected, and indeed there would be many in the future, but this detachment set the standard by which all future operations would be judged.

Several other casual detachments were deployed to the South Pacific area, principally for sentry duties. On March 21, 1943, 120 dogs along with a veterinary detachment arrived in New Caledonia. Subsequently, dogs were also dispersed to Guadalcanal and Espíritu Santo. Much of the work entailed sentry duty at airfields and depot facilities. The efficiency of these sentry dog detachments was rather poor, due mostly to the declining medical condition of the dogs. By November 1943, they were no longer used, just cared for, and the detachment disbanded about a year later.

Veterinary reports indicated several problems with working the dogs in the tropical climate. Most were attributed to heat exhaustion and hookworm infestation. A severe form of canine filariasis, better known today as heartworm, resisted treatment and caused most of the dogs to be euthanized in late 1944 instead of being returned home to the United States.

These first detachments of men and dogs to enter combat represented a pioneering achievement. Mistakes would be made, but the experience enabled the army to adapt training to meet combat requirements. Because the function of these first scout dogs was to provide early silent warning, it took time and experience to learn the basics. Like students in a classroom, few handlers totally understood all the concepts involved in the deployment of the dogs. Wind direction and velocity, heat and humidity, and the concentration of human scent were factors that had to be learned chiefly while on the job.

As more dogs began to deploy overseas, there were other considerations beyond training. For dogs to work effectively they needed the proper food and equipment. The United States did not have an inexhaustible supply of materials, and dogs were fairly low on the pecking order. Still, under the conditions of war the QMC and the Army Veterinary Corps fared well in maintaining the dogs in a healthy condition in battle areas. Many people at the time did not realize how important nutrition for dogs was, often believing that canines could exist on table scraps and other garbage. For a household pet, this may hold true to a certain extent—but such a dog would not be subject to the rigors of sentry duty or combat. The intestinal abuse many canines suffered came from a combination of ignorance, superstition, and lack of nutritional requirements. The same held true for many humans. In Alaska, for instance, many dogs were being fed raw rabbit meat, which caused a serious outbreak of taeniasis, commonly known as tapeworm.

The army veterinarians understood this problem and quickly went to work to develop a program for the proper feeding of dogs and for general enlightenment throughout all the services about its importance. Veterinarians dictated the proper feeding requirements for dogs. The quality and variety of foods varied significantly from within the continental United States (CONUS) to the jungles of the Pacific and to the desert of North Africa. Commercial dog food of the time did not meet daily nutritional requirements, and supplements were required.[9]

By 1943, certain aspects were made clear to handlers, despite the combat situation. Topping the list was water: always available, cool, and replenished daily, with the water dish to be boiled once a month. Meat would be the predominant staple of canines, and one meat readily available was horsemeat. The basic rule of thumb at the time was for a daily ration of one to one and a half pounds of meat for each fifty pounds of dog weight. Condemned horses and mules were tested for glanders, an intestinal contagion, and then slaughtered under veterinary supervision. All horsemeat transported was specifically labeled "Horse Meat for War Dogs Only." Other approved meats included beef, mutton, and well-boned chicken. Expressly forbidden were veal, Spam, raw fish, bacon, canned ham, and pork. Vegetables and cereals were also recommended to balance the meat protein with vitamins and minerals. Well-mashed tomatoes, spinach, carrots, cabbage, string beans, and peas were all used. But even in the best of times some of these foods would be hard to locate, particularly at the front lines and in remote areas. Type C rations, a staple of infantrymen, were then used, supplemented by canned salmon and evaporated milk.

Now that more tactical dogs would be delivered to the field, other conditions also needed to be met. Once concern was the possible use of chemical gases by both the Germans and the Japanese. Clearly this was an issue to be taken seriously based on the use and effects of these gases during World War I.

During World War I, with the advent of phosgene and mustard gas, suitable protection was needed for the dogs participating in the war. At the time a mask was developed for dogs; it was made of eight layers of cheesecloth and was treated with chemicals called Simplexene and Complexene. Eyepieces were manufactured from cellulose acetate and a rubber seal fitted comfortably around the dog's neck. This mask provided protection for about one hour during a gas attack. Nothing was done to improve on this design until 1926, when a similar unit was developed and sent to the chemical officer in the Philippine Department. Since the army had no tactical dogs at this time, no other development work was undertaken.

In April 1940, the Chemical Warfare Service (CWS) asked the Adjutant General's Department about the possible use of dogs in warfare. The CWS received the following reply: ". . . the use of dogs in the theatre of operations was not contemplated."[10] Two years later, the situation changed radically.

The QMC contacted the Chemical Warfare Service in August 1942 and asked it to begin developing a canine gas

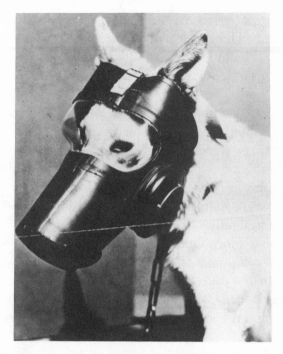

Lassie gets fitted with a gas mask. The M6-12-8 mask weighed slightly over two pounds and could fit about 97 percent of the dogs in service. *(Carlisle Barracks)*

mask. Work started in 1943 at Edgewood Arsenal, Maryland, and resulted in the development of a prototype model designated E.12 R.8. This bulky unit was made from a stiff rubberized canvas that covered the dog's face from the nose to the ears, and a molded plastic eyepiece that could be attached separately. Air entered through a small metal container at the tip of the nose. As the dog exhaled, the air flowed back and exited the mask via two tubes.

The prototype mask had several problems. Most of the weight was up front, making it uncomfortable for the dog and potentially damaging to the filter canister if the dog's head dropped to the ground. Another problem was that the mask would not fit the larger dogs in the army's inventory, including many German shepherds, which outnumbered all other breeds by this time.

This early prototype led to a one-size mask that weighed

A handler places a gas mask on his dog. Tactical dogs could wear the mask for about an hour but were not expected to work with it on. *(National Archives)*

two and one half pounds and could fit 97 percent of the dogs in the army.[11] Designated the M6-12-8, it became standard in August 1944 after an initial production of five hundred units. The mask also had a fixed eyeshield and covered the entire head of the dog. One mask accompanied each tactical dog that was sent overseas. It was not intended that the dog be worked while wearing the mask, but that the mask provide the same level of protection the handler had.

While the mask was under development, it was found that dogs needed training to become accustomed to wearing it. For the first week, trainers had dogs wear the masks for five to fifteen minutes a day and lengthened the duration thereafter.

Precautions were needed to ensure the dogs' health with the mask on during hot weather. Since dogs have few sweat glands, most heat is dissipated through convection, the vaporizing of large amounts of water through the respiratory system—in other words, by heavy breathing with their mouths open. The gas mask severely restricted this means of losing heat, and if not monitored, a dog could easily suffer heatstroke, especially at temperatures greater than eighty-five degrees Fahrenheit. Given the short period of time the CWS had in which to develop a mask, it did quite a remarkable job and came up with a model for all known chemical gases and smokes.[12]

Broadening the tactical roles of dogs sent the QMC off down several other avenues of exploration and research. Recognizing the possibility of chemical warfare, a "gas detection dog" was studied by the Army Veterinary Corps. Little progress was made and the project was soon abandoned. Another experiment harkened back to World War I and the use of Red Cross dogs, now called the "War Casualty Dog."

Once again it seemed desirable for dogs to find wounded men on the battlefield and then report their location. The first test for these casualty locators took place on May 4, 1944, at Carlisle Barracks, Pennsylvania, under the direction of Col. Frank L. Carr, former commander at Fort Robinson. As with most military demonstrations, this one went off without a hitch. The dogs had three months of training and wore a harness emblazoned with a small red cross on each flank, indicating their function. Once a few of these dogs were tested under actual battle conditions, they failed to differentiate casualties, unwounded, and dead personnel. The AGF promptly rejected the dogs and turned them into messengers.[13]

The AGF had more immediate problems than searching for casualties on the battlefield. Japanese-built pillboxes and bunkers on Pacific islands posed a serious threat and were difficult for American soldiers to attack. Artillery and aerial bombardment alone could not guarantee the destruction of these fortifications since many were dug to one story beneath the ground.

A German shepherd participates in a chemical gas exercise. The Red Cross insignia indicates that the dog is a casualty locator. The mask is of an unknown type, probably experimental in nature. *(National Archives)*

Tanks, flamethrowers, and rockets were then the preferred choices of weapons. But not all infantry units had these weapons available to them. This meant that they needed to be attacked in hand assault and with placed charges. Many Americans lost their lives in such attacks, cut down by deadly machine-gun fire.

To help alleviate this situation the New Developments Division, a research-and-development group located at Fort Belvoir, Virginia, suggested that dogs be used. In theory, it was believed that dogs could be trained to attack fortified bunkers with explosives attached to their backs. These charges would be set off by a timer and calculated to explode once the explosive was inside the bunker. For the dogs it would be a one-way suicide run.[14]

Many lower-ranking officers on the front line favored the idea. This should not be considered a callous attitude but the desire to have every possible weapon at their disposal in order to save lives. Higher-ranking officers viewed the problem differently and could see numerous supply problems with such a program. Still, it sounded like a good idea for jungle operations, and during November 1943 Lt. Col. Daniel S. Spangler, 220th Armored Engineers, sent a secret memorandum stating in part, "The dog-placed charge is desired if it works. It is a special purpose weapon which might be the only means [to destroy a bunker] in certain places."

The training of the bunker dogs took place at Fort Belvoir. A small supply of dogs was made available by the Quartermaster Corps for both training and tests to be conducted around fortified concrete bunkers. Training was rather easy and superficial since it only required the dog to carry a satchel charge with a timer to the bunker, enter it, and sit. In actual combat, the dog would probably be dead from enemy gunfire before the charge even exploded. These tests used only simulated explosives, and no canine deaths occurred during this period.

Several problems surfaced immediately during testing. In a few cases a dog turned around and headed back for his master. At the front, carrying live charges, this could lead to disastrous consequences. Also, under actual combat conditions, several bunkers would probably be located within 150 yards of each other. Some of these could already be occupied by friendly troops, and the dog might inadvertently run to one of them.

Either for security reasons or to soothe their own consciences, army personnel began to refer to these suicide dogs as "demolition wolves." The project garnered enthusiastic support from Col. E. M. Daniels, chief of the Remount Branch, who felt that this special-purpose "weapon" should be made available immediately.[15] Daniels never consulted with representatives from Dogs for Defense, who would ultimately

supply the "demolition wolves." There was an obvious reason—DFD would never approve of such a project, even during
times of war. What the American public felt can only be spec-
ulation. Suicide, even in battle, has no place in American cul-
ture. The army did make note of possible public backlash
against such a plan if word got out, and the whole project was
kept secret during its short life span. The idea of American suicide dogs probably emanated from captured German papers
that documented Russian dog attacks upon their tanks. It remained to be seen under the given circumstances if American
soldiers would relish the task of ordering out a suicide dog.

As the war progressed, tanks and flamethrowers remained
the weapons of choice in attacking these fortified bunkers. The
"demolition wolf" proposal would surface later in the war,
when the army's commanding general of Pacific Ocean areas
asked Gen. William Borden about the disposition of the program. A secret communiqué sent in May 1945 stated in part,
"Information is requested on the status of the project for the
possibility of obtaining units of this kind [suicide dogs] for use
in future operations." The New Developments Division sent a
memo indicating that the program had been terminated on
December 17, 1943, but kept open the possibility of reactivat-
ing the project.[16] Fortunately this never took place, and one
can only imagine what might have happened. Although some
researchers in later years recommended similar programs, this
is the closest the United States would come to what could only
be referred to as kamikaze dogs. Some of these ideas were
only minor diversions as the army began to send more and
more dogs into combat areas.

In March 1944 the War Department, recognizing the
promising future for tactical dogs, took the next step beyond
experimentation by authorizing the Quartermaster Corps to
establish war dog platoons. For this purpose specialized Tables
of Organization and Equipment (T/O&E) were developed for
standard platoon strength. Initially, a platoon consisted of one
officer, twenty-six enlisted men, twelve scout dogs, twelve
messenger dogs, and one mine-detection dog.

Based upon a review of the overseas operations to date,

the T/O&E was amended ninety days later to delete the mine-detection dog. It also increased the number of scout dogs to eighteen and reduced the number of messenger dogs to six, with a contingent of twenty enlisted men. By the end of 1944, the Quartermaster Corps had established fifteen platoons, dispatching eight to the Pacific and seven to the European Theater. Any casual detachments in the field remained there for the duration.

Although there was intensive training between the handlers and the dogs, several problems surfaced involving the personnel. The handlers and officers all came from the QMC, and there was little advance training with the AGF. Many handlers were physically unfit for the rigors of tactical operations in combat areas. Infantrymen tended to distrust anyone with a QM patch on his sleeve. After all, the responsibility of the Quartermaster Corps was to supply the materials to support combat troops, not to actually participate in the fighting. To overcome this deficiency, the War Department shifted responsibility for the training and activation of dog platoons to the AGF. The QMC still retained control over the procurement and initial training of the dogs.

Along with the shift in handler responsibility, the usefulness of messenger dogs did not warrant their continued use; they were just not as valuable a commodity as the scout dogs. As the war progressed, electronic communication became increasingly reliable. In December 1944, the T/O&E was changed again, dropping the messenger dogs and increasing the platoon strength of scout dogs to twenty-seven. The fifteen Quartermaster War Dog platoons were redesignated at this time to Infantry Scout Dog platoons to reflect these changes. The AGF established an additional six platoons during 1945, but only one completed training and shipped overseas before VJ Day. Though the QMC platoons had their weaknesses, they did a commendable job in a short time with limited resources.

Besides the fifteen war dog platoons deployed during the war, about nineteen hundred dogs trained in the United States saw service in practically every combat theater around the world. Because of the quarantine restrictions enforced by the

United Kingdom and Australia, hundreds of other dogs were procured and trained locally. Most of these dogs were in casual detachments, since the only organized programs involved the QMC and Marine War Dog platoons. Large casual detachments, accompanied by veterinary personnel, were sent to the China-Burma-India (CBI) Theater, New Caledonia, and the Mediterranean Theater. Smaller detachments were placed in Puerto Rico, the Panama Canal Zone, and western Canada.

The use of dogs in combat began to escalate dramatically at the beginning of 1944 and continued for the balance of the war. Thousands of patrols would be mounted in both Europe and the Pacific Theater of operations. Focus is now given on the general deployment of dogs to these areas, with highlights on some of their accomplishments and failures with different endeavors. The reader will find a marked difference between

War dogs at Berth 177 in Los Angeles are carefully transported in their shipping crates to an awaiting Liberty Ship. *(National Archives)*

how dogs were utilized in Europe as compared with the Pacific; two entirely different environments but with the same goals, and a stark contrast of how to achieve ultimate victory.

The first casual detachment to use scout dogs returned from New Britain during February 1944. Seven war dog platoons were then assigned to the Southwest Pacific Area and participated in campaigns in New Guinea, the northern Solomons, the Philippines, and the Ryukyu Islands. Following the first two war dog platoons into action sets the table for all the war dog operations conducted later during the war. In many cases the army capitalized on the lessons learned by these two platoons, and probably just as many were disregarded.

M-DOGS: EXPERIMENTAL FAILURE

During the spring of 1943 in North Africa, the German army periodically slowed the Allied advance by strategically placing nonmetallic mines in the ground. Since mechanical and electronic mine detectors were ineffective against them, a suitable countermeasure needed to be found.

The British, along with several other European countries, had some success using dogs to detect these mines. When Captain Garle, from England's War Dog Training School, visited several remount stations, one stop was made at Fort Belvoir, Virginia. Here, he suggested to members of the New Developments Division that the United States begin a mine-detection dog program. The QMC took Garle's suggestion and naturally reasoned that if dogs could instinctively find buried bones it would be a simple task to train them to locate mines encased in plastic or wood. The dogs were designated M-dogs, and two methods—called "attraction" and "repulsion"—were used to train the dogs to find buried mines. Neither method turned out to be effective.

With the attraction method a dog would be rewarded for locating a mine, yet few dogs were trained using this method. The foundation of the repulsion method, the one most dogs were trained under, resided with the dog's inherent sense of safety—during training the mine or trip wire would give the dog an electric shock if touched. This simple technique taught the dog that anything buried in the ground or suspicious by its very nature could hurt him. Once the dog found a buried device he showed its presence by halting and refusing to advance. Using these techniques, it was reasoned, M-dogs could detect the presence of minefields and skirt the area safely, or the handlers could probe a clear passage for the accompanying soldiers. Both training methods mandated that the dog be worked on a six-foot leash.

A crash program involving several civilian trainers and one hundred dogs was started at the Cat Island facility during May 1943. A demonstration was then held at Fort Belvoir, Virginia, on September 7, with more than twelve officers present. Two weeks earlier a dummy minefield consisting of wooden, plastic, and metallic mines was laid out with a gravel road running through the middle. Engineers sowed the mines in an area measuring about twelve feet square with the mines planted eighteen inches apart. Over one hundred vehicles had passed over the road since the mines were laid out and considerable rainfall had also fallen.

The dogs moved quickly and began working the minefield, as handlers marked each device with a small stick. Once finished, three officers then used metal probes to locate the missing mines. The dogs missed 20 percent of the buried mines, and another 20 percent of the marked spots showed no mines. It was also noted at the time that the dogs uncovered a minefield planted by engineers about eight months earlier, and this impressed the reviewing officers greatly.

For those observing the demonstration, this was not only a promising development but was considered an overwhelming success. As would be seen later, these test results were skewed, and essentially the dogs were not trained properly. The officers might have been elated at the results achieved in the dummy minefield; however, it would be enlisted men and their dogs walking into a live minefield at the front. At the time few seemed worried about the 20 percent of mines not discovered and the consequences of a dog or handler stepping on one.

Based on this single demonstration, Col. Lee A. Denson Jr., of the General Staff Corps, War Department, authorized the QMC to train at least 500 dog teams for mine detection. During November 1943, the QMC activated the 228th Engineer Mine Detection Company (Dog) at the Cat Island Dog Center. The company, consisting of 120 men and 100 dogs, a far cry from Denson's requirements, shipped to North Africa attached to the Fifth Army Combat Engineers.

The handlers and dogs assembled on May 5, 1944, to prepare for the trip overseas. The men and dogs were shifted among different boats, finally arriving at Oran, Algeria, on May 30. Six days later the 228th arrived in Naples, Italy. Little or no refresher training had been done with the dogs since the end of March, more than ninety days earlier. The M-dog program quickly disintegrated soon after their arrival; as the dogs began probing minefields, a substantial number of casualties resulted.[17]

At this time, the company went to the Combat CE School for further training and testing. Here the results were indeed dismal, as the dogs accounted for only about 30 percent of planted mines during testing. Most dogs were quickly withdrawn from active service, and the program languished until September 1944. The Fifth Army decided to abandon the 228th at this time and call it quits. The Seventh Army, led by General Patton, briefly acquired the orphan group and soon decided it was useless, sending its personnel back to Naples. In February 1945 the 228th Mine Detection Company returned to the United States, where it was deactivated.

During their training the dogs were not exposed to artillery or even small-arms fire. It was believed that their employment would be in relatively quiet areas after a battle had ceased—but this was not true at all. Furthermore, their training did not allow for the rubble and human bodies often present on the battlefield. These distractions would prove too much for the dogs. Field commanders were also expecting dogs to locate 100 percent of the mines. This was unreasonable; nothing could guarantee such success. To expect that kind of efficiency from the dog teams was ludicrous. The failure of this ambitious program should not be placed on the handlers or their dogs–it was doomed even before the first dog started training. Essentially, the dogs were not trained to locate buried ordnance itself but to find soil turned over by humans in the process of burying the mines. The dogs were sniffing for human scent in turned earth, a difficult proposition at best and obviously unreliable.[18] At the time, no one realized that dogs could detect the chemical explosive present within the mines. Decades later this unique sensory capability would be discovered and exploited.

The repulsion method is also not a viable training technique–dogs always respond better, generally speaking, to positive reinforcement. Like other crash programs instituted during the war, the M-dog program was hastily conceived without sufficient background knowledge to implement the program–finding bones is entirely different from locating an explosive mine. In retrospect, there was no one within the army who was qualified to oversee a program of this scope.[19] Too often the military wanted (and needed) results that showed immediate benefits. Unfortunately, the M-dog program had little information to work with and not enough time and thus was unable to succeed. It also contributed to the failure of the military dog program as a whole throughout the European campaign as rumors spread about how ineffective the war dogs were. Decades later, the M-dog would be resurrected and provide outstanding service. The differences were time, money, and solid information combining for the big payoff.

BOUGAINVILLE

The Japanese maintained a strong defense along the shoreline of Bougainville since this was their last stronghold in the Solomons. At dawn on November 1, 1943, American forces began their attack by softening up the defenders with naval gunfire. Despite a twenty-minute bombardment, every man who was about to assault the beaches knew that enemy resistance would still be stiff. The initial assault by Marines included the First Marine War Dog Platoon, attached to the

Second Marine Raider Regiment (Provisional). The platoon separated and boarded three Higgins landing craft. It was scheduled to land on the beachhead one hour after the first wave of Marines went ashore. Even then, mortar fire from enemy positions only several hundred yards inland pounced on the landing craft during their approach.

Several hours after landing, CO Capt. Clyde Henderson located the unit's command post and began coordinating offensive strategies. For the first eleven days, tropical downpours continued almost nonstop, and for the men and dogs this meant conducting operations in a swamp. Even though this did not provide the best environment for the dogs to work in, the platoon achieved success from the very first day.

Fearing the Japanese would try to reinforce their position around Empress Augusta Bay, a 250-man patrol, tagged M Company, was ordered to penetrate inland, led by a Doberman named Andy (71) and two handlers, Pfc. Robert Lansley and Pfc. John Mahoney. It was expected that Japanese reinforcements would be brought up along two possible trails: the Numa-Numa and the Piva. The Numa-Numa connected farther inland with the Piva, and if the Marines could reach this critical junction, reinforcements could be blocked.

Lansley and Mahoney worked Andy off-leash; he was one of the few dogs in the platoon with this ability. With Andy about twenty-five yards ahead of the column, they moved inland. Three times the dog alerted to enemy positions, the short hairs on his back bristling. He was considered an easy dog to read, and his advance could be checked if he moved too fast or too far ahead by Lansley's making a clucking sound to get the dog's attention. Lansley could then motion him back with hand gestures. All enemy positions were routed by this method, and no Marine casualties ensued, as they achieved their objective. M Company also had the distinction of having the farthest penetration during the first day of the invasion.

The first canine casualty of the campaign occurred on the third day. Caesar (05H), a German shepherd dually trained as a messenger and as a sentry, was handled by Pfc. Rufus Mayo

Private First Class Robert Lansley and Andy, an off-leash Doberman, on Bougainville. Andy broke up several Japanese ambushes on the very first day of the invasion. *(National Archives)*

and Pfc. John Kleeman. The heavy rains disabled most of the walkie-talkies, dense foliage limited their range, and telephone lines had yet to be established. Caesar provided a vital communications link, handling eleven missions before exhausting himself. The big German shepherd also distinguished himself as a sentry and during one episode probably saved Mayo's life. On the morning after the third day of the invasion, the dog jumped from the foxhole he shared with Mayo and ran toward the unseen enemy. Mayo called the dog back, and as Caesar was returning an enemy sniper felled him with a shot to his shoulder. During the firefight that followed, Caesar disappeared, but he was soon found near Battalion Command with his second handler, Kleeman. Several Marines rigged a stretcher and took turns carrying the wounded dog to the regimental first-aid station. With the bullet too near the heart to operate, the regimental surgeon believed the dog would pull through despite the position of the wound. Caesar returned to active duty in about three weeks, with the extra weight of a bullet in his chest.

The first newspaper accounts wired to the States indicated that Caesar had grabbed a Japanese soldier's arm, forcing him to drop a grenade and run away. But this was strictly propaganda for a home front looking for some good news. However, he did alert Mayo of the enemy's presence and might have attacked the enemy had he not been called back. In his diary, Henderson recorded the event, writing: "Caesar made nine official runs carrying messages, overlays, and captured Jap papers. On at least two of these runs he went through sniper fire. Caesar and his handlers are real heroes."[20]

Private First Class John Kleeman and messenger dog Caesar on the west coast of Bougainville. Notice the bullet wound in the dog's left shoulder, received during a Japanese attack. *(National Archives)*

If Henderson was impressed by the actions of Andy and Caesar, that judgment was tempered by problems with other dogs. Six of the dogs, including all the bitches, became overly gun-shy and nervous, forcing them to retire from the front. Other dogs picked up the slack—like Jack, a Doberman who alerted to a sniper in a tree, or Otto, another Doberman who scented an enemy machine-gun placement one hundred yards distant. Another Jack, a German shepherd messenger, received two bullet wounds but still completed his mission.

Only two dogs would be lost on Bougainville by the Marines during their three months on the island. Kuno, a Doberman pinscher, suffered a critical injury from a mortar shell explosion. After several hours, it was decided to stem the dog's suffering, and a medic administered an ether injection into the dog's bloodstream. The other dog fatality coincided with the death of his handler.

After completing nearly two months of patrolling activity, Rolo, along with Pfc. Russell T. Friedrich, was introduced to a new handler: Pfc. James M. White. White replaced Pvt. Stephen M. Linnicus as Rolo's second handler only three days before the ill-fated patrol. The two handlers and the dog accompanied an army unit temporarily attached to the Marines. Their objective was to ferret out Japanese positions along the Torokina River. The patrol advanced about three thousand yards into the jungle, with Friedrich and Rolo on the point, when the dog gave a strong alert. The army patrol leader pushed the pair farther on, disregarding this information, and into a Japanese ambush.

Stumbling into a group of soldiers, White later stated that the Japanese spotted Rolo and began hollering, "Doggie, doggie." Friedrich whistled the dog back, and then the shooting began. Friedrich then sent the dog back to White, only eight feet away. The bullets progressively came closer to White, so he sent Rolo back to Friedrich. Just as the dog reached his handler, he was hit. "Rolo whined a minute and then died," White said. Several minutes later Friedrich was shot, and the patrol withdrew. During the withdrawal a bullet creased White's scalp. They regrouped later and the patrol searched for

Friedrich, but found only Rolo's body. Believing him to have been taken prisoner, they listed Friedrich as missing in action, never to be seen again.[21]

In three months on Bougainville, the First Marine War Dog Platoon proved the possible scope and tactical advantages offered by scout dogs in a jungle environment. Although Friedrich never returned from the army patrol, no handlers were killed while leading Marine patrols. According to a report endorsed by both Maj. Gen. Roy S. Geiger, USMC, commander of U.S. ground forces on Bougainville, and Maj. Gen. Allen H. Turnage, USMC, Marine Division Commander: "The War Dog Platoon has proven itself to be an unqualified success, and the use of dogs in combat was on trial. This first Marine War Dog Platoon was admittedly an experimental unit and minor defects were found that need to be remedied. But the latent possibilities of combat dog units proved itself beyond any doubt."[22]

The success and press accounts of the First Marine War

Marine combat artist Elmer Wexler depicts several Doberman pinscher war dogs and their handlers on a jungle island in the Pacific. *(USMC)*

Dog Platoon bolstered the ranks of Dogs for Defense, who had fought to have dogs join in the battle only a year earlier. But it was on the front lines where the war dog platoons were appreciated. When a handler and dog appeared, foxholes were dug immediately for them. The old adage in the Marines is "If a man will dig a foxhole in the front line for another guy, he wants that guy around"—even if the other guy is a dog.

CBI DETACHMENT

On January 24, 1944, 108 dogs, 100 enlisted men, and 2 officers boarded the Liberty Ship *Benjamin Ide Wheeler* in Wilmington, Louisiana. The vessel was bound for Kanchrapara, India, located near Calcutta. It seems the dogs had the better deal during the trip, housed topside in two sheds located just aft of the midship house on both the port and starboard sides. The handlers, along with another 100 enlisted men from the AGF, spent the next seventy-two days housed in the number-three hold during the tortuous journey. The vessel made the unescorted trip across the Pacific to its first scheduled stop at Fremantle, Australia. It was in the Tasman Sea that a tremendous typhoon pounded the overloaded freighter for three days, threatening to send the dog sheds over the side. The storm cost the ship five days' traveling time, and another reality set in—dogs can easily get seasick and create quite a mess.

After arriving in Fremantle on March 4, the *Wheeler* refueled and departed after only two days in port. The extreme heat turned the metal decks into hot stove tops, blistering the pads of the dogs' feet. Handlers tried to fashion canvas boots, which did not work out, and then simply kept flushing the deck with saltwater to keep it cool. This had its own consequences for the dogs' feet, forcing the soft blisters open. Taking care of the dogs to the best of their ability, the handlers lost only two animals, both due to heatstroke, during the journey.

The *Wheeler* arrived in Colombo, Ceylon, on March 21, stayed for three days, and continued its journey to Calcutta, arriving on April 4. Trucks immediately transported the detach-

Corporal Charles Williams shows off a pair of leather boots fashioned for his scout dog while on station in Burma. The dogs found them uncomfortable and usually tore them off in a short time. *(National Archives)*

ment to Kanchrapara, and there they spent two weeks with no assignments. An additional twenty-five dogs and handlers arrived during the month to support the initial contingent. The rest of the detachment gave the dogs refresher training and provided demonstrations for Calcutta Command officers.

Within a few weeks everything would change, as the men and dogs of the casual detachment scattered across the entire China-Burma-India theater of operations. A few teams began guarding the main supply depot in Calcutta, and the theft problem there diminished abruptly. Officers noticed this immediately and began to demand the services of the dogs. The group separated and deployed to the Assam area, which included Thanai and Raidang, to guard airstrips, ammo dumps, and other outposts. Dogs entered combat in the Burma campaign as part of the 5307th Composite Regiment (Galahad Force) and the 5332d Provisional Brigade (Mars Force) with a

A German shepherd crosses a narrow footbridge somewhere in Burma. There were few places that dogs could not travel, and this added to their versatility during the war. *(National Archives)*

small group attached to the Office of Strategic Services (OSS) Detachment 101 in China and Burma.[23]

Finally twelve men and dogs flew to Myitkyina, assigned to Merrill's Marauders on an experimental basis, where they were used during the last month of the operation. Although used sparingly, the dogs were so successful that any future plans included their use. On three separate occasions they alerted to a superior enemy force without the enemy's noticing the patrol. In seven incidents, patrols were unable to locate snipers that picked off men with impunity until scout dogs were brought in. Each sniper was not only located but eliminated with no further loss of American lives.

One night at the command post (CP), as the men slept, Wotan, a scout dog handled by Cpl. Delton Armstrong, was staked outside and off-duty. A lone Japanese soldier infiltrated the perimeter of the CP with a bag of hand grenades. He then crawled too close to Wotan, who promptly jumped the man and mauled both of his legs. The soldier, unable to escape, pulled the pin on one of his grenades and rolled over on it. The explosion woke the men, who were surprised to find the dead infiltrator—yet relieved to find Wotan unharmed.[24]

As troops mopped up scattered areas of resistance around Myitkyina, two Japanese soldiers were seen crossing a rice paddy and entering the jungle. A patrol, with a scout dog and handler, immediately started a search for them. A couple of hours later the dog alerted, yet nothing could be seen. The patrol leader remained skeptical but ordered the handler to shoot where he thought the enemy might be. A short burst from the handler's Thompson submachine gun killed one Japanese soldier and flushed out another, whom the patrol quickly cut down. The patrol leader thereafter requested scout dogs and handlers to accompany the men into the jungles.

These incidents and many more were a learning experience for the neophyte detachment, both dogs and men alike. Some of the dogs had been trained by the agitation method. Once they alerted they would invariably attack their prey. This caused numerous problems, as the dogs barked during their pursuit, thus giving away the position of a patrol. Other dogs, trained by praise after an alert, proved to be far superior and much quieter. But all their training still did not prepare the dogs for actual combat conditions. No one considered, for example, that a dog would alert to a herd of wild elephants—and, in fact, the first dog killed in action was not killed by the Japanese but by a tiger.

The same problems facing the dogs in the Pacific operations plagued the animals in the Burma campaign, although heat exhaustion was far less prevalent. Besides the common parasitic problems, skin diseases such as dermatitis and eczema cropped up. Numerous tick-transmitted diseases also surfaced. Stomach distress bothered many dogs, often on a daily basis, due principally to poor-quality food and water. The handlers themselves were not immune and were subject to malaria, typhus, and dengue, all of which accompanied sol-

Jesse Cowan and Kane on patrol somewhere in Burma. Kane belonged to Cowan's sister. The two enlisted together. *(National Archives)*

diers throughout the duration. Since the detachment split up, with small groups dispatched on various assignments, its members were often considered curiosities by infantrymen. Typically they were asked who they were and what the dogs were for. As transients, they referred to themselves as war orphans and took up the slogan "Nay Momma, nay Poppa," as though they did not feel at home with anyone.

Even as transients they proved themselves time and again. Perhaps one of the best examples, and perhaps the most bizarre one, involved not the enemy but Americans. Richard Zika, a former CBI veteran handler, relates a tale told to him by Calvin Reister, a handler who was in the original group sent to Assam and, along with several others, who had been assigned to patrol a small ammunition dump in the Ledo area. Zika states:

. . . the overall area was not completely stable. Just across the Burma boundary some of our supply troops ran into opposition from enemy forces who had worked their way around the front's flank and into a position to direct machine gun and mortar fire on ammunition and other supplies being brought forward. Located on two knolls with extremely heavy jungle growth, these emplacements were so well concealed that to return fire with any degree of accuracy was almost impossible, so Reister and Ted Both were directed to use their dogs in an attempt to pinpoint location.

On the morning of their arrival conditions were quiet, so the two worked their way toward the ominous knolls. The breeze, though variable, was generally favorable as it traveled through the already overheated air, and shortly Reister's dog alerted, quickly followed by Both's dog doing the same. Working their way through the dense growth they began hearing voices and, strangely, some words sounded familiar. As they came within a few feet of a small clearing they were greeted with a sight as unbelievable as it was shocking. Seven heads protruded grotesquely from the ground in a horrible condition of bruises, open sores, and covered with flies. They were Americans!

As these men were being dug out and given rudimentary first aid and water, their story came out. They came from several different small units which had been scattered by the Japanese raiding forces flanking attack and been captured. Forced to dig chin-deep foxholes, they had been buried in them with only their heads above ground for several days and had been in this helpless position with their captors periodically urinating on them accompanied by kicks and clubbings; a not unusual treatment of POWs by the Japanese.

Realizing the Americans would soon be coming in force, the Nips simply withdrew, leaving their prisoners to die a horrible death, which would have been inevitable had the dogs not located them. Another day or so and none would have survived. Incredibly, once evacuated all seven recovered, albeit not without lifelong aftereffects. One lost the sight of an eye, another deafened for life, while none escaped the emotional scars which would be theirs to the end of their days. But all of them grateful for the keen sense of scent God bequeaths on dogs.[25]

Only a handful of people realize the value of war dogs, and few episodes of this nature ever reach a wartime press; most become just faded memories of a war fought a long time ago. The ability of dogs to scent both enemies and friendlies reinforces the argument that dogs saved numerous lives, as shown in this extraordinary case. It is also interesting to note that casual detachments like the one in the CBI theater never earned the Combat Infantry Badge because they were part of the Quartermaster Corps—although without a doubt they engaged the enemy on numerous occasions.

Of course, there were several factors that limited the use of war dogs in the CBI theater of operations. As casuals, the handlers and dogs could not be added to the units unless they released some of their own men. Few were willing to do this. Also, no one knew how to obtain additional or replacement dogs and handlers. The fact was, there were not enough to go

Technician Fifth Grade Lester Shattuck helps place a gauze muzzle over his dog at Battalion Aid. Both were wounded during a Japanese mortar attack. *(National Archives)*

around, and the CBI commanders would have to make do with the one casual detachment. Considering the conditions prevalent at the time, it is surprising that about eighty-five dogs survived the war and were returned to the United States. The handlers themselves became custodians of many of the dogs, and they often contacted the original owners in an effort to keep the dogs they had fought beside. Their experiences with the dogs earned them that right, and most of the owners understood that.

EUROPEAN OPERATIONS

On June 6, 1944, Allied troops completed the largest amphibious assault in history, crossing the English Channel to the beaches of Normandy. Within eight days the beachhead was secured and Allied forces moved inland, liberating Paris on August 25. The Allied advance in France slowed somewhat at this time due to a severe gasoline shortage. Earlier in the year Allied troops had landed at Anzio, just thirty miles south of Rome, for the continued push northward through Italy.

During this time, in the middle of 1944, seven QMC War Dog Platoons, the 33rd through the 38th and the 42nd, were readied for action and deployed to the European theater of operations. All platoons were structured for scouting and messenger work except the 36th QMC War Dog Platoon, which consisted solely of mine-detecting dogs.

Scout dogs would see very little activity in the war against Germany. From the few experiences related here, it is easy to see that infantry units had no idea how or when to use them effectively. All too often they were thrust into heavy combat, neutralizing their specialty of detecting the enemy with early, silent alerts. In general, conditions were unfavorable for their employment: soft, deep snow and slippery trails often precluded their use; heavy rains and mud made scenting difficult; open country made their use conspicuous. Seldom was there a static front, and rapid troop movements and heavy artillery limited their roles dramatically. By far, gun-shyness proved their greatest weakness, most dogs having been exposed to only small-arms fire in training. Some patrols were mounted, but overall the scout dog platoons fell into disfavor with the infantry units, and they were soon ordered to rear areas as sentries.

The 33rd QMC War Dog Platoon, under the command of Lt. Austin A. Risse, would be the first to see action in Europe, arriving in Italy during August 1944 and joining the 6th South African Armored Division. During the fall, the platoon went out on forty-one scouting and reconnaissance patrols before heavy winter snows limited the use of the dogs. Open country and heavy combat in the immediate area usually limited the use of scout dogs, but under the right circumstances there was still no substitute—as was demonstrated on the night of December 20, 1944.

Corporal Robert Bennett and his dog walked point for a small reconnaissance patrol leaving a forward outpost to check a village about a mile into enemy-held territory. The pair had walked only a few hundred yards when the dog suddenly stopped and alerted. Bennett's dog pointed straight ahead, and the hairs bristled along his back. Not sure what to expect, the patrol leader crept forward alone, discovering a large group of Germans sitting in ambush two hundred yards away. As the patrol withdrew, the CO radioed instructions for mortar fire to be directed at the German position. The 33rd then spent several weeks giving the dogs a refresher course before moving up to the front with the 34th Division. Here another twenty-five patrols were conducted, and the dogs helped by alerting to several ambushes.[26]

Another platoon, the 37th, was activated on May 5, 1944, at Fort Robinson, Nebraska, under the command of 1st Lt. Archer Ackers. After finishing training, the platoon departed for Naples, Italy, aboard the Liberty Ship S.S. *James Monroe* on August 22. The trip took twenty-nine days, and a rigid schedule of exercise was maintained for both the men and the dogs. After arriving in Naples they quickly departed for Bagnolia, in the northern part of Italy, but were not allowed at this time to recondition the dogs. On December 19, they left Bagnolia and arrived in nearby Pistoia, where they billeted in a rural area just outside of town.[27]

Here there was ample space to give the dogs a refresher course, desperately needed after three months of inactivity. Finally, orders were received on February 15, 1945, giving operational control of the platoon to the 87th Regiment, 10th Mountain Division. Two days later four scout dogs and their handlers made preinvasion nighttime reconnaissance patrols into enemy-held territory, but no enemy contact was made at this time.[28]

Two nights prior to the planned offensive, scout dogs went into action again as T5 Clifford Mortensen and his scout dog, Tarzan, led a reconnaissance patrol of a position to be overtaken and occupied by C Company. Tarzan alerted twice to enemy gun positions, allowing the patrol to remain undetected. On the night that the offensive was to be launched, Mortensen and Tarzan led a forward element to their reconnoitered position. A second patrol was led by T5 Orville Wilson along with his dog, Champ. Both patrols worked well with the dogs, and patrol members were satisfied with their performance.[29]

Things did not go as smoothly for the other two scout dogs and their handlers. Both Sgt. Himberger and T5 Whitaker were given only ten minutes' notice prior to the start of their patrol, and neither handler was briefed by the patrol leader about what to expect. Both handlers told the CO that the dogs were of no value since there was a quartering tailwind. This information was disregarded, and a short time later the entire patrol was pinned down by machine-gun fire, which lasted for more than two hours. Scout dog Skippy began whining and started barking. Whitaker was forced to release the dog, who scampered away for a short time but came back. Enough was enough, and both handlers took their dogs to the rear while under fire.

The same company also botched the use of a messenger dog—with nearly disastrous repercussions. The handlers and dogs were taken along for the attack even though they were normally brought forward only after a position had been overrun and secured. A German 88mm artillery round landed only

Prince, a messenger dog, carries a dispatch in the Sassonero area of Italy. Conditions in Europe did not favor the use of scout and messenger dogs on a wide scale. *(National Archives)*

thirty yards from one handler, knocking him out and leaving the messenger dog with no handler.[30]

Both of these situations were easily avoidable if there was time for the handler and patrol leader to brief each other properly. The patrol leader would have provided the essential details of the operation, and the handler could then in turn give the limitations and expectations of the dog. As often happened, when this important briefing was not held, the lives of not only the handler and dog but of the entire patrol hung in the balance.

The platoon was then held in reserve until March 19, when four scout dogs and their handlers moved to the bivouac area of the 10th Reconnaissance Troop, 10th AT Battalion, attached to the 85th Mountain Infantry Regiment. Technician Fifth Grade Ray Fultz and Magsie worked point on a nighttime patrol comprised of forty men whose mission was to take prisoners. They covered about six miles during their patrol, scouting several villages but with no enemy contact.

On the invasion night, Cpl. W. D. Davis and T5 H. Spencer, with their messenger dogs, Rex and Mack, were ordered to set up reserve communications between F Company and the battalion command post. On at least two occasions the dogs provided vital communications, traveling a distance of about three quarters of a mile. The dogs were held over sixteen hours and made their runs through dug-in troops and two active mortar positions. Within a day, wire communications had been established, and the messenger dogs were put in reserve. Just to keep the dogs in condition, their handlers had them deliver the morning report and the daily G-1 report to Battalion Command.

On the night of February 25, Cpl. Cecil Brown and Buddy led a patrol of seven men from E Company, 87th Regiment. In an area near Rocco Coroneta, Buddy alerted and a patrol member went forward to investigate. A German sentry challenged the man, who spoke the enemy's language fluently. But the sentry soon became suspicious and began firing. A firefight followed and Brown caught a fragment from an enemy grenade. The patrol retired under heavy enemy machine-gun fire with no further casualties. Buddy made no sound at all during this time, and when Brown crawled, Buddy would crawl automatically without command.

The 37th also made two other short reconnaissance patrols with dogs alerting both times. The patrols withdrew and did not investigate the alerts. By February 28, all men and dogs were bivouacked between the artillery and frontline positions near Vidiciatico. This exposed the dogs to the heavy artillery barrages. Since they were not working, they grew accustomed to the loud battle noises.

During the next night another patrol went out, but this time with very serious consequences. Sergeant Severance and

Peefka worked an area comprised of several small villages. The conditions were favorable for the scout dog, but as they approached one building a German sentry opened up with automatic rifle fire. The patrol hit the ground fast and the sentry threw a hand grenade that landed near the dog. Under enemy fire and with Peefka seriously wounded, Severance had no choice—he turned the gun on his own dog and fired a single shot. The patrol gave covering fire to the four men in the forward position, which allowed them to withdraw. No one was killed during the brief fight, but two men were wounded.

Why Peefka did not alert was discussed after the patrol returned. Severance felt that since the patrol was a long one, the dog might have tired and stopped working. The patrol leader just chalked it up as "one of those times that a dog chooses not to work." In any event, Peefka failed. Officers and patrol leaders were then asked about their estimate of the value of scout dogs in combat. Even with Peefka's failure to alert, all were enthusiastic about the dogs and believed they aided the patrols. But Peefka's failure added a dose of reality to those who believed dogs were infallible.

Most scout dog platoons in the European Theater did not see much, if any, frontline action. The bulk of their time was spent in rear areas as sentries around ammunition depots or guarding POWs. Generally the terrain and fast-moving forces provided an unsuitable environment for scout dogs. Few commanders even knew how to employ them effectively. Also, quartermaster personnel in fighting positions were always held suspect by the ground forces. In open areas scout dogs were easily visible, and in heavy snows they were almost useless. When employed in static fronts and under the right conditions, scout dogs proved very effective. Their true payoff, however, would take place in the Pacific.

WAR CAN BRING OUT some of the strangest stories, and this holds true for one unique group of war dogs. There is some evidence to suggest that at least a few dogs participated in several airborne assaults in Europe by jumping into combat. One German shepherd named Jaint de Mortimorney, reputedly made more jumps during World War II than any man. Although no training was ever formally adopted for parachuting dogs during the war, the QMC did develop a special harness for them at the San Carlos War Dog Training and Reception Center. This idea originated with the search-and-rescue dog teams, but the harness was not placed into the army's general inventory.

Former paratrooper William Kummerer, from New Rochelle, New York, was with the 463rd Parachute Field Artillery and recalls making a jump on August 14, 1944.[31] This was in southern France as part of a post–D day mop-up mission. Jumping along with the fourteen men was a Doberman pinscher unceremoniously kicked out the door with a special

Lieutenant Peter Baranowski with Jaint de Mortimorney, one of the few scout dogs to actively participate in airborne assaults during the war. Note the U.S. flag paratrooper insignia on the dog's side. *(National Archives)*

parachute attached to a static line. Kummerer stated, "About three hours after we landed he [the dog] turned to the left a little bit and growled. The men quickly cranked around their fifty-caliber machine gun. Sure as hell, over the rise came four Krauts in a wagon. We cut loose with everything and they never got back to the Rhineland, don't you know."

In a spirit of thanks, Kummerer went to pat the dog and nearly lost his hand as the Doberman bared all his teeth. After that day he never saw the handler or dog again. Where they came from and went to remains a mystery. Most Dobermans served with the Marines in the Pacific, so it is likely that this dog and Jaint de Mortimorney were probably part of a casual detachment in Europe, much like Chips had been, and not one of the formally established QMC War Dog Platoons.

THE PACIFIC BATTLES

America's war dogs in the Pacific, unlike their counterparts in Europe, proved to be an overwhelming success in most cases, although some problems did arise. Many difficulties could be overcome in the field, while others required long-term solutions that had to be addressed during a dog's initial training period. Most of the battles in the Pacific presented a tropical or semitropical environment and terrain steeped in vegetation. This changed dramatically as the Allies advanced closer to Japan.

Without doubt, the Battle of Midway, on June 2, 1942, was a turning point in the naval war and placed Japan in a defensive position. In the months to follow, Marine and army forces would launch counteroffensives as islands in the southwest and central Pacific lay wide open for Allied attack. Much of the Pacific campaign consisted of island-hopping, with some smaller ones being bypassed altogether. Army and Marine War Dog Platoons were deployed as required, but often at a disadvantage. As dog casualties mounted, fewer dogs were available for patrols, and dogs often became hot property once their limitations were understood and they were used judiciously by knowledgeable commanders.

Dogs and handlers board a warbound ship in Los Angeles for some unknown overseas destination. *(National Archives)*

Beginning in 1944 and lasting until the end of the war, army and Marine War Dog Platoons conducted thousands of patrols scattered throughout the Pacific theater of operations. An overall view is given in the following pages for the general movements of these platoons and how they conducted themselves in key situations. Background on some major engagements is furnished so the reader can appreciate the scope of each operation and the role in it of the war dogs and their handlers. As in any war, numbers alone do not tell the whole story. Comparatively speaking, war dog platoons were a unique, albeit tiny, component of all the fighting forces involved. For that reason alone they bear closer scrutiny.

The first army platoon to go overseas in the Pacific was

the 25th QMC War Dog Platoon, under the command of 1st Lt. Bruce D. Walker. When they left San Carlos, California, on May 11, 1944, none of the handlers knew what their final destination would be. Unfortunately, the platoon was hard hit when it had to leave several highly trained dogs behind due to heartworm infestation. At San Francisco, men and dogs boarded the Liberty Ship *John Isaacson* to begin their twenty-two-day sea voyage. Unlike many ships bound for the war, the *Isaacson* had plenty of room for the men and the dogs. Deckhouses were built, which meant the platoon could remain topside, where the only things to do were care for the dogs and get a suntan. Others opted for poker, and no doubt a lot of money changed hands during the next three weeks.[32]

On June 2, Guadalcanal came into view, but it was another four days before the platoon could leave the ship. The men loaded themselves and their dogs onto a truck at the Kukum dock and began a short trip inland to camp with the 314th Baking Company. About a quarter of a mile from their destination the truck hit a soft shoulder and overturned, scattering the men and dogs. Three men were hurt, but none seriously, and the platoon finally managed to gather themselves together and reach camp. Two nights later, Mickey, a scout dog, disappeared. He was found three weeks later at a local water-cooling unit, taking refuge from the heat.

On the second day in Guadalcanal, Colonel Fredricks, commanding officer of the 37th Division, paid a surprise visit and asked for a scout dog demonstration. The dogs had not been worked for a month, and no one knew what to expect. With fingers crossed, the platoon worked on problems set up by the colonel. The months of training back in the States paid off, and the demonstration went off without a hitch. This left Colonel Fredricks with a good appreciation of everyone's capability, and he said that the handlers and dogs would be immediately deployed to an island where they would be put to good use.

The handlers gave their dogs refresher training in earnest, and on June 25 the platoon left aboard the freighter U.S.S. *Taganak*, arriving at Bougainville three days later. The first week was spent on orientation, further training in jungle warfare, and a short course on the island's geography. It was only a matter of days before the 25th went into its first combat, and the platoon stayed wired in anticipation. Although the initial assault by Marines had occurred over seven months earlier, the island was not yet completely secured.

The 25th saw its first action on July 16, as a truck brought two scout and two messenger dog teams to a command post located on the Numa-Numa trail. The platoon, along with the 164th Infantry, started to push entrenched Japanese soldiers from a strategic hill. One patrol was sent out to ambush fleeing Japanese soldiers, but it soon became evident to Command that they in turn might be walking into an ambush. Since there was no radio communication at the time, Champ, a messenger dog, was dispatched with orders for the patrol to return immediately. Champ located his second handler and the patrol returned promptly.

During the battle for this location, Private Simpson and his dog volunteered to lead a patrol to an important position. Simpson got the patrol to the desired spot and also accounted for the first enemy kill by a member of the 25th. This action earned Simpson a recommendation for a Bronze Star. After that, requests for dogs came more frequently from both the 164th and the 182nd Infantry.

It was also during this same period that another handler, Private Cramer, and his dog, Beauty, volunteered for a reconnaissance patrol. Beauty alerted to some Japanese soldiers after their patrol returned to base camp, allowing everyone to retire safely with no casualties.

The first bad news for the 25th came on the morning of July 29, when Walker told the men that Private Barker had been killed during a patrol the previous afternoon. The first death in a tightly knit group such as the 25th brought the reality of war very close. Several days later, news of two more casualties, this time dogs, was given to the men. Rex, known as Eightball by everyone, and Prince, handled by Simpson, were both killed in action during fierce firefights. These dogs had worked perfectly up to that time and had also alerted to hidden Japanese personnel on numerous occasions. It is at times like this, often in war, that a combination of pride and sadness intermingles with the news of such losses.

The 25th received its new T/O&E, increasing the number of scout dogs and reducing the number of messenger dogs. The men came to understand this as better radio communications became available, and the requests for messenger dogs dropped off dramatically. This started the men working to convert most of the messenger dogs to scout duties. This conversion training not only took time, but proved very difficult in a frontline position. The platoon's morale remained high, and refresher training continued fervently for several reasons: the dogs had already performed outstanding service, saving numerous lives, and many battles remained to be fought before everyone went home.

Back in April, the War Department was still queasy about using dogs in frontline positions and had asked for regular reports on the "usefulness, capabilities, and limitations of war dogs, particularly in combat." Interviews were conducted with patrol leaders, because platoon handlers and officers had a natural bias. Overall, the reviews of the 25th on Bougainville were mostly favorable. A captain with the 164th Infantry reported on several occasions when he had the opportunity to employ scout dogs between July 16 and July 27:

> The patrol leaders of two different three-day patrols reported that the Scout War Dog was very helpful. Both patrols were alerted by the dogs in plenty of time to enable them to have the upper hand with the enemy and in both cases Japanese soldiers were killed. Talking with the lead scouts of our infantry patrols, the individual reports that he feels much more confident when operating with the dogs. This battalion would like more training with scout dogs and patrol leaders in our area of operations state that they would like to have Scout War Dogs to use on all patrols in enemy territory.[33]

The few dissenting reports indicated that the dogs sometimes slowed the pace of a patrol. Others stated that a few dogs would whine at night if not staked near their handlers. Still

Dog handlers were always able to rest comfortably with their dogs. The dogs gave the men an extra sense of security, especially at night. *(National Archives)*

others mentioned that frequent alerts made some patrol members edgy, although these alerts were often abandoned enemy bivouac areas or friendly patrols. As one sergeant put it, "Better to err on the side of caution."

There is no doubt that the scout dogs would have been even more effective if the patrol leaders had been indoctrinated and briefed beforehand on their capabilities and limitations. This appears to be one of the weakest links in the development of scout dogs at the time. Handlers and dogs often traveled to different commands as required, and hence no training ever developed between the handler and dog and patrol members. Since a common thread of knowledge did not pass through every infantryman, scout dogs would never truly reach their full potential during the war.

THE SECOND QMC PLATOON to enter into the Pacific campaign was the 26th, arriving in New Guinea on June 16, 1944, under the command of 1st Lt. James Head. Two weeks later the platoon accompanied the 41st Division to Biak Island, just

The 26th Quartermaster War Dog Platoon starts out on a patrol on Aitape, New Guinea. *(National Archives)*

north of New Guinea, and shortly thereafter moved on to Aitape with the 31st and 32nd divisions. During the Aitape operation, the platoon, minus one squad, worked both scout and messenger dogs. Handlers had a hard time in the heavy jungle growth, since they were working the dogs on leash, and the messenger dogs were found to be ineffective when required to run considerable distances through heavy mud. Still the platoon boasted several good alerts to ambushes, and the messengers made quick runs from patrols to command posts.

In September, the 26th joined the 31st Division for the assault on Morotai Island in the Netherlands East Indies (also known as the Dutch East Indies). The operations conducted on Morotai helped to further develop the basic principles for successfully using scout dogs on patrol. Here the Japanese offered only token resistance to the Americans landing on the beaches and withdrew to the mountainous jungle terrain of the interior. Small enemy parties would continually harass the Americans, causing an inordinate amount of time and men to be spent on reconnaissance and combat patrols. These patrols were often made in dense jungle vegetation that offered only semidarkness even during periods of brilliant midday sun. Poor lighting and thick growth provided excellent cover for enemy ambushes and infiltration. Japanese snipers took advantage of terrain that varied from marshy low-lying areas to the hillier areas that were rough underfoot.

The 31st Division of the Sixth Army used the 26th QMC War Dog Platoon to provide a tactical edge in the heavy jungle environment that had to be dealt with. From September 17 to November 2, 1944, the 26th conducted over 250 patrols on the island. Typically, there were three daily patrols that ranged to eight thousand yards and four weekly patrols that lasted two

Nompa, a scout dog, checks a hidden cave on a coral cliff on Biak Island, Dutch New Guinea. Dogs proved invaluable in mopping-up operations on small Pacific islands. *(National Archives)*

days or longer. The success of these operations proved outstanding, as no patrol was ever ambushed. Scout dogs alerted to the enemy at no less than seventy yards and often scented at distances greater than two hundred yards.[34] One weakness did manifest with the dogs when there was no trail to follow on cross-country patrols: handlers found that the scout dogs made considerable noise moving through the underbrush and were difficult to keep headed in the proper direction.

The scope of the patrols ranged from small five-man reconnaissance units to rifle companies with over two hundred men. Initial estimates showed approximately 75 percent of all the enemy killed were taken by surprise. Lieutenant Colonel Walter J. Hanna, commanding officer of the 155th Infantry Regiment, stated in one report: "Of equal importance is the ability of the dog to pick up enemy bivouacs, positions, patrols, troop reconnaissance, etc., long before our patrol reaches them. This advance warning has frequently enabled our troops to achieve surprise and inflict heavy casualties on the Japs."[35]

Messenger dogs were also employed advantageously on Morotai. Initially they accompanied short patrols of several thousand yards and could be worked reliably for fifteen hundred yards. This avoided the need for the patrol to carry radios or to lay wire. Used daily, these four-footed messengers were eventually worked to distances of three thousand yards as they gained experience and grew accustomed to their chore.

On longer patrols where radio equipment was necessary to maintain contact with rear command posts, messenger dogs provided the first link in the communications chain. The radio unit and its accompanying riflemen would remain well back from the main body of the patrol unit. The messenger dog, accompanying the lead group, would be sent back a thousand yards with a dispatch. This enabled the radio link to be well protected in cases where the patrol made enemy contact, yet still provided little delay in communicating with rear support areas.

The high humidity and heat wreacked havoc with the tube-type radio gear, and often the messenger dog would be the only reliable communications link. During one patrol, a dog made three round-trips within an hour, covering a total distance of about nine thousand yards. The patrol had ambushed a Japanese party, killing four of them, with the survivors fleeing into the jungle. The patrol broke up to recon the remaining enemy, while the messenger dog relayed vital information to the rear area.

Prominent among the messenger dogs that operated on Morotai was Buster (A684). This collie was directly responsible for saving the lives of seventeen men of F Company, 155th Infantry Regiment when the patrol was surrounded and outgunned. Buster avoided heavy machine-gun and mortar fire to complete a round-trip. The return trip brought the message for the men to hold their position. Having done so, reinforcements were quickly brought up and were able to rout the enemy forces and relieve the patrol.

The fact that the dogs could not distinguish between friend and enemy was turned around to an advantage. By far, most patrols operated in hostile territory, and it was preferred that the dog alert to anyone. The resulting feeling of security boosted troop morale and allowed the patrols to work efficiently and to cover greater distances. This posed no problem, except at those times when overconfidence in the animal extinguished common sense. The 26th gained invaluable experience—in the next few months it would make over 850 patrols without the loss of a single man. Still ahead lay many more deadly island clashes as U.S. forces worked their way toward Japan.

THE UNITED STATES INVADED the Mariana Islands on June 15, 1944, setting up a position from which to retake Guam. Finally, on July 21, 1944, the invasion force landed near Apra Harbor at a location almost identical to the one the Japanese had used three years earlier. Almost nineteen thousand Japanese defended Guam, and the Marines would be held on the beaches for four days.

Twenty dogs and twenty-six handlers and NCOs went

ashore with the First Marine Brigade on the first day of the invasion. The Second War Dog Platoon was commanded by 1st Lt. William T. Taylor and the Third War Dog Platoon by 1st Lt. William W. Putney. A graduate of a school of veterinary medicine, Putney also served as veterinarian for both platoons and established a field hospital, the first in Marine Corps history, for the dogs on Guam. To take care of the dogs Putney often scrounged material from the navy and also equipment from captured Japanese medical units to augment his veterinary supplies.

Guam proved to be an ideal environment for the use of dogs by the Marines. During the liberation, both Marine War Dog Platoons participated in over 450 patrols, and alerts by scout dogs were made in 130 of them. This resulted in 203 enemy killed. The dogs also did double duty by providing nighttime security and alerting to enemy activity at least forty times. These actions accounted for an additional 66 of the enemy killed, as reported by Gen. A. H. Noble in his report of activities of the war dog platoons.[36]

Five days after the invasion, the largest skirmish between the enemy and the war dogs and their handlers took place. A group of Japanese managed to skirt the Marine lines on the hills overlooking Assan and attack the division hospital, a short distance from the beach. About twenty-five of the enemy began bayoneting wounded Marines in their stretchers and also killed several doctors and corpsmen. Lieutenant Putney led a counterattack with a complement of war dogs and handlers, and managed to kill all of the enemy marauders.[37]

During the initial fight for the island, the Japanese realized that once a dog was spotted the Marines were not far behind. For that reason about ten dogs were killed by rifle fire, as the enemy soldiers believed they could escape detection by killing the dogs. After the island was declared liberated, on August 10, hundreds of Japanese continued a guerrilla campaign, many of them fighting until the war was declared over. Fifteen other dogs died during mop-up operations on the island, and other dogs suffered from malnutrition, tropical diseases, and filariasis.

The Marines honored their war dog dead by building this cemetery on Guam at the close of the war. In 1994 the entire cemetery was moved and rededicated through the efforts of William Putney, D.V.M. *(National Archives)*

Once control of the island was wrestled from the Japanese, Americans built a large base to support B-29 Superfortress attacks against Japan. The island also became the central point for receiving and dispersing war dogs for the Marine platoons throughout the Pacific. At least 350 dogs spent some of their time on the island. Two major events also centered on the war dogs operating on Guam: the determination that messenger dogs were no longer required and the decision not to accept Doberman pinschers as replacements in the future.

The commanding officers of both platoons, Taylor and Putney, furnished a report to the commander of the Marine Corps providing a basic overview of operations and future recommendations. Because the Marines maintained excellent communications during the invasion, only one messenger dog, a Doberman bitch, was used. Future operations could expect to have good communications as well; therefore it was believed that the messenger dogs were no longer needed. Messenger dogs did provide excellent nightly surveillance and could also be retrained as scouts. It was noted that German shepherds, Doberman pinschers, several mixed breeds, and one Labrador retriever were employed. Each sex seemed to work equally as well, with little difference also between purebreds and mixed breeds. However, Taylor emphatically stated:

> Although a few of the Dobermans performed in an excellent manner, it is considered that this breed is, in general, unsuited for combat duty due to its highly temperamental and nervous characteristics. They also failed to stand up as well as the other types under field conditions. On the whole, the Doberman proved to be more excitable and nervous than the other breeds under combat conditions, and required much time and effort on the part of his handler at all times in order to keep him properly calmed down and under control. Although admirably suited for certain types of security work, dogs of this breed are not desired as replacements for the 2d and 3d War Dog Platoons.[38]

In stark contrast to his views on the abilities of the Doberman, Taylor then went on to highlight the attributes of the German shepherd:

> They [German shepherds] stood up excellently under field conditions; and throughout, their health average has been very high. Possibly the fact that this group were not so highly bred may have had some bearing on their more stable qualities and better stamina. All German shepherds were available for front line duty at all times.

The report also explained the advantages of training scout dogs to work off-leash, noting that some could work up ahead of their handlers by 150 feet. Working on-leash, Taylor noted, made noise, wore the dog out, and reduced his senses of smell and hearing and his general alertness. A Labrador retriever also worked well, but one collie, Tam (404), died of pneumonia and was buried at sea before his performance as a combat dog could be determined. Taylor's report, accepted on face value, meant the beginning of the end for the Doberman pinscher as a military working dog.

AFTER GUAM AND OTHER BATTLES in the Mariana Islands, the Palau Island group became the last stepping-stone for the eventual invasion of the Philippines that lay five hundred miles to the west. One island, Peleliu, was only six miles long and two miles wide, yet it held more than ten thousand Japanese. Entrenched in more than five hundred caves, most of which were connected by tunnels, the Japanese defenses were formidable. It would turn out to be a bloody assault.

On September 15, 1944, the First Marine Division landed on the southwest corner of the island with three regiments abreast. After four days of heavy fighting they captured the airfield, but the entire island would not be secured for another two months. In the end, the First Marine Division had 1,152 men killed and over 5,000 wounded. The Japanese death count stood at 13,600, with only 400 captured.

On the second day of the invasion, the Fifth War Dog Platoon, commanded by 2nd Lt. Grant H. Morgan, left the U.S.S. *Acquarius* for the island with a squad of twenty men and twelve dogs. Arriving at night, the entire platoon was placed around the command post (CP) for security. The platoon went into immediate action the following day as two patrols left at dawn's light in an attempt to locate snipers. A call also came in for the use of a messenger dog. Duke (Z876), a German shepherd, traveled about one and a half miles across the airport under mortar attack to deliver twenty pounds of enemy maps and papers to the CP.[39]

Other dogs made alerts during the night, and the Marines laid down a curtain of automatic rifle fire in the direction in which the dogs pointed. Marines found clusters of enemy bodies the next morning. The continuous mortar fire, both

Fifth Marine War Dog Platoon's Cpl. William Scott and Prince on Peleliu. More than ten thousand Japanese soldiers were entrenched in caves and bunkers; it took over two months to secure the tiny island. *(National Archives)*

friendly and enemy, caused Hans, a Doberman pinscher, to snap and attack his handler, Cpl. Bernard G. Passman. The handler had to shoot his own dog to stave off the attack. The dogs continued to work patrols each day and were then placed on night security. No successful infiltrations were reported at any of the positions held by dogs. But after a week of continuous duty the dogs were becoming exhausted. At least four were characterized as "shell-shocked." Many had suffered cut feet from walking about on the coral along the shore.

One night a handler, his dog, and another Marine slept alongside a gun emplacement, exhausted from an all-day patrol. A common fallacy that circulated throughout the front lines was that dogs are indefatigable, and even when sleeping can sense the approach of an intruder. In this situation, a Japanese soldier crept up to the men and grabbed their rifles before scurrying off. Fortunately, another Marine heard the intruder and shot him. The apparent lesson is that dogs do tire, and a fresh sentry dog is required at night if dogs have been out on patrol during the day. Dogs bordering on exhaustion lose interest in working, just like any human being, and their great sense of smell is also compromised as they begin to breathe more heavily through their mouths.

The coral surrounding the island tore to pieces the pads of the dogs' paws. Often a handler could be seen carrying his dog over a nasty stretch of coral. Although many handlers attempted to get their dogs to wear boots, the footgear did not stay on for long. Once the dog stopped working he would immediately begin to chew the leather boots.[40]

The Fifth War Dog Platoon worked almost constantly, and the fierce battle for the small island decimated the group. Three of the platoon handlers were killed in action, and another eight were seriously wounded. Eight dogs were wounded and another three were killed. The last patrol for the platoon took place on October 18, 1944. Eight dogs and their handlers went to Ngesebus Island with the 5th Marines to look for snipers. Handler Cpl. Charles Linehart and Blitz alerted to several Japanese, who were quickly cut down by automatic fire. After this action, the entire platoon returned to Pavuvu, in the Russell Islands, at the end of the month for a breather. The Fifth Marine War Dog Platoon was only one tiny group of Americans determined to take Peleliu. The statistics told the entire story: Based on the number of Japanese dead, it took 1,600 rounds per person of both heavy and light ammo to accomplish the job. With the Palau Island group secured, the United States turned its attention toward the return to the Philippines.

The first dogs entering the Philippine Campaign came from the experienced 25th and 26th Quartermaster War Dog Platoons. They were followed by the 39th and 43rd, and then by the 40th and 41st. The 26th went ashore at Luzon on January 9, 1945. Originally assigned to the 43rd Infantry Division, the platoon was attached to the 169th Infantry once on the island. Several problems immediately popped up as the 169th began making rapid advances inland with patrol leaders not previously oriented to the use of scout or messenger dogs. Small wonder the animals displayed mediocre performance during the few patrols they accompanied.

Two weeks later, the 26th became attached to the 27th Infantry, where commanders were more familiar with the tactical advantages of the dogs. The platoon worked continuously until the beginning of April 1945. Essentially the main problem was the inadequate number of dogs available for patrol work. Everyone wanted to use them, yet there were not enough to go around. When dogs were available, they could not be brought to the staging areas fast enough for them to be used with the patrols. Typically during the Philippine operation, when dogs were needed they always seemed to be somewhere else. When faced with combat activity they were often highly successful, and line officers voiced their enthusiasm after seeing the dogs work. It was recommended that each rifle company have one messenger dog, who is valuable only if available immediately. Messenger dogs were also prized for other reasons, as they often alerted to enemy troop movements when not "officially" working. With losses mounting in the campaign, the 26th retired on April 7, to be used on special assignments only. By the middle of June the platoon was only at 25 percent of its designed strength in combat situations.

In a report to the commanding general of the Sixth Army, the 26th's CO, 1st Lt. James S. Head, stated: "The dogs of this organization are directly responsible for the saving of a considerable number of American lives as well as the destruction of the enemy. Had more dogs been available for deployment, the number of lives saved and the number of enemy destroyed would have been proportionately larger. The 6th, 25th, and 21st Infantry Divisions have each requested permanent assignment of a very much greater complement of War Dogs."[41]

Lieutenant Head was probably the most knowledgeable officer in the field about the employment and care of war dogs. In a letter to the CO of the War Dog Reception and Training Center in San Carlos, sent several months earlier, Head listed a number of recommendations that would pass the test of time. He suggested that portable kennels be used in lieu of

The 26th Quartermaster War Dog Platoon assembles for a briefing prior to going out on patrol. These were the first dogs to see action on Luzon. *(National Archives)*

shipping crates and that they be well ventilated with an opening at the bottom of the exterior walls. This space would allow better ventilation and facilitate the hosing down of the kennel floors. Head even noticed that because the prevailing winds in the Pacific were from the south, crates should be located on the port side of the transportation ship.

Head's concern for the care and well-being of the dogs is nothing short of extraordinary. In lieu of exercise, Head had his men massage the dogs daily for thirty minutes; he noted that this helped the dogs sleep and also relieved those with constipation. No sore feet or skin problems surfaced while the dogs were transported. Extra care ensured that the shipping crates remained dry and well off the ground. Head also checked to make sure that dogs staked outside were in well-drained areas.

Head also helped to treat several cases of moist eczema the dogs suffered with. He believed the condition was caused in part by excessive protein intake. This meant cutting back on the horsemeat and using a canned dog food more often. The young lieutenant strongly disliked one of the vet techs attached to his unit and chastised the man for cutting too much hair from the dogs, noting how hair helps keep insects away and protects against the heat.

Obviously the commander respected his men and dogs. He even managed to maintain a sense of humor in a letter mailed earlier while in the Solomons. After getting thirty-six inches of rain in just thirty hours, Head said of the experience, "It's not so bad after you get used to being wet all the time."

THE LAST PLATOON TO BE ACTIVATED and sent overseas during World War II was the 44th. It left Seattle, Washington, on March 29, 1945, and arrived in Honolulu on April 7. After taking additional training at the Jungle Training Course on Oahu, the platoon boarded the Liberty Ship *Burnett* on June 9. The next day the 44th left for Saipan. The handlers pulled extra duty for ship security during the voyage, manning the eight 20mm machine guns.

After its arrival on Saipan, the 44th, along with the 811th MP Company, completed mopping-up operations all over the island. Small pockets of Japanese soldiers, mostly individuals, remained hidden in caves and bunkers. The scout dogs helped to locate many of these underground sanctuaries, and patrols either attempted to force the Japanese to surrender or cleared them out with grenades and flamethrowers. The platoon remained on Saipan until the war was over and left for home on December 12. A month later the men and dogs arrived at Camp Anza in Wilmington, California.

FOR THE INVASION OF IWO JIMA, on February 19, 1945, the Marines split their Seventh War Dog Platoon into three sections, with the first squad hitting the beaches on the first day of the assault. The other two squads landed two days later. Their duties varied little from those of the army dogs: nighttime security at the front, mopping-up operations, and rear area sentry duty. They gave the men on the front an added sense of security and alerted frequently to enemy infiltration parties.

A war dog lies dead in the mud of Okinawa, killed by enemy artillery fire. His handler escaped injury. *(National Archives)*

The 6th Marine War Dog Platoon also split into three sections, with the first group departing the U.S.S. *Whitley* on D day. Four days later the second section left the U.S.S. *Stokes,* and the third group went ashore from the U.S.S. *Tolland.*

It soon became apparent that the dogs would be best used for nighttime security. Private James E. Wallace was killed by mortar fire the first night, and his dog, Fritz (255), was wounded. Where the third group operated, string was laid out as a signaling device between the foxholes of the Marines. Carl (441), a Doberman pinscher, alerted his handler, Pvt. Raymond N. Moquin, a full thirty minutes before a Japanese attack. Fully prepared, the Marines wiped out the attacking Japanese. The third section, situated around the division command post, saw no action.

The next day King (456) was wounded by shrapnel and Duke (330) was killed by a sniper. That same morning near the command post, Jimmy (384) alerted his handler to three infiltrators. Private W. T. Davis tossed two fragmentation grenades, killing the three Japanese. A short time later, Hans (340), a Doberman, alerted the Marines to four Japanese who had crawled from a tunnel on the beach. They were quickly killed by Hans's handler.

Conditions on Iwo did not warrant the extensive use of

dogs—owing to the extensive artillery and small-arms fire across the wide-open terrain. Because of the noise and confusion, dogs on patrol alerted not only to the enemy but also to the Japanese dead who littered the landscape. First Lieutenant William Taylor, the CO of the 2nd Marine War Dog Platoon, and with the experience of Guam under his belt, noted: "Marine handlers have to stand with the dogs and their use at the front in the usual scouting and patrolling capacities limited. Anybody in an upright position on Iwo's front line gets hurt, and there is no sense in sacrificing our dogs needlessly." Taylor soon turned his efforts to security watches and mopping-up actions to locate hidden tunnels and pillboxes.[42]

Iwo Jima would not be completely secured until March 26, 1945. The tiny volcanic island cost the Marines more than 6,800 dead and a staggering 18,000 wounded. Iwo was taken to serve as an emergency landing field for battle-damaged and fuel-starved B-29 Superfortesses returning from attacking Japan. Over 2,200 planes, carrying 24,000 crewmen, would make emergency landings on Iwo before the war ended.

PRIOR TO THE INVASION OF OKINAWA, 1st Lt. Wiley S. Isom, QMC and 45th War Dog Platoon, arrived on the island of Espíritu Santo, New Hebrides, on March 8, 1945. At this time the platoon was assigned to the Tenth Army and attached to the 27th Infantry Division. The handlers worked the dogs for the next two weeks, giving demonstrations and providing refresher training. They then departed to participate in the invasion of Japan's last island possession. Although it was not known at the time (because everyone believed an invasion of the Japanese homeland would be necessary to win the war), this would be the largest land battle in the Pacific.

Okinawa represented the convergence of Allied forces from both the central and southwest Pacific. Covering 794 square miles, it is the largest of the islands in the Ryukyu chain and is similar in terrain to Iwo Jima. Platoon leaders would soon find out that their men and dogs would play limited roles in this engagement. Three army war dog platoons—the 40th,

The 45th Scout Dog Platoon on Okinawa. The 45th mostly conducted mopping-up actions on the island and sentry detail for Japanese POWs and civilians. *(National Archives)*

41st, and 45th—participated in the Okinawa campaign along with the Marine Fifth War Dog Platoon.

About five days before the invasion, several handlers and dogs from the Fifth War Dog Platoon went ashore with a detachment of Marine scouts. Dropped off by two destroyer escorts at night, the men made their way to the island in rubber rafts. Patrols were established to probe Japanese defenses and reconnoiter shoreline installations. The scout dogs alerted their handlers numerous times, and the Japanese never spotted the patrols.

At Okinawa, the 41st disembarked from the U.S.S. *Fondaulac* and moved swiftly to the vicinity of Futema. The platoon provided security for the 96th Infantry Division MPs, who were guarding POWs and civilian internees. Sentry service was also provided for the Quartermaster Corps dump. No battle casualties for handlers are recorded, and only one dog was killed. The 40th also remained in the rear, serving in the same capacity as the 41st.

In August, the question arose about the value of the scout

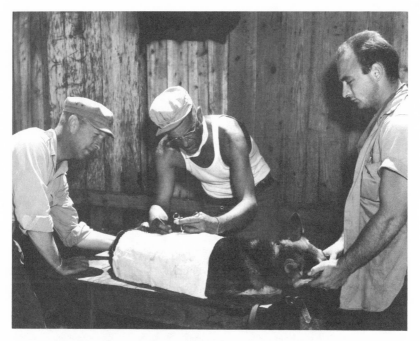

A veterinarian officer removes shrapnel from a wounded war dog on Okinawa. *(National Archives)*

dog platoons, since they participated in no combat patrols on the island. The AGF also disliked the amount of refrigeration equipment required to provide fresh meat for the animals. But this recommendation was based on activities of the 40th and 41st, whereas the 45th and the Seventh Marine War Dog Platoon saw limited combat action with scout dogs and then later used their messenger dogs advantageously. The report also disregarded the hazardous operation that the Fifth Marine War Dog Platoon participated in several days before the actual invasion.

Arriving thirteen days after the initial assault, Lieutenant Isom was ordered to provide fourteen dogs for frontline duty. One dog was assigned to each company set to assault a strongly defended Japanese position. As Isom later stated, "... upon entering enemy territory the Japs opened with everything they had, including small arms, machine guns, mortar, and artillery. There was so much confusion, so many people moving around, that our dogs were of no use whatsoever. Immediately our dogs were ordered to report to the rear."[43]

These problems arose simply through a lack of understanding on the part of field commanders as to the proper deployment of dogs. On this type of terrain, wide-open daylight operations were senseless. On their second trip to the front, with just four dogs, Isom's team worked more effectively. Two of the dogs had an opportunity to work, and one alerted to four Japanese approaching from a hill who were cut down by a man with a Browning automatic rifle. The other two dogs were of no value since they were continuously under mortar attack.

Marine Pfc. Hallet McCoy and his dog, both veterans of Peleliu, take a break on Okinawa. The wide-open terrain of the island meant that most dogs were used for sentry duty or mopping-up operations. *(National Archives)*

A third attempt to field eight scout dogs yielded no results due to heavy artillery fire.

Then it was time for mop-up operations to find the enemy hidden in scattered caves. Here, without the noise and confusion, the dogs checked the many caves and bunkers. But this work was also foreign for the dogs, and the smart ones refused to enter any dark place. Isom recommended further training if these types of operations were to be conducted, and noted, ". . . with artillery in the background. Dogs cannot get too much training under guns."[44]

The Japanese were subdued on Okinawa by July 2, 1945, and the Allies began preparing for the projected invasion of Japan itself. Six weeks later—on August 6—a B-29 bomber took off from Tinian and dropped a single atomic bomb on the city of Hiroshima. Three days later another bomb, the last one in the U.S. inventory, was dropped on Nagasaki. Five days later an eight-hundred-plane B-29 strike pounded Honshu. After three and one half years of war, Japan finally accepted unconditional surrender.

The army and Marine war dogs had done remarkably well, considering the fact that just about everything was a new learning experience. The two soft spots on their record are probably the operations conducted on Iwo Jima and the ones on Okinawa. The use of dogs in these two places, particularly in the early stages of the invasions, was probably unwarranted, based on the geography and the sheer number of men fighting. Although dogs participated in the mop-up of both islands, they were not trained to check caves. In the future, specific dogs were developed just for this function.

Scout dogs could not be used indiscriminately, and most of the negative results from Europe and the Pacific stem from this practice. When the need was specific and within the capabilities of the dogs, there was no question of their effectiveness. This is supported by the fact that the QMC had plans to establish sixty-five scout dog platoons. The close of the war meant that more scout dog platoons would not be necessary, and the army's attention was diverted to what needed to be done with its dogs.

RETURN OF THE CANINE VETERANS

A more ambitious plan than even the recruitment and training of thousands of war dogs was the decision by the army to return K-9 veterans to a civilian role. This respectful gesture toward war dogs and the service they had provided was the first and final time such large-scale action would be taken by the military establishment, which ultimately classified dogs as equipment. A great number of unexpected problems appeared; the army and Marines spent thousands of hours of labor and dollars to retrain the dogs and return them to civilian life. Although simple in concept, the idea of returning dogs to civilians was no easy feat.

Not every dog was requested to be returned. Those who originally wanted their pets returned might have had a change of circumstances, no longer wanted the dog, or were dead. Other dogs, acquired from pounds and various kennels, had no original owners. Many surplus dogs presented serious health risks, not only for other dogs but for humans as well. By far the army spent the majority of time demilitarizing the dog, so its behavior in a civilian environment was both safe and acceptable.

In April 1945, the War Department stated that the dogs would be disposed of through one of the following methods:

1. By issue to the Seeing Eye, Inc., as a prospective Seeing Eye dog.
2. By issue to a military organization as a mascot.
3. By making available to the servicemen dogs they had handled in the service.
4. By sale through negotiation of the Procurement Division, Treasury Department.

Colonel George Parker, who issued the summary, further stated, "In no event will dogs go to undesirable individuals or to laboratories or institutions."[45]

Two bills surfaced in Congress during 1945 that addressed the surplus dog situation. Bill H.R. 543 stipulated its purpose as to "provide for the gift of war dogs to servicemen who trained them for their war tasks." The War Department had no objection except for the time that a dog could be held for someone. The army opposed another bill, H.R. 3687, which ordered the military to retrain war dogs (which it was already doing). It also established a commission headed by two members of Congress and another member appointed by the president to oversee the return of the war dogs. Secretary of War Stimson objected, stating that retraining was already in progress and that the War Department was "fully conscious of its obligation to the donors of these dogs and is providing for their utmost care and treatment under all circumstances." Effectively H. R. 3687 was unnecessary, just adding another financial burden on the taxpayer.

The return of the K-9s involved the services of Dogs for Defense, the Quartermaster Corps, and army veterinarians: DFD terminated procurement of dogs for the service branches on March 1, 1945. Before the conclusion of the war DFD believed that K-9s should be returned to civilian life wherever possible. According to a DFD spokesman, "We feel that the place for a K-9 veteran is in a home and not in some kennel or an Army post. To say that a dog should be kept confined to a kennel, robbed of the pleasure of companionship only to be found in a home, seemed to us just like arguing that the soldier for whom no job is in sight should be kept in uniform indefinitely."[46]

Although DFD offered its services to place all surplus dogs not returned to their original owners, by law, as government property, they needed to be sold. Depending on the distance the dogs were shipped, the price varied from fourteen to twenty-four dollars. For the person receiving the dog, this was indeed a bargain, considering the expense the government had absorbed for the dogs' reprocessing and for veterinarian care. In an effort to keep costs down, everyone was expected to return the shipping crate and feed pan at their own expense.

Often an owner received a dog that was in better physical condition than when it first "enlisted." And these former war dogs were certainly better trained than when they had "enlisted."

How the dog would fare in the future, from a behavioral standpoint and considering its medical condition, could not be warranted by the army. The detraining process alone took about the same amount of time as the original training had when the dog first entered into service. Detraining began by allowing the dog to be handled by several people. The dog was encouraged to play, and reinforcement was given to teach the dog that everyone was his friend.

Eventually the dogs would be confronted by a person who exhibited combative behavior. Even with this extreme irritation, trainers made corrections if the dogs displayed any aggressive behavior. As the process unfolded, the dogs gained more and more freedom, and handlers tested them in several

These dogs were well along in their detraining and would soon be discharged and returned to civilians. The army and Marines made an extra effort at the end of the war to send as many dogs home as possible. *(National Archives)*

ways to check their progress. One test was to have a dog walk beside a secluded building on a leash, and then have an aggravator jump at him, waving a stick and shouting. If the dog tried to make friends, and was not unduly alarmed, the handlers believed the dog was ready to be returned to civilian life. Only a few dogs could not be detrained and needed to be destroyed.

The veterinarians ensured that dogs returning to the civilian quarter did not carry any diseases that could be spread among the dog population. Diseases that could not be treated, such as leptospirosis, dictated that the dog be euthanized. Dogs having filariasis were originally allowed to be returned to their owners, once the owners were notified of the probability of recurrence, the unsuccessful history of treatment, and the possibility of spreading the disease to other dogs. Few owners decided to keep dogs affected by this disease, and after January 1944, all dogs found to have filariasis were destroyed.[47] Other dogs, particularly those in the southwest Pacific area, who were infected with filariasis or had been exposed to scrub typhus were destroyed locally. In late 1945, the army dictated that any dogs returning to the United States be vaccinated for rabies prior to reentry.

One problem the army anticipated was a shortage of homes for the former war dogs. Actually the opposite came true, as the DFD received over fifteen thousand applications for the K-9 veterans–many more than the number of dogs available. These applications still streamed into DFD headquarters years after all the dogs had been dispersed. Special consideration was given to veteran handlers who wanted the dogs they had worked with and to people who had donated a dog or had a family member die in the service. Those who were fortunate enough to get a canine veteran received a certificate of faithful service, an honorable discharge certificate, a collar, a leash, and an army manual titled *War Dogs*. The DFD continued to offer support to the owners by establishing obedience training classes, films, and lectures about continuing the adjustment of war dogs to civilian life.

Overall there were few problems once the dogs were returned. Without exception, every dog still recognized its owner, even after an absence of over two years. Of the approximately three thousand army dogs discharged to civilians, only four needed to be returned. The myth of the belligerent and vicious war dog that could not be accepted in the civilian world would not surface for another twenty-eight years. The Quartermaster General and Dogs for Defense received numerous unsolicited letters during the program that ensured this continued success. Typical of the hundreds of letters received is one from Maj. V. E. Reemes of Oakland, California, who purchased a German shepherd. Reemes wrote:

> Fritz was not our dog when he was entered in Dogs for Defense. Therefore, we are not able to compare the change, if any, in the dog now and prior to his Army training. As his new owners, we are most satisfied. He is very affectionate, gentle with every member of the family, courteous to strangers, not antagonistic toward men making deliveries to the home, as newsboy, garbage or milk men. He is friendly with the other dogs in the neighborhood (which certainly is an asset in community living). In fact, having him has been nothing but a pleasure. He has no objectionable habits at all. We are most grateful to the organization of Dogs for Defense and the patient men who trained these dogs; and for the opportunity to own one of these splendid animals![48]

The Marine Corps also established a dog return policy that mirrored the efforts of the army. Approximately 1,047 Devildogs served with the Marines during World War II in the Pacific. After the fall of Japan, the Marines returned home 232 dogs aboard the S.S. *Merrick* and another 259 through other channels. Incredibly, only 19 of the returning dogs from this group needed to be put to sleep. Four were impossible to detrain and the others had serious diseases that necessitated that they be destroyed. Of all the dogs returned to civilian life after the war, the Corps never received a report of anyone's being attacked, injured, or dissatisfied with a dog.[49] With no future wars on the horizon, the Marines dismantled their war dog program in September 1946.

Well before the Quartermaster Corps and Dogs for Defense formulated plans for the return of the war dogs, considerations were made for the establishment of a national memorial to honor these canine veterans. Harry Miller, an executive secretary at the Gaines Dog Research Center, put forth one idea.

In 1944, Miller tried unsuccessfully to have a memorial placed in front of the Pentagon to honor the dogs serving–and those that died, and will die, while in service to their country. Like others before him and those yet to come, he found that the labyrinth of bureaucracy could not be breached. It was all too easy for government officials to just say no. In this case, Brig. Gen. Edward Witsell passed the buck to the Commission of Fine Arts, stating that this department had jurisdiction over all memorials erected on public lands.[50] The proposal died quietly with no government support. Inexplicably, DFD did not propose or endorse any memorial honoring the contributions of dogs.

The Quartermaster Corps issued two paper certificates honoring war dogs. One was called the Certificate of Merit; it was given to owners of dogs killed in action. The other was a Discharge Certificate for canines mustered out of service. Other paper honors could be presented to dogs, but after the award fiasco with Chips, no standard medals would ever be placed on a canine again.[51] The army did relent in another area, however, and allowed the commendation of dogs in general and unit orders. This practice continued for dogs that served in Korea and later in South Vietnam.

Many dogs also died in service to their country, and this was recognized by the War Department, which would send a telegram to the dogs' owners, stating, "It is with regret that I write to inform you of the death of _____ donated by you for use in connection with the armed forces of the U.S. It is hoped that the knowledge that this brave dog was killed in the service of our country will mitigate the regret occasioned by the news of his death."

World War II marked not only the beginning of the U.S. K-9 program but also the end of an era. The entire effort to place dogs in military roles had started as an experiment initi-

World War II Canine Discharge Certificate. The army recognized the war dogs by issuing a discharge certificate upon their return to civilian life. This practice was discontinued shortly after the war when Dogs for Defense disbanded and the government prohibited the return of dogs into the civilian sector.

ated by civilians. Many lessons learned in World War II would be reinforced during the Korean conflict and forgotten during the Vietnam War. For the dogs, things would also change dramatically in the future with the departure of civilian interests. Since 1945, canine recruitment has meant servitude for life—no longer would dogs leave military service. This policy change would spin off other repercussions, particularly in Vietnam, when it was time for the United States to leave.

5.

POSTWAR AND KOREA

OFFICIAL CHAOS

The demilitarization of the armed forces following the world-wide conflict of World War II was both sweeping and deep. This became apparent as various dog programs in the different branches of the armed services disappeared and scout dog platoons were deactivated. Although a number of subtle enhancements were made, the development of scout dogs was largely ignored.

The War Department had intended that scout dog platoons be continued in the postwar establishment. During a conference held at Fort Benning during June 1946, the army's Committee on Organization met to debate the situation. Committee chairman Brig. Gen. Frederick McCabe discussed the contributions dogs made during the war and recommended that "Infantry War Dog Platoons be retained and be attached to infantry training units for training and operations." McCabe made clear recommendations when he stated that "experimentation be continued with dog units along all lines, especially breeding, improving techniques of training, and extending the the scope of usefulness of the dogs."[1]

As is often the case, implementing a plan can be much more difficult that just bringing forth recommendations. A general lack of interest, fiscal cuts, and manpower reductions snuffed the keen attention the army once held for dogs during times of war. By the time the Korean War flared up, only one active scout dog platoon (26th Infantry Platoon Scout Dog) could be found in the world.

In 1946 the Quartermaster Corps discontinued its program of acquiring dogs on loan from U.S. citizens, initiating the beginning of the end for civilian involvement with military working dogs. It was much more efficient and cost-effective for the military to purchase the dogs directly from breeders. This practice is nothing new and has been used for years in acquiring horses and mules. The direct benefit is the ability to acquire the best possible dogs with the lowest possible rejection ratio. Based on some of the problems Dogs for Defense had in procuring suitable military dogs, the Quartermaster Corps launched a new program beginning in the latter part of 1945, a short time before Dogs for Defense dissolved. Thus began the short life of the Army Dog Association, Inc. (ADAI).

Commercial breeders and responsible individuals became part of ADAI; their intent was to have a pool of readily available dogs for training. An individual would agree to purchase a dog for one dollar and begin a very careful breeding process. The military retained the prerogative to select one male puppy (between twelve and fifteen months old) from each of the first three litters produced. The program intended that the breeder make a profit on the sale of the other dogs to private citizens. By this time the army had limited the breeds of choice to German shepherds only. With their ability to adapt to hot and cold climates, they could readily meet any demands of the services around the world. The initial breeding stock, acquired in Germany in late 1945, consisted of seven bitches and one male puppy.

For the next five years the program languished. The Quartermaster Corps lost interest since it no longer was involved in training, and in reality it had no facilities in which to house the newly acquired dogs. Since there was little or no demand, and no replacements called for, the entire program was quietly terminated in 1950.

The army still purchased dogs directly from citizens and kennels on occasion, although these too were limited to German shepherds. Physically the dog had to be between twenty-two and twenty-eight inches in height at the shoulders and weigh between sixty and ninety pounds. Females were also accepted if they were spayed, and all dogs needed to be between nine months and three years old. The basic temperament requirements remained unchanged in that the dog had to be alert and moderately aggressive, display no nervousness, and, of course, not be gun-shy.

The responsibility for training within the dog program also became a hot potato, one that no one was keenly interested in handling. In 1948 the Quartermaster Remount Depot System was discontinued, and training responsibility was transferred to the Army Field Forces and the 26th Scout Dog Platoon, located at Front Royal, Virginia. Just a couple of months later, the platoon picked up and moved to Fort Riley, Kansas. On December 7, 1951, dog training was transferred to the Military Police Corps and the 26th moved again—to Fort Carson (formerly Camp Carson), Colorado.

Fort Carson could educate 86 sentry dog handlers and 380 dogs during any training cycle, now set at eight weeks. Newly arrived handlers came from the army, the Marine Corps, the navy, and the air force (six enlisted men). With the country at peace, the army figured that scout dogs were no longer required, but sentry dogs were still a valuable commodity for every branch of the military.

Sentry dogs provided base security, but the biggest advantage to be gained from their employment came from deterring pilferage. In 1949, for instance, it took an entire infantry battalion to guard several warehouses and supply depots in Japan. Yet within a four-month span, over $600,000 worth of material was lost through theft. When 125 handlers and 65 dogs took over the same guard responsibilities, not a single dollar's loss could be attributed to theft during the next twelve months. This accomplishment also released 600 men from guard duties, netting the government millions of dollars in savings.[2]

In 1953 yet another military study recommended that all war dog training be returned to the Quartermaster Corps. The report also recommended the activation of a new installation at Fort Lee, Virginia, and the subsequent phaseout of the Army Dog Training Center at Fort Carson. These ideas were rejected in May 1954, but a new directive once again changed the responsibility of war dog training. Even though the Quartermaster Corps would still be responsible for procuring the dogs, the training shifted from the Military Police Corps to the Chief of Army Field Forces at Fort Monroe, Virginia. This shuttling around of training duties is perhaps the overwhelming reason only one war dog platoon would see service during the Korean conflict and consequently tax their resources to the limit. The constant shift in responsibilities also meant command and doctrine changes in training, resulting in an inherently weaker sentry and scout dog program. In the higher echelons of the military, confusion reigned supreme—within a few short months the Quartermaster Corps had publicly stated:

1. It was discontinuing the K-9 Corps.
2. It no longer accepted donations.
3. It still accepted donations.
4. Dogs would be purchased only from breeders.
5. The army would begin its own breeding program.

Such were the circumstances surrounding the development (or lack) of a military working dog program within the United States during the late 1940s and early 1950s. The role of the military at this time was to prepare for a possible nuclear confrontation with the Soviet Union. There was no foresight of any conflict that would require the use of tactical dogs, even though General McCabe had recommended their continued development back in 1946. All the necessary ingredients were available for a cost-effective and efficient canine program. The only thing standing in the way was the military.

INTO BATTLE AGAIN

Before hostilities began in Korea, the army maintained about a hundred sentry dogs, mostly around Seoul and at other strategic locations. Most of these dogs were killed or starved to death as North Korea launched a major attack against South

Korea on June 30, 1950. In quick fashion, the Communists took over the capital, Seoul, and pushed toward the southern port of Pusan. Within days, the United Nations agreed to bolster the defenses of the faltering South Korean forces. A month later, the first Americans entered the conflict.

On September 15, 1950, with the American forces cornered in the Pusan area, Gen. Douglas MacArthur directed a bold strike. A large amphibious landing took place at Inchon, behind enemy lines, cutting off their supplies. Weeks later, troops advanced across the 38th parallel and overwhelmed the North Koreans. But on November 26, some two hundred thousand Chinese Communists entered the battle, pushing the United Nations troops back across the 38th parallel and recapturing Seoul.

At this time there were no American scout dogs in Korea, and with mechanized military units on both sides moving swiftly, there probably was no need for them. There remained only one active scout dog platoon, the 26th, stationed at Fort Riley, Kansas, and even it did not possess a full complement of trained handlers and dogs. The primary mission of the platoon consisted of official demonstrations, touring the country for television appearances, and occasionally accompanying infantry units during maneuvers.

Since World War II, the army had relied solely on German shepherds for scouting and ambush patrols. Their heavy coats withstood severe weather, a prime consideration for Korean winters, and the dogs displayed a good overall demeanor in the field. Although no particular bloodline was required, field work was limited to males only. Males tended to be more aggressive since they were not neutered. Female dogs were spayed according to regulations, which led them to be less aggressive.

In May 1951, orders alerted the entire 26th Scout Dog Platoon to embark for Korea. The United States managed to push back the Communists to the 38th parallel, and the war stalemated at this point. Each side launched massive attacks but the battle lines remained relatively stagnant. With neither side gaining any ground, the war now offered a good opportunity

153

to test the abilities of scout dogs and their handlers once again. Only a single squad, consisting of seven handlers and six dogs, was ready to ship out. After arriving in Korea in June, it was attached to the 2nd Infantry Division. The balance of the platoon was promised to arrive in September; however, its training was not completed in time, and its departure date was pushed back until January 1952. Two months later, recognizing the need for additional dogs, the army responded by activating a War Dog Receiving and Holding Station at Cameron Station, in Alexandria, Virginia. Here dogs were purchased and received veterinary examinations prior to their shipment to Fort Carson, Colorado, for training.

On January 25, 1952, thirteen enlisted men, twenty scout dogs, and an officer left Fort Riley by railcar for San Francisco to await the next available freighter sailing to Korea. The shipping crates for the dogs would also serve as portable kennels once they arrived. Dogs had been placed in one railroad car and then attached to the Pullman where the handlers were quartered. This allowed the handlers to easily exercise the dogs at various stops during the three-day journey. Upon their arrival in San Francisco, the dogs were placed at a veterinarian's facility for a final inspection before leaving on February 3 on a freighter bound for Pusan.

The only reported problem during the eighteen-day sea voyage was with the dogs' diet, as many of them showed stomach distress during the voyage and after arriving in Pusan. When the dogs left Fort Riley they had received frozen canned horsemeat, but they were switched to fresh horsemeat at San Francisco and back to frozen canned horsemeat on the freighter. Their stomach distress can probably be attributed to the switching between fresh and frozen horsemeat. In Korea, fresh meat was next to impossible to get, even though it was more beneficial for the dogs. Supplements such as cod liver oil could be acquired easily, and this was added to the dogs' diet on a daily basis when feasible.

Commanding officer for the platoon 1st Lt. Bert M. Deaner departed Pusan to meet with James A. Van Fleet, commanding general of the Eighth United States Army, Korea

(EUSAK), and G3 (army intelligence) to discuss the deployment of the platoon to its best advantage. The platoon left for Chunchon and then on March 1 left by truck for the headquarters of the 224th Infantry Regiment, U.S. 40th Infantry Division. Here it joined the original squad that had arrived ten months earlier.

For its duration in Korea the platoon was never sent into reserve. Although it did receive thirty days off, it was always kept on call. While at the front, the platoon never received all the equipment it was entitled to. For instance, although authorized to have three two-and-one-half-ton trucks, instead it made do with six quarter-ton trucks. Basic items such as choke chains, harnesses, dog dishes, and grooming supplies were very difficult to locate and obtain. The dogs would be kenneled in their respective shipping crates for the duration of service.

With the experience of World War II and continuing success in the Korean conflict, basic policies involving the handlers and the dogs evolved. In Korea, the biggest distinction was that most of the dogs participated in night patrols, and the handler was usually given twenty-four to forty-eight hours' notice. This would give him ample time to prime the dog for the mission. On the day of a proposed patrol, a morning meal was given to the scout dog, followed by a light workout. The dog was fed no other food until the patrol was completed. This allowed the dog to remain at a high level of alertness and alleviated the torpidity that frequently manifests after a full meal.[3]

The handler and dog met with the patrol members at least one hour before the start of a mission, giving him ample time to brief the members on the different aspects of the operation. If the group had not worked with a dog before, the handler told them what could be expected from the dog—just as important—what he expected the patrol to give him in return. The dog also became better acquainted with the members of the patrol and more familiar with their individual scents.

Although furnished with an M-2 carbine, the handler relied on the patrol members to provide protection for himself and his dog. Most of the time the handler was fairly well occupied with watching the dog during the course of the patrol and looking for any telltale signs of an alert. With the handler intimately familiar with his dog, he could determine accurately and quickly if the dog was giving a "strong" or "hard" alert and thereby determine the direction and distance to the enemy. There are no hard-and-fast rules, and the dogs' responses were subjective. Therefore, the more experienced the handler and the longer the time he had spent with the dog, the better the interpretation of the dog's signaling he could make.

If the handler and dog were working the patrol downwind from the anticipated position of the enemy, the dog would work on the leash and the pair would be in the point position. If the wind was blowing on their backs, the scout dog team might be placed in the rear or the middle of the patrol. The most critical stage of a patrol was when the dog gave an alert and the patrol leader had to take firm, decisive action. Most casualties involving the handler and dog typically occurred at this point. One Silver Star was awarded in Korea posthumously to a handler killed along with his dog. Even though the dog alerted three times to the enemy, the patrol leader disregarded the information and did not halt the team to evaluate the situation before deciding on the next course of action.

By the end of 1952, the 26th Scout Dog Platoon had achieved great success and obtained significant experience in the field working the dogs. Peace talks continued, and President-elect Dwight D. Eisenhower visited Korea in December, attempting to break the stalemate that bogged down the bargaining. In March 1953, China and the United States agreed to exchange sick and wounded prisoners. The end of the conflict was near at hand. Three of the original dogs had that shipped over were still in service at this time, and First Lieutenant Deaner later pointed out, in a report generated in February 1953, several strong points and some weaknesses in using the dogs.[4]

Deaner noted that the dogs could scent best on level terrain. Mountains and hills tended to make the wind swirl, and an alert at one hundred yards from the enemy in these locations was considered very good. Still, there were times when the dog did not scent until thirty feet from his quarry. It was also difficult for the dog to scent someone on higher ground than the patrol, since scent often rises like smoke. But although the dog might not pick up a scent due to the terrain, his keen sense of hearing would also provide an alert—perhaps not as reliably, though.

The dogs employed by the 26th were considered ready for patrol work every four days. After the patrol they were given a day of rest, and then the daily routine of training would resume, to keep the dog fresh. It is often noted that they got bored on long ambush patrols, and handlers would comment that the dogs missed the excitement of the chase whereas, in training, once someone was scented they would begin running and provide evident excitement for the dog. In combat situations, the Chinese Communists usually shot back before they considered running away.

Members of the 26th Scout Dog Platoon were awarded a total of three Silver Stars, six Bronze Stars of Valor, and thirty-five Bronze Stars for meritorious service. On February 27, 1953, the Department of the Army also recognized the accomplishments of the platoon in General Orders No. 21 as follows:

> The 26th Infantry Scout Dog Platoon is cited for exceptionally meritorious conduct in the performance of outstanding services in direct support of combat operations in Korea during the period 12 June 1951 to 15 January 1953. The 26th Infantry Scout Dog Platoon, during its service in Korea, has participated in hundreds of combat patrol actions by supporting the patrols with the services of an expert scout dog handler and his highly trained scout dog. The members of the 26th Infantry Scout Dog Platoon, while participating in these patrols, were invariably located at the most vulnerable points in the patrol formation in order that the special aptitudes of the trained dog could be most advantageously used to give warning of the presence of the enemy. The unbroken record of faithful and gallant performance of these missions by the individual handlers and their dogs in support of patrols have saved countless casualties through giving early warning to the friendly patrol of threats to its security. The full value of the services ren-

dered by the 26th Infantry Scout Dog Platoon is nowhere better understood and more highly recognized than among the members of the patrols with whom the scout dog handlers and their dogs have operated. When not committed to action, the soldiers of the 26th Infantry Scout Dog Platoon have given unfailing efforts to further developing their personal skills as well as that of their dogs in order to better perform the rigorous duties which are required of them while on patrol. Throughout its long period of difficult and hazardous service, the 26th Infantry Scout Dog Platoon has never failed those with whom it served, has consistently shown outstanding devotion to duty in the performance of all of its other duties, and has won on the battlefield a degree of respect and admiration which has established it as a unit of the greatest importance to the Eighth United States Army. The outstanding performance of duty, proficiency, and esprit de corps invariably exhibited by the personnel of this platoon reflect the greatest credit on themselves and the military service of the United States.

General Orders 114
Headquarters
Eighth United States Army
Korea
January 18, 1953[5]

YANKEE–TAKE YOUR DOG AND GO HOME!

One thing was for certain: the Chinese did not like the American dogs. Many handlers found that in close-quarter fighting, the Chinese or North Koreans would try to kill the dog immediately. Sometimes the Communists attempted to unnerve the American soldiers by setting up loudspeakers and making short propaganda broadcasts during the night. On at least one occasion the loudspeakers blared forth, "Yankee–take your dog and go home!"[6] Perhaps if they had utilized scouting dogs themselves, the Chinese would not have felt that way. By all accounts, the success of ambush and reconnaissance patrols at night struck a certain fear in the Chinese and North Koreans alike.

During the war the 26th Scout Dog Platoon[7] employed

scout dogs almost exclusively at night. When it was desired to take prisoners, patrols were sent out along suspected routes in an effort to intercept the enemy. If the dog alerted, the patrol then deployed and set up an ambush. If the enemy was moving away, the patrol attempted to intercept them. An alert to an enemy patrol that was not moving allowed them to be encircled and the trap set. None of this would have been practical or effective without the services of a scout dog.

Most of the scout dogs were kept in the Far East Command after the conflict and retrained for sentry duty. The army intended to keep the K-9 Corps active, but a series of botched press releases linked the demise of the military dog program to the deactivation of Fort Carson. Letters of protest from across the country flooded the army, and several, like the following, were addressed to the secretary of defense.[8] Even active members of the 26th Scout Dog Platoon were confused.

Corporal Max Meyers wrote: "I am in the Army and was

In Korea, a quick and efficient method was found for moving scout dogs and handlers into areas where they were needed. *(National Archives)*

put into the scout dog platoon and trained dogs for nine months in the states and have had the same dog all the time. This dog 'Star' has saved my life and about 12 other men's lives. I would like to know if there is any way I could have him discharged the same time that I am. I would gladly pay the government for the dog and take all responsibility for him. I would appreciate it very much if you could help me in any way so I can take him home with me. This dog is not dangerous and would be suitable to civilian life."

A veteran of Korea, Frank Conanno of West Babylon, New York, wrote: "I strongly request you to reconsider demobilizing the K-9 Corps. These dogs performed a very useful service during the war as I can personally attest to. I owe my life to one of these dogs. While fighting in Korea I was attacked and one of these dogs took over my attacker and I was able to recover my footing and escape. Please reconsider."

Not all protests were from veterans. Wendy Bogue, from Eau Claire, Wisconsin, succinctly stated: "There isn't a thing on this old Mother Earth that is so faithful, so loyal, so willing to give his life for his master than a dog. Disposing of these dogs would be the greatest mistake the Army could make."

The army was not about to "dispose" of the K-9 Corps, but it sure would make a few mistakes in the upcoming years. The limitations and performance of the dogs in Korea paralleled the experiences of their World War II counterparts. The overriding concern surfaced in a memo from the Seventh Infantry Division, stating, "Several instances have been noted wherein maximum benefit was not obtained due to improper utilization of the dogs and a lack of understanding as to their capabilities and limitations."[9]

This "understanding" is the linchpin of using dogs in combat. Although dogs have come to be regarded as equipment in later years, it has to be understood that dogs are living and thinking animals and that each is an individual in its own right. The military, in general terms, had a terrible problem accepting this. All other equipment, be it an airplane or a tank, will act the same and work the same under a given set of circumstances. Within the entire arsenal of the American combat mil-

itary structure, only two distinct creatures did not fit this profile—man and dog.

Success depended on both the handler and the dog working together as a team. As one veteran scout dog handler
pointed out, "You can have the best dog in the world. But if
the guy on the other end of the leash doesn't understand his
dog, cannot pick up the subtle alert, then someone is going to
get killed."[10] Even after undergoing the same rigorous training,
dogs differed dramatically in not only what they alerted to but
how they displayed it. Some dogs of the same breed scented
from the ground, yet others favored an airborne scent. Others
alerted to suspicious sounds, whereas others might be oblivious, checking for any type of movement.

One dog who proved an outstanding success with the
26th Infantry Scout Dog Platoon in Korea was York (011X).
Between June 12, 1951, and June 26, 1953, York completed
148 combat patrols, the very last patrol coming one day before
the armistice was signed, officially ending the war. For this outstanding performance Gen. Samuel T. Williams awarded him
the Distinguished Service Award. No patrol member was ever
killed while York led point.

On May 8, 1957, York received orders to return from the
Far East to the dog training center at Fort Carson, Colorado.
Here the German shepherd became a member of the demonstration team, to improve public relations and to foster interest
in the recruitment and procurement of military working dogs.
When the training center at Fort Carson deactivated on July 1,
1957, York was transferred to Fort Benning, Georgia, where he
was once again attached to the 26th Infantry Scout Dog Platoon.[11]

ENTER THE AIR FORCE

During the years following the Korean conflict, several distinct
factors took place to alter the shape of the war dog program.
By 1957 there were fewer than 1,000 dogs in the military, and
most were in sentry positions. This included 500 in Europe,

250 in the Far East Command, a handful of sled dogs in Alaska, and 250 dogs scattered about in CONUS.[12]

With a nuclear buildup under way, the Strategic Air Command (SAC), as part of the now independent air force, increased in size dramatically during the early stages of the Cold War. In 1955, SAC representatives began an aggressive procurement program to obtain sentry dogs for airfields, equipment storage facilities, and specifically for missile sites. Many air bases were being developed and expanded at this time, but the massive fencing projects surrounding these facilities lagged behind. Sentry dogs helped to plug this security gap. During 1956, the Quartermaster Corps obtained an additional 593 dogs, with ongoing training at Fort Carson.

The next year, an additional 382 dogs were received, but the program came to an abrupt halt with the closure of the Colorado training facility. The air force now needed to estab-

The proliferation of missile sites across the country and their security requirements spurred the air force into adopting its own sentry program. *(National Archives)*

lish its own procurement and training location to continue the program. The army, in an abrupt shift in policy, cited little need of the animals for its own use and said it wished to demobilize the entire canine force. This was presumably an economic gesture only—and a surprising one, since it cost only about fifty-five cents a day to maintain a dog. It also coincided with the army's attempt to abandon horses for military funerals, preferring instead to use motorized carriages.[13]

With the army's position well stated, on March 22, 1957, the air force launched it own pilot program using ten dogs and their handlers at several Nike sites for a trial period. If this was successful, the plan called for procurement of thirty dogs per month until a full operational complement of three hundred was reached. While the air force continued to expand its sentry dog program, the Department of Defense (DoD) began an austerity program by scaling back the number of Infantry Scout Dog Platoons. The DoD deactivated the 25th IPSD (Fort Ord, California) on September 23, 1957, and eliminated the 44th IPSD (Fort Benning, Georgia), 48th IPSD (Fort Riley, Kansas), and 49th IPSD (Fort Lewis, Washington) two months later. The 26th IPSD once again remained the sole survivor as a training and demonstration unit at Fort Benning.

By the end of the decade the army, relegated to procuring dogs for the air force, now found itself scrambling to secure sufficient quantities of dogs for itself as air force requirements increased. The QMC announced the need to acquire one thousand dogs in September 1957, followed by an urgent appeal to the public in January 1960. The army offered up to $150 for German shepherds or mixed-breed shepherds to fill the air force quota.

Sensing it was time to take matters into its own hands, in October 1958 the air force established the Sentry Dog Training Branch of the Department of Security Police Training at Lackland Air Force Base, near San Antonio, Texas. Eventually over seven hundred acres were set aside for training dogs and handlers, and more than seven hundred kennels were built to house dogs in training and those newly procured. By February 1962, a shortage still existed, with another urgent appeal by the QMC for 560 dogs. This was followed by an attempt to recruit an additional 1,700 German shepherds during the remaining ten months of 1962. The QMC fell well short of this goal; it purchased only 524 dogs and received another 92 through donations. In June 1964 the air force relieved the Army Quartermaster Corps of procuring all "live animals not raised for food."

In attempting to obtain the necessary number of dogs to fill its assigned quotas, the air force began to send recruiting teams to military bases across the country. These twelve-man teams were comprised of a team leader, a procurement officer, a veterinarian and assistants, and several dog trainers and handlers. Although this endeavor proved beneficial, because the dogs were sorely needed, it also proved expensive.

The air force recruiters first contacted the local media and either through donated or paid advertising called on owners to bring in their dogs—it was the patriotic thing to do. Examinations were given on the spot, which meant the owners did not have to wait to get paid. With the air force's stringent requirements, about 40 percent of the dogs were rejected outright—the reasons were split evenly between physical problems and improper temperament. Most physical rejections were due to hip dysplasia and heartworms. Each dog was purchased at an average of $150. Some owners would hold out for more, but in general, higher prices did not make the dogs any more desirable for military service. Contract breeders also contacted the air force, and though not turned away, they were often discouraged because of the strict military requirements, which probably cut into their profit margins.

The weakest point in the entire system was an inability to recruit a sufficient number of dogs. Besides the air force, police departments and private security firms also desired the versatile canines and often outbid their military counterparts. The army had to compete with the air force for dogs, and it considered establishing its own independent procurement arm. But soon it realized that it could not do a better job (or a more economical one) than what the air force was presently doing. The army purchased its German shepherds from the air force for only $175 each–truly a bargain, based on the time and effort it took to recruit them. Recruiting a sufficient number of dogs turned out to be an annual headache for both the air force and the army for many years to come. No longer did the military have the resources of an organization like Dogs for Defense to fall back on.

6.

THE VIETNAM SAGA

WAR ON THE HORIZON

President Dwight D. Eisenhower not only administered the Korean armistice, he can also be given credit for introducing the first American military component to the Republic of Vietnam (RVN). In May 1960 he increased the total number of allowable military "advisers" to 685. In two years, with John F. Kennedy at the helm, that number increased to over 10,000. Labeled "advisers," they acted and dressed the same as combat troops.

In 1960 the Vietcong (VC) ran rampant throughout South Vietnam. Long before the involvement of American fighting troops, the Military Assistance Advisory Group, Vietnam (MAAGV), recommended the establishment of a military dog program for the Army of the Republic of Vietnam (ARVN). Some American advisers were familiar with the British use of dogs to put down Communist insurrection in Malaysia. A simple premise surfaced: to provide sentry and scout dogs for the ARVN. The sentry dogs would guard key installations, with the scout dogs keeping ARVN troops from being ambushed and in turn aiding in the hunt for the VC. Like many ideas, it looked great on paper, but in practice it was a disaster from day one.

The first entry of American dogs to Southeast Asia began in 1960 as the air force began a research-and-development project to expand on some new ideas, believing that South Vietnam provided an excellent proving ground. The project was split into four distinct areas: first, to see if military working dogs were practical in such an environment; second, to begin experimenting with a combination sentry/scout dog. The third phase decided which breed would be most suitable in a tropical climate. The final objective was to see if dogs could be bred in-country.[1]

Air force personnel set up shop at an old French dog compound in Go Vap, on the western outskirts of Saigon. The French had left behind some bloodhounds, German shepherds, and a couple of Doberman pinschers. Most of the work done by this team was a rehash of knowledge already gained from World War II and by civilians decades earlier. The small group plugged away for about a year and then disbanded, since MAAGV had already established the requirements of an ARVN dog program independent of this experimental venture.

The ARVN officials led the MAAGV advisers to believe that veterinary support would be no problem. In reality, only about twenty veterinarians existed in the entire country. Most of them were elderly and no longer practicing, with only four in uniform as members of ARVN. Not even one Vietnamese veterinarian, military or civilian, had experience with dogs. And why would they? This was a country where people often ate dogs. No one ever paid to have a dog treated in Vietnam— not when people couldn't even pay for their own basic health care.

In the fall of 1961 MAAGV further recommended that 468 sentry dogs and 538 scout dogs be sent to RVN. These dogs were purchased privately, since the United States military did not possess the required number in its inventory. The DoD figured that 300 dogs were sufficient to start the Vietnamese program. These dogs could be purchased in West Germany and then transported by airplane. The army maintained a Dog Training Detachment in Lenggries, West Germany, under the command of Capt. Barton H. Patterson. Patterson and veterinarian Capt. William E. Callahan crisscrossed the country in search of German shepherds to be sent to Vietnam. They were purchased for about $40 (American) each, and Callahan gave each dog a brief physical before acceptance.[2]

In May 1962, Brig. Gen. Russell McNellis, chief of the U.S. Army Veterinary Corps, assembled a team of three officers and three enlisted men to pull six-month temporary duty in Vietnam. Their job was to establish veterinary support for the new dog program. One team member, S.Sgt. William J. Kadic, would eventually earn the Army Commendation Medal for his accomplishments in beginning a "successful" program.

The military press can put the spin on anything, turning disasters into glowing achievements. For example, after Kadic's return and medal award, a military reporter asked about the special effort to keep the dogs in top physical condition. Kadic responded that it was partly due to their "special" diet, saying, "Such foods as rice, buffalo meat, carrots, tomatoes, local vegetables, salt, meal, duck eggs, and chicken kept the animals in good condition."[3]

In truth, the dogs had a hard time of it from the day they arrived in-country. While advisers were present, the dogs appeared well treated and fed. In practice, the recommendations for the dogs' basic diet was ignored by ARVN officers. That minimal diet would cost more than what was being provided to the average soldier on a daily basis! The suggestion by MAAGV members to feed a dog better than an ARVN soldier flew like a lead balloon. In the years that followed, even with support from U.S. Veterinary Corps members, nearly 90 percent of ARVN dog deaths would be attributed to malnutrition.

By the middle of 1962, ARVN soldiers began assembling for training as handlers and veterinarian technicians. Among the veterinary advisers present at the time was 1st Lt. Willard "Greg" Nelson. In a letter to Col. William H. H. Clark, author of *The History of the United States Army Veterinary Corps in Vietnam,* Nelson related the first major meeting between South Vietnamese handlers and dogs newly arrived from the heart of West Germany: "When the dogs first arrived they were scared to death of the Vietnamese. They would break away from them and run to us for protection. They had never seen Orientals and just didn't understand them at all. The dogs had German names and listening to the Vietnamese trying to pronounce

Rolf, Rex, and Arco was quite an experience. Later, the dogs gave their complete allegiance to their Vietnamese handlers and became wary of Caucasians."[4]

For tactical training the army sent four instructors to South Vietnam in April 1962. Among the group was SFC Jesse Mendez, who started to train ARVN soldiers at Go Vap while a larger training facility was being built at Thanh Tuy Ha. Mendez found a number of unexpected problems no one had even considered:

An ARVN veterinarian inspects a scout dog. Few veterinarians familiar with dogs could be found in South Vietnam before American intervention. *(Carlisle Barracks)*

There were many difficulties encountered in getting the ARVN handlers to accept their dogs. Of course many Vietnamese were Buddhist, who believed in reincarnation and none of them wanted to come back as a dog. It was very difficult to show how valuable the dogs were for security and scouting purposes. When we first got there, we had a heck of a mess. The air force had trained many sentry and attack dogs and ARVN was trying to use them with infantry units out in the field. These dogs would bark on patrol missions, posing a serious problem. On top of that, they wanted to attack and chew up friendly patrol members. The only type of dog that would work out on patrol was a silent scout dog. It took a while to get these dogs exchanged out. Eventually we got trained dogs to each of the five ARVN scout dog platoons.

But the biggest problem was trying to get the ARVN handlers to praise their dogs if they performed well or did what was expected from them. Perhaps they were reluctant because of their

An ARVN handler and scout dog cross a river about forty kilometers north of Can Tho, in the Vinh Long Province. *(National Archives)*

dog's size—after all, many handlers only outweighed their dogs by a few pounds.[5]

By September 1964, the ARVN had amassed 327 dogs, some of them obtained from the early U.S. Air Force (USAF) research-and-development project begun in 1960. Disease and accidents soon decimated the ranks of scout and sentry dogs. Although authorized to have 1,000 dogs, by 1966 the population had dropped to just 50 scout and 80 sentry dogs. The United States continued to prop up the ARVN dog program over the next few years in an effort to overcome their high mortality rate. The biggest boost came from the American withdrawal that began in the latter part of 1969. The military decision to turn over *our* dogs actually gave the ARVN forces a surplus. With the fall of South Vietnam in 1975, the dogs were abandoned, along with helicopters, tanks, and the other articles of war. Officially, no one really knows what happened to them—the only questions that really remain are how many were killed, eaten, or just simply starved to death.

The U.S. program would fare much better, although it too would be hampered by the same problems that had been around since World War II. Sentry and scout dogs anchored the military dog program in Vietnam. In a short time, Americans would also develop a tracker dog program, introduce a dog trained to detect tunnels, and resurrect the M-dog—all with excellent results.

ON GUARD AGAINST THE VC

At first there was little thought given by the United States to using sentry dogs in Vietnam, although they easily proved themselves in overseas duty at air bases in nearby Korea and Japan. In March 1961, the air force sent two instructors, along with ten sentry dogs, to assist the Vietnamese air force to establish better base security. Little supervision and support were given to the project, and the program deteriorated quickly. Veterinary care was next to nonexistent at this time, and no one expressed an interest in establishing a training regimen. The concept disintegrated entirely as the dogs became pets and mascots, losing completely their worth as sentries.

Four years later, sentry dogs were still not part of any American security plan in Vietnam. The director of security and law enforcement for the air force believed that the tropical climate would be too oppressive for the animals and they would be ineffective.[6] Obviously he had not been informed that ARVN forces were already using German shepherds extensively as scouts and sentries. Opposing their use on these grounds meant that once again not everyone was acquainted with the capabilities of the German shepherd. Clearly the history of their deployment in tropical climates, particularly in the China-Burma-India theater of operations during World War II, proved they could adapt to the climate of the area. The belief of the security director also reveals that information about dogs and their capabilities and weaknesses did not circulate throughout the military establishment to any great degree.

On July 1, 1965, a sapper (Vietcong combat engineer) raid against the Da Nang air base changed all that. The VC engineers managed to enter the base past security guards and an assortment of electronic detectors. Two days after this enemy penetration, the USAF quickly launched Project Top Dog 145.[7] This hastily conceived plan called for the deployment of forty handlers and forty dogs to Vietnam for a period of four months. The teams quickly assembled at Lackland Air Force Base and arrived in Vietnam two weeks later. The air force dispersed these sentry dog teams to the Tan Son Nhut and Bien Hoa air bases near Saigon, and to the Da Nang air base, near the demilitarized zone (DMZ).

After a successful four-month trial period, the handlers returned to the United States while the dogs stayed on duty. Trained handlers already in Vietnam took over their places. This trial period proved beyond any doubt, for the air force at least, that German shepherds could acclimatize to the heat and provide an effective deterrent against air base attacks.

With Project Top Dog over, the next phase, dubbed Project Limelight, acquired more dogs at Lackland for base security and began the escalation of canines shipped to Vietnam.

Although the majority of these additional dogs came from Lackland, others came from the Pacific Air Force Sentry Dog Center at Showa, Japan, and Kadena Air Base, on Okinawa. During the early days of our involvement in the war, most of the air bases weren't even expecting the arrival of sentry dog teams. A case in point was the arrival of the 633rd Security Police Squadron (SPS) at Pleiku in the Central Highlands, on October 29, 1965. Airman First Class John Risse recalled getting off the C-130 transport that day:

> Upon our arrival we were told we were unexpected. We just laughed and took our dogs off the plane, staking them out between the runway and rice paddies. There wasn't a place for our dogs to stay, so the first day we began making temporary kennels for them. We put the shipping crates in two lines and staked the dogs between them. Within a couple of days we had our dogs settled in and we began guard duty at the ammo dump, fuel storage area, and the perimeter of the base between the runway and the rice paddies.[8]

The air force continued to increase its German shepherd sentry dog force for the next two years, reaching a peak of 476 in January 1967. These dogs maintained perimeter watches at Bien Hoa, Binh Thuy, Cam Ranh Bay, Da Nang, Nha Trang, Tuy Hoa, Phu Cat, Phan Rang, Tan Son Nhut, and Pleiku. The number of air force dogs declined after 1967. One reason is that the bases were becoming very congested and so noisy that the dogs could not be worked effectively. In 1969 the U.S. forces also began their planned gradual withdrawal, and consequently fewer handlers were available or required.

FOLLOWING CLOSELY ON THE HEELS of the air force, the army began deploying its sentry dogs to Vietnam during September 1965. The army sentry dog teams originally comprised several military police detachments until formally organized as the 212th Military Police Company (Sentry Dog) in January 1966. This initiative formed the first of three companies under direct command of the 18th Military Police Brigade. With 250 officers and men, and about 200 dogs, they provided security protection for fifteen different locations.

In February 1967, the 981st Military Police Company (Sentry Dog) was activated at Fort Carson, Colorado, and arrived in Vietnam in November 1967. And in January 1970, the 595th Military Police Company (Sentry Dog) arrived, bringing the army sentry dog population to a wartime high of approximately three hundred. Beginning in April 1966, the Marines and navy each had one sentry dog unit stationed at Da Nang.

Most of the dogs and handlers for the army and Marines were trained at the U.S. Army Pacific Sentry Dog School in Okinawa. Other handlers completed courses at the military police school at Fort Gordon, Georgia, and then obtained their dogs and an additional eight weeks of training at Lackland. Some handlers were yanked from different security positions in-country and given on-the-job training (OJT).

In just a few months the sentries proved their worth, as Vietcong forces began probing various air bases. In February 1966, three attempts were made by the VC to infiltrate the air base at Pleiku, in the Central Highlands. A couple of weeks

Sentry dog refresher training in South Vietnam. Most training took place in the early morning or evening hours, when the cooler air helped to prevent possible heatstroke for the dogs. *(Carlisle Barracks)*

later several probers were routed from Bien Hoa, and two months after that several attempts to enter Tan Son Nhut were circumvented. The dogs proved to be a frustrating experience for the VC attempting to infiltrate different installations. Through the end of 1966 no successful penetrations were made at Phan Rang, Qui Nhon, or Ban Me Thot by guerrilla forces. These successes prompted the 1st Cavalry Division (Airmobile) to also request sentry dogs to secure its firebase facilities at An Khe.[9]

With the succession of failed attempts, the VC tried to infiltrate by using different sprays and pepper. Before going into action, most of these sappers spread a garliclike herb called *toi* all over their bodies in an effort to disguise their human scent.[10] Failing at these efforts, sporadic mortar attacks were directed at kennel areas at several air bases in an attempt to reduce the sentry dog population. On April 13, ten mortar rounds were directed at the Tan Son Nhut kennels, but all missed their mark. Sentries were still able to capture twenty-five suspected VC near the base perimeter.

At Tan Son Nhut Air Base on December 4, 1966, one handler and three sentry dogs were killed during a VC penetration. This would be the largest battle involving sentry dogs, their handlers, and the Vietcong during the entire American involvement. Tan Son Nhut, bordered by metropolitan Saigon to the east and south, was a huge facility and the largest air base in South Vietnam. The base was designed for 3,000 people but had 25,000 and swelled to over 50,000 during the day as civilian and military personnel came to work. This posed serious security problems, and the first major attack is thought to have come from VC who infiltrated the site during the day.

It began just after midnight as A2C. Leroy E. Marsh and his dog, Rebel, detected a group of at least seventy-five VC less than one hundred yards away. Marsh released Rebel, who was quickly cut down by automatic fire. This gave Marsh enough time to radio for a reaction force and to make his way to the next sentry post, about three hundred yards away. About an hour later A2C. Larry G. Laudner's dog, Cubby, alerted to the same group. Laudner released Cubby, and the dog was then shot and killed.[11]

The raiding party was still in the vicinity as dawn approached. Once again a sentry, A1C. Dale Sidwell, with his dog, Toby, alerted to the infiltrators. The VC opened up and Sidwell returned fire, killing one VC. One handler was then killed trying to rescue a wounded officer, and another handler pursued a six-man VC mortar crew. The VC then went to ground and tried to hide in the immediate vicinity and wait for nightfall before attempting to escape.[12]

Early in the evening, A2C. Robert Thorneburg and Nemo alerted to several VC hiding in a cemetery within the base perimeter. Thorneburg released Nemo, heard several shots, and could hear his dog crying in pain. Thorneburg went looking for him and killed one VC before being wounded by return fire. Before the reaction team reached them, Nemo had crawled across his master's body and refused to let anyone get near him. Finally Nemo was persuaded to leave Thorneburg as other handlers administered first aid.

Shot in the face, Nemo lost sight in one eye despite the quick efforts of base veterinarians. Nemo would no longer walk sentry duty, but returned to Lackland in July 1967 as an air force canine recruiter. As part of the air force dog recruitment drive, he made numerous television appearances across the country and helped to maintain an adequate supply of dogs for all the armed services. Nemo died on March 15, 1973, from a combination of his original war wounds and natural causes.[13]

Attacks by the VC in superior numbers did not always lead to success. In January 1967, at a construction area near Pleiku, an army handler armed with only a .45-caliber pistol and his dog repelled twelve VC armed with automatic weapons. Penetration of air base defenses required stealth and luck for the enemy, both of which were often in short supply when sentry dogs walked a nighttime perimeter. The sentry dogs provided a psychological boost for the handler on nightly patrols and a deterrent to enemy infiltrators. A common

Nemo, wounded at Tan Son Nhut Air Base in 1966, returned to Lackland AFB as a canine recruiter. Nemo toured the country, making numerous television appearances and helping the air force fulfill its canine recruitment quota during the war. *(Mary Thurston)*

phrase heard throughout Vietnam was "The night belongs to Charlie." And in this war of attrition with the VC this was often true. Contributions by sentry dogs helped to even the playing field.

With the vicious nature of the sentry dog at this time, little bonding occurred with the handler, who often had a hard time controlling his own dog. This contrasted sharply with scout, mine/tunnel, and tracker dogs, who maintained milder dispositions. Even as ferocious sentinels, they still remained self-appointed guardians for their handlers, providing a margin of safety on remote nighttime perimeter walks. Sentries not only had to worry about VC infiltrators but also had to remain alert to the presence of poisonous krait snakes underfoot. For humans a snakebite meant almost instantaneous death, prompting many guards to carry antivenom serum.[14]

Airman Second Class Robert Horen's first encounter with this dangerous snake came only one hour after the start of his first patrol. While walking along a remote perimeter of Pleiku Air Base with his dog, Mac, Horen heard an almost inaudible hiss. Mac then pushed his handler aside, taking the bite in his shoulder. Dogs are more resistant to the snakebite than humans. Horen kept his composure and administered the antivenom to Mac. Quick intervention by base medical technicians saved the dog's life, and within three days Mac was back on duty with Horen. Not all dogs were so lucky, and carrying antivenom serum was not standard operating practice at every air base in Vietnam.

In February 1969, air force sentries captured a sapper in an attempted penetration at Phu Cat Air Base. In the subsequent interrogation he related that his company commander had discussed the dangers involved with these dogs and what steps could be taken. The VC engineer stated, "The commander stressed that they [dogs] were very intelligent and were to be respected. If any man heard or saw one he was to lie down immediately, hold his breath, and remain motionless until he left."[15]

Few people, if any, believed that sentry dogs did not provide outstanding service in Vietnam. Captain Stephen A. Canavera, Security Police Operations officer at Binh Thuy Air Base, stated: "of all the equipment and methods used to detect an attacking enemy force, the sentry dog has provided the most sure, all inclusive means."[16] Canavera certainly believed in the value of sentry dogs and their handlers, but that does not mean they were always congratulated. In some cases, the men and dogs alerted to problems that the higher echelon refused to acknowledge. During October 1967, on a routine night patrol, SP4 James Kelley, assigned to the 18th MP Brigade, walked patrol at the U.S. Army Long Binh Ammunition Depot with his dog, Rock. Kelley relates:

> At the corner of the dump I was talking with another dog handler named O'Neil, underneath the guard tower. As we were talking, my dog Rock suddenly alerted and I looked out over the

wire and I saw somebody. I can stand here and swear to God I saw this guy. So O'Neil sees him, and both of our dogs are going crazy and I yell up at the guard tower, "Do you see him out there?" Well these guys are smoking dope and one of the guys says he sees something.

I have this pencil flare in my pocket. I popped the flare, which comes up red, which means (and I found out later because no one ever told us), that you mobilize all these goofy things and all of a sudden all these helicopters are up in the air. In the meantime before any of this happens, I see this guy running. So I flip the selector over [M16] to full automatic and start popping caps out. The guys in the tower turn a 60 [machine gun] on him, and they start letting go. Well, the next thing I know we have helicopter gunships in the air, flares, and all this, and I'm being yelled at by a Major that there wasn't anything there. I'm relieved on the spot and sent back to headquarters to make out a firearms use report. Now I thought that was kind of strange—after all we were in the middle of a war.[17]

Kelley and his dog obviously alerted to either a sapper or a VC infiltrator. The next day, no body had been found, and neither had any tunnel, further discrediting Kelley, even though several others saw a figure running. No one at the time had any inkling as to just what the VC had accomplished at every air base in South Vietnam with respect to their elaborate and numerous tunnels. Many of these intricate tunnel systems were never detected during the course of the war. Sentry dogs proved themselves time and again by alerting to infiltrators on the ground. Below the surface, a surefire method had yet to be established to detect these tunnels, which many commanders just refused to believe even existed.

The last battle death of an air force canine sentry took place on January 29, 1969, at Phan Rang Air Base. The majority of sentry dog deaths during the war did not come from the enemy. In the early years of the American buildup in Vietnam several fatalities were attributed to spoiled food. By far the biggest factor accounting for most deaths and injuries was heat-induced illness and snakebites; these were two enemies the animals could not cope with on their own.

By 1967, the military had close to thirty years of sentry dog experience, both in training and in deployment. Common sense dictated that this background would translate into progressively superior sentry dogs. Yet the air force continued on a route that made these dogs a severe risk and an increasing liability to both handlers and any other personnel who came in contact with them. The original concept of having the most vicious dog at your disposal, both as a psychological and as a physical deterrent, backfired in alarming ways. In one sense it can be considered the supreme abuse, breaking the human-animal bond.

Sentry dogs became an inherent physical risk for handlers, veterinarian technicians, and kennel maintenance personnel. One case occurred on a road on the outskirts of Saigon. A sentry dog was riding in a jeep that passed another vehicle with several army personnel on board. The dog quickly lashed out and mangled the ear of an unfortunate infantryman in the passing jeep. If a fence or wall happened to be between the dog and his prey, he would do almost anything to get through. And as handlers rotated from service, went on leave, or became sick, the new handlers often found themselves in the impossible situation of trying to convince a snarling beast to accept them.

These problems (and it should be noted that they are always attributed to the dogs, never to their masters) and many others forced the air force to begin experimenting with a new category of sentry dog. In 1968 a program began to recruit and train patrol dogs, canines adapted to working in a variety of situations and with different people. The air force hired the Metropolitan Police Department of Washington, D.C., to train four patrol dog teams. Their initial trials began at Andrews Air Force Base, Maryland, and these were wholly successful.

Replacing the almost uncontrollable beast was now a dog that could work perimeter defense unmuzzled and even off-leash. But the handler could easily command it to attack an intruder. This meant that the dog could achieve a multipurpose role such as crowd control, tracking, and escort service. Stationed worldwide, some of these dogs did find limited service with both the air force and the army in Vietnam.

The Strategic Air Command (SAC) came to the same conclusions at the end of a 120-day test in March 1969 that involved thirty patrol dogs. Six of the dogs had been formerly trained as sentries and twenty-four were new recruits. After completing tests at Castle AFB and Vandenberg AFB in California and Davis-Monthan in Arizona, observers stated that they were "far superior to the sentry dog." One adviser involved in the new program said, "With the sentry dog, the handler could only look forward to spending his time in isolated areas. With the patrol dog a much broader spectrum of security police activity is open to him."[18] Shortly after these tests the air force adopted the patrol dog as the standard military working dog.

RETURN OF THE SCOUT DOGS

In 1965 a turning point, one of many that surfaced throughout the torturous conflict in Vietnam, occurred. With the military situation in South Vietnam deteriorating rapidly, the United States faced two choices: either call it quits and pull out, or up the ante. President Lyndon Johnson chose the latter, escalating the fight and taking a more offensive posture. General William Westmoreland figured he needed 275,000 troops to halt the degenerating tactical conditions in the south. By the end of the year, 183,000 Americans had been deployed.

For the Vietcong this made little difference in their tactics. Since the Americans had intervened, they always attacked when everything was to their advantage. A quick strike and they melted back into the jungle or the countryside. The VC ambushes on American patrols increased dramatically. Trip wires, bamboo whips, and punji pits took their toll both physically and psychologically. The Vietcong were everywhere—yet often nowhere to be found.[19]

Viewed on the large scale, the United States conducted

the war based on World War II tactics. Yet the VC fought a guerrilla action, requiring an appropriate response with effective countermeasures. For that reason, the army decided to reactivate its scout dog program in 1965. "Ever since the Vietnam War began, Charlie has been hitting only when everything has been to his advantage," said Sgt. Jesse Mendez, lead

In 1969, SFC Jesse Mendez, a scout dog instructor at Fort Benning, Georgia, departs a plane with Pal, a forty-six-pound scout dog, in the first military parachute free fall involving a working dog. *(Jesse Mendez)*

scout dog instructor at Fort Benning, Georgia. Mendez had already spent two and a half years in Vietnam helping to build the ARVN scout dog program. He returned in time for the reemergence of the American version.

To support Vietnam infantry operations, an initial request for scout dogs arrived at Fort Benning in September 1965. This was planned as a one-time training expansion for the 26th IPSD along with an increase in both kennel and veterinary facilities. Considering the tactical situation in Vietnam at the time, this initial requirement was deemed inadequate, and in December an additional thirteen infantry scout dog platoons and three Marine platoons were added.[20]

Meanwhile, the DoD established its annual dog recruitment quota at 1,000, and it soon became evident that a serious shortage would occur as the war escalated. Even with the established quota, only 761 dogs were obtained in 1965. This problem could be attributed to a high rejection rate of 30 to 50 percent of the potential canine recruits. Competition with civilians and private security firms also hampered military procurement. The DoD doubled the annual quota in January 1966, and the army again toyed with the idea of establishing its own breeding program.

A start-up shortage also existed between handlers and instructors. The twelve-week course for new handlers and their dogs taxed the few qualified instructors, only 40 percent of whom had been to Vietnam. Officially, all personnel entering the scout dog program were to be either "volunteers or selected individuals." Although this was desired, since proper motivation in handlers could only be achieved if they truly liked dogs, it was not a fact of life. As a crash program, this was probably the weakest point in the army's attempt to field effective scout dog teams.

During the winter of 1965, the Marines again entered tactical dog training with an interservice training pact with the 26th IPSD. This would be the first time since World War II that the Marines would use scout dogs. The indomitable spirit of the Doberman pinscher gave way to the more versatile German shepherd for this fight. First Lieutenant Robert

Wilder commanded the group of thirty-six Marines and twenty-eight purebred German shepherds scheduled to participate in the 540-hour training course at Fort Benning. Captain Arthur Blair, who had recently returned from Vietnam, became project officer, assisted by Lt. John Clark, commander of the 26th IPSD. The Marines began with fresh dogs, having no obedience training at all. According to Sgt. Charles Paris, a training NCO for the joint effort, "These dogs are just like humans. Some are quick to learn and others are slow-witted. Some cooperate and others are stubborn. You just don't know what to expect until the dog and man start working together."[21]

Two Marine scout dog platoons deployed to Vietnam in February 1966 under the command of Wilder. The Marines kenneled their fifty-six dogs near Da Nang at Camp Kaiser, named after the first Marine scout dog to be killed in action. Kaiser and his handler, Lance Cpl. Alfredo Salazar, had participated in a dozen major operations and thirty patrols. On their last patrol together, the VC hit them with automatic fire and hand grenades. Kaiser took the first hit. Salazar knelt beside his dog. "He tried to lick my hand," he said, "and then he died."

Wilder immediately reported some problems with the dogs, especially with their acclimatization to the heat. He suggested more time be spent conditioning the dogs. Handlers also needed to quickly recognize the onset of heatstroke, which could occur after only a few hours on patrol.[22] Some problems arose simply because dogs were unfamiliar with certain situations, such as the use of shotguns and flares. No one needed a dog to start barking after a flare popped up during a nighttime ambush.

"Everyone wants our scout dogs," stated 1st Lt. Ronald Neubauer, who had replaced Wilder within a few weeks after arriving in-country. "Although people have to be convinced that the dogs will be a positive use to them, once a unit uses dogs, they always come back for more. At times requests have to be turned down because of the limited number of dogs available," Neubauer reported.[23] In the first year of Marine operations, twelve dogs in the first platoon had been wounded and two killed, while the second platoon had seven wounded. Although handlers from both platoons had been wounded, none had been killed.

When they first arrived in Vietnam, dogs were considered just a curiosity and another unnecessary burden. But Neubauer stated, "We've never had a patrol ambushed that has had a dog along. The dog has always managed to sniff out the danger and force the VC to show his hand before he wanted to."[24] Patrol commitments for the dogs and handlers lasted from two hours up to five days. But, as in World War II, many field commanders did not always know the best tactical advantages for employing the versatile scout dogs.

The first opportunity to employ U.S. Army scout dogs in Vietnam came in June 1966, as Lt. Teddy Hampton and the 25th IPSD arrived at Tan Son Nhut, just outside of Saigon. Here they acclimatized to the tropical climate, continued their training, and then moved to Phuoc Vinh, north of Saigon, in III Corps as their base of operations. A month later the 38th IPSD, commanded by Lt. Ralph Harrison, arrived at Cu Chi, near the infamous "Iron Triangle," an area of high-intensity VC activity. Harrison expected the platoon's twenty-seven dogs to be used immediately for combat and recon patrols, village-clearing missions, and security. "Our main concern now is to prove the value of the dogs," Harrison said. "We want the rifleman to have confidence in the dog's performance."[25] The platoon soon entered its baptism of fire during operations in Ia Drang Valley.

During one operation, a scout dog, named Tiger, with the 25th IPSD gave his handler a strong alert. He prevented the company from walking into a battalion-size VC ambush three hundred yards away. Lieutenant Hampton later stated, "After Tiger gave the alert, the company swung left and hit just the trailing edge of the ambush." A firefight erupted with only light casualties on the company. Tiger fell from one of the first shots, and his handler was wounded during the exchange of small-arms fire that followed. Within two months, the 25th IPSD conducted 310 patrols as part of the Ia Drang Valley action. They accounted for the capture of forty-one North Vietnamese Army (NVA) soldiers and seventy VC suspects.

By November 1966, the two Marine scout dog platoons had participated in eleven major operations, which characterized both the strengths and weaknesses of the dogs. Lieutenant Neubauer, reporting on activities, stated, "It has been estimated that well over two thousand Marine lives have been saved since the insertion of the 1st Scout Dog Platoon into Vietnam."[26]

The Marines ran into several problems that could easily be corrected. During training, all personnel ahead of the patrols were considered hostile. In Vietnam, especially when entering a village, dogs alerted to civilians and VC alike. This meant that the patrol leader needed to clear the village of civilians first for the dogs to effectively alert to the enemy. The

A scout dog departs a UH-1 Huey to participate in a search-and-destroy mission in the Northwest Kantum Province. *(National Archives)*

training at Fort Benning also had not considered the possibility that domestic and farm animals would be present in villages. Some dogs became easily distracted, while others wanted to cut loose and give the animals a good chase.

The early success of the army and Marine scout dog teams did not go unnoticed by the air force. By the end of 1966, the air force had firmly established its security ground forces at all the air bases in Vietnam. The air force did not want to count on the army or the Marines to defend against battalion-size attacks from the VC or NVA, and it decided that a quick reaction force composed entirely of air force personnel could handle any threat. A decision was made that scout dogs would be one component of this mobile force.[27] This effectively took the static perimeter defense into a new dimension—outside the bounds of the air base in search of the enemy and early interdiction.

The Safe Side evaluation was a hastily conceived operation. Fort Benning could not accommodate the air force for scout dog training, given the little time available. An interim program was established at Lackland AFB with fourteen German shepherds that were originally intended to begin routine sentry training. Three army instructors assigned to the USAF sentry dog course who had previous scout dog experience took responsibility for the new training program. The handlers selected were former honor graduates of the USAF sentry dog handlers course. After twelve weeks of training they joined the 1041st USAF Police Squadron at Schofield Barracks in Hawaii, where the entire Safe Side unit assembled.

From January to July 1967, the 1041st evaluated the use of scout dogs at and around the Phu Cat Air Base on the Vietnamese coast in the II Corps area. Although thirty days was set aside for the dogs to acclimatize, it was found that most were ready to work after only four to six days. During this six-month period, the scout dog teams conducted 30 patrols, 54 ambush/blocking force positions, 430 outposts, and 152 camp security patrols.

A review of this scout dog detachment proved again the desirability of having the dogs accompany the security unit.

Their employment at listening posts during the night made these positions attain the same effectiveness they had during the day. Safe Side, as a crash program, had no definite goals, and the true capability of the scout dog teams would never be realized. Therefore, security forces had little background on employing scout dogs to their best advantage and most han-

The air force demonstrates a rappelling harness made from a poncho. When helicopters couldn't land because of the terrain, scout dogs could still accompany patrol members using this method. *(National Archives)*

dlers considered these scouts the same as sentry or patrol dogs. Although the initial training was given by army personnel with scout dog experience, air force commanders really had no idea what role scout dogs should play and should have been satisfied with the capabilities of sentry and patrol dogs.

In 1967, as the war dragged on, American involvement escalated at breakneck speed, and seven more scout dog platoons joined in the fight, bringing the total number to seventeen by year's end. The army started the year with about 380 dogs but within twelve months that figure jumped to more than 1,000. These scout dog platoons had the responsibility of covering the 65,726 square miles of South Vietnam, an area roughly the size of Oklahoma.

SOUTH VIETNAM WAS BROKEN into four military zones known as Corps Areas. Nearly half of the scout dog platoons were in III Corps, an area surrounding Saigon that was the most populated region within the country. Known as the Piedmont, this area comprised many rolling hills and flat plains and held most of the sanctuaries for the Communists. It also bordered the major supply stations for the VC and NVA along the Ho Chi Minh Trail in Cambodia. Scout dogs assisted infantry units for supply and personnel interdiction. Small wonder that this area would host the most scout dog teams and consequently see most of the missions during the war. The terrain of III Corps also lent itself to a great number of search-and-destroy missions, and scout dogs provided an effective, although low-tech, approach to stemming the Communist infiltration routes. For all their worth, scout dogs and handlers were often scarce, as the military concentrated on sophisticated weaponry and heavier firepower.

Handlers put great stock in a dog's capabilities, but a wise one always tempered that judgment. "One eye was on my dog and the other was on the terrain around me, because I didn't trust the dog completely," said Sgt. Robert Kollar, 58th IPSD. Based at Phuoc Vinh, Kollar worked Rebel (M421) beginning in September 1968. "As far as I was concerned," Kollar stated,

A scout dog from the 25th IPSD and patrol members take a break and relax in Quang Nai Province as part of Task Force Oregon in 1967. *(National Archives)*

"he [the dog] had the mind of a four-year-old. If a human being can screw up, and enough of them did, I sure as hell know a dog can."[28]

Many handlers bonded emotionally with their dogs as if they were their own—as they should, since their lives often depended on them. This gave each person a good understanding of the advantages and limitations of the animal in his charge. Some men were killed trying to save their dogs' lives, and many canines took the brunt of booby trap explosions, saving the lives of their handlers. In 1968, for example, Sgt. Robert Himrod and his dog, Miss Cracker, 49th IPSD, worked a recon patrol just six miles south of Saigon. Attached to Company A, 2nd Battalion, 3rd Infantry, 199th Infantry Brigade

(Red Catchers), the two worked near a river that bordered Hun Village, just south of Saigon. As the pair approached a low limb, a slight popping sound could be heard. "We both knew it was a booby trap," Himrod recalled.[29] "I jerked back on the leash frantically as I hit the ground. She [Cracker] reeled back, but the leash caught on the limb as the bomb exploded."

Miss Cracker took the full force of the blast and Himrod's foot got nailed by a piece of shrapnel. The pair were quickly dusted off by a medevac helicopter. Though injured, Himrod tended to Cracker's wound; suddenly she stopped breathing. Without hesitation he grasped her snout and applied mouth-to-mouth resuscitation in a vain attempt to keep his canine comrade alive. Cracker died a short time later. "I'm not sure if I missed her alert, it happened so fast," he later stated. "It may sound funny to someone else, but she was more than a dog. She was also a close friend and the only reason I survived that day." Himrod's experience is just one example of the stories repeated on hundreds of occasions throughout the war.

Of course, all handler deaths could not be avoided, and as in all wars past and those to come, letters of condolence were sent to the families of men killed in the line of duty. The following letter was sent to the parents of Pvt. John Kuefner, 37th IPSD, who arrived only a few months before his death. It is typical of the thousands of letters that originated from Vietnam.[30]

> Dear Mr. and Mrs. Eugene A. Kuefner,
>
> I wish to extend the sincere condolences of myself and the men of this unit on the recent loss of your son, Private First Class John A. Kuefner, who died in action in the Republic of Vietnam on 14 August 1969.
>
> On the evening of 14 August 1969, John and his scout dog KING were leading a patrol in the vicinity of firebase Claudette. John's scout dog gave an alert, the patrol moved on. Again, KING gave a second alert. John notified the patrol leader, and at this time, the patrol leader halted the element. He then assembled one fire team, his radio operator, and John and his scout dog KING.

Approximately 15 meters further ahead, fifteen Viet Cong fired on them with automatic weapons. John died of small arms fire.

It may be of some comfort to you to know that John died instantly and was not subject to undue suffering. A memorial service was held 18 August 1969 at the platoon's base camp at Phu Loi.

I sincerely hope that the knowledge that John died in the service of his country will be of some comfort in your hour of bereavement. It might also comfort you to know that John and his scout dog KING probably saved the lives of all the other members of the patrol. We all admired and respected him and share with you the great loss of a close comrade. Again, I wish to extend the sincere sympathy of the men of this unit as well as my own personal condolences.

Sincerely,

Richard D. Bruce

2LT. INFANTRY

Commanding Officer

Bruce said within his letter that Kuefner and his scout dog had probably saved the lives of the patrol members. This scenario took place often during the Vietnam conflict, and before the end of the war more than one hundred handlers would be killed and numerous others injured. There is no doubt that more scout dog teams could have prevented even more casualties if they had been given a higher priority in the army.

To support the teams sent out into the field, Bien Hoa, located a few miles from Saigon, was home to the USARV War Dog Training Detachment and was set up as the nerve center for the training and deployment of all dogs and handlers in South Vietnam. The official motto of the twenty-nine-man detachment was "Forever Forward." This related to all the dog teams in Vietnam, since it meant they were always out in front of a patrol, commonly referred to as "walking the point." In the next few years, as the war widened and spread into Laos and Cambodia, the patrols numbered in the tens of thousands.

Army scout dog teams peaked on January 20, 1969, with the arrival of the 37th IPSD in Vietnam. This become the twenty-second platoon deployed, along with the four war dog

Scout dog Duke alerts Pfc. Elisha Walker to a Vietcong spider hole. The spider hole was a VC version of the American foxhole, but was usually well camouflaged. *(National Archives)*

platoons of the Marine Corps. On November 10, 1969, the 55th IPSD was activated for deployment to an undisclosed overseas area, presumably Vietnam.[31]

Since the beginning of the war the army had sent over a total of 1,387 dogs for both scouting and sentry duty. In 1969 alone, 210 on-leash dogs and another 137 off-leash were shipped out to Vietnam. They proved reliable and successful, particularly on the guerrilla war level that the VC had mastered. When the scout dog program began, instructors wanted volunteers only as handlers. This could not be accomplished because of the high demand for scout dog teams and the fact that there were few volunteers. Consequently, new handlers were recruited in-country who were either sentry dog handlers or pointmen with rifle platoons. This meant on-the-job training, and the effectiveness of some of the scout dog teams diminished accordingly.

The effectiveness of the platoons also varied with the "type" of scout dog used. When the war first started, all scouts were worked by the handler with a fifteen-foot leash. This had its good points and bad points. Tha handler could easily control the dog and could use a minimum of hand and voice signals while the patrol worked in "Indian country." It also meant that the handler would be in close proximity should the dog trip a booby trap. The natural progression was for the army to train dogs to work off-leash and allow them to range a short distance in front of the handler. This is nothing new; the same efforts had already been accomplished during World War II in the Pacific.

Off-leash dogs began to be trained at Fort Benning toward the end of 1968 and would be in the field by the beginning of 1969. The off-leash capability gave the handler a bigger margin of safety, kept one hand free, and meant that he didn't have to worry that the leash would get caught in heavy vegetation, a major factor should the patrol encounter an enemy element. The dog was trained to sit for his alert, and the handler would have to determine the direction and range to the enemy from a distance. If the dog needed to be recalled, a "silent" whistle would be used. The entire scenario sounded okay—until the army decided to start playing around with electronics that would allow the dog to range even farther ahead of the handler, and sometimes out of his sight.

Researchers developed a radio transmitter that could be easily attached to a dog's collar. As the dog moved through the brush, the handler could listen to a receiver that emitted an oscillating tone when the dog moved. When the dog stopped and sat down for an alert, the oscillating tone would change to a steady tone. When this occurred, the dog could be completely out of sight of the handler. Hence there could be no read on the alert and absolutely no idea where the enemy might be. The patrol would then have to locate the dog's position and, of course, possibly trip a booby trap or even encounter the enemy while doing so.

Why the army decided to continue this training practice is unfathomable. When tested in the field, the same conclusions were drawn if the dog went out of the handler's sight. What good is a dog when you couldn't see him and had no idea of what he was doing? Perhaps with the advanced electronics of today a miniature camera could be rigged, and then the handler could view what the dog could see—but this type of technology did not exist in 1969. This is another example of where the army tried to improve on something that just did not need further enhancement.

The scout dogs would soon be supported by mine and tunnel dogs, and further extended with the addition of tracker dogs. Scout platoons stayed mobile and moved around quite a bit in the corps area that they operated in. Until the army de-

The army experimented with off-leash scout dogs by attaching transmitters to their collars. This allowed the dog to range far ahead of the main patrol element and out of sight of its handler. *(National Archives)*

cided to wage war on the same terms as the Vietcong, a guerrilla war, scout dog teams could never possibly reach their full potential. When paired off with the mine/tunnel dogs or the trackers, the combination proved highly successful. Even with all the limitations imposed upon them, the scout dog teams earned a good amount of respect for their work. Of course, as in previous wars, they still remained a small element that could provide only a limited impact. Viewed on the grand scale of the war at large, their accomplishments remained minor. When analysis is made based on their numbers in the field, their impact was significant. Deploying more scout dog teams would have made absolutely no difference in the final outcome of the war, but additional teams would have meant a lot more boys returning home. As scout dog instructor Sgt. Jesse Mendez would later state, "They are the only weapon system we ever devised to save lives." Here again the military needed to cope with a concept it was unfamiliar with: scout dogs enabled the army to locate and kill the enemy, but at the same time save Americans from being killed.

THE M-DOG RETURNS

Science and technology advanced tremendously in the detection of explosive mines since World War II. But little could be done electronically to detect many types of explosive booby traps effectively used by NVA and Vietcong forces in Vietnam. Although the United States fought with considerable technological prowess, the enemy maintained a very primitive arsenal. The military soon realized that the cruder the device, the more difficult it was to detect. Booby traps posed an unseen terror for the American soldier, and the ingenuity that the VC displayed cut deep into the soldier's psyche. Not all booby traps were set to kill immediately. The VC often set shrapnel explosives aimed for the head or groin, with enough explosive force to provide a lifetime of disfigurement or blindness, often a fate worse than death. Punji pits featured sharpened stakes of bamboo, capped with feces, leaving a gangrenous wound that eventually dictated amputation. Such is the backdrop of activity in the jungles of Vietnam during 1967.[32]

To cope with the insidious problems associated with such devices, several U.S. agencies scrambled to find suitable countermeasures. In May 1967, the U.S. Army Limited Warfare Laboratory (USALWL) at Aberdeen Proving Ground, Maryland, decided to check the feasibility of employing mine-detection dogs (M-dogs).[33] It believed that new techniques and advances in training methods could overcome the earlier disappointments in developing an M-dog that the army experienced during World War II and during the 1950s.

Previous attempts to train dogs during World War II centered on the concept of fear motivation or food reward. Although initial results were encouraging, once deployed in the field under actual combat conditions, M-dogs proved to be very disappointing and were quickly withdrawn. Parts of the problem were the sights and sounds of large-scale conflicts, and battlefields littered with the bodies of the dead and burning vehicles. After the war, the British conducted similar tests at the War Dog Training Center at Melton-Mowbray, England. These tested the motivational inspiration of food rewards for finding buried mines. But here too the results were inconclusive. Also, in these earlier attempts dogs were trained more to indicate where soil had been turned up by a person planting the mine rather than to locate the device itself.

In 1952, the military hired Stanford Research Institute to study the means by which dogs could locate buried mines. Based on their experience, researchers concluded that the fear motivation method offered the greater chance of success. Researchers conducted several tests under a variety of conditions. The basic premise was that the dog was given an electric shock if he should contact a mine. The results were still inconclusive, and the percentage of mines located ranged from a dismal 18 percent to 72 percent. This performance was still not high enough for any tactical advantage. The problems were that at times the dogs did not locate a mine or booby trap, and that they sometimes gave a false alert to a mine where none existed.

The USALWL based its training on food motivation, but altered the concept subtly. In the past, the dog would be rewarded with food if a mine was located. Now, the behavior modification method dictated that if the dog wanted to eat, he would have to locate buried devices. This positive stimulus and conditioned response showed the most promise. Besides the food reward, the dogs received praise and affection as positive reinforcement.

In the early training period, researchers placed the food directly on the mine. As the program advanced, trainers removed the food but still rewarded the dog upon locating the buried device. The regimen was enhanced even further by teaching the dog to sit about two feet from the device and wait for his reward. Besides buried mines, the program also emphasized the detection of trip wires, booby traps, and other ordnance—in other words, any planted manufactured object. The USALWL sought a return to the original 90 percent detection rate objective, attempted during World War II.

Of course, the USALWL didn't have to worry about the 10 percent of undetected mines and booby traps—but the handlers and dogs did. Vietnam would ultimately prove the dogs' ability, although the mine/tunnel dog teams received less-than-enthusiastic support when first introduced, mostly from witnesses to casualties incurred from undetected devices. But men who were saved by the dogs' detection of explosives and booby traps were understandably loquacious with their praise.

The USALWL did not possess the resources or the expertise to initiate an advanced program involving many dogs. In the early part of 1968 the agency contracted with a civilian company, Behavior Systems, Inc., to develop dogs to detect booby traps, mines, trip wires, and tunnels. The company operated in Apex, North Carolina, near Raleigh, on property with an ideal variety of terrain. Within a few short months the company had trained fourteen dogs to detect mines, booby traps, and trip wires, and another fourteen dogs to specifically locate tunnels only. The final test of the new mine/tunnel dogs took place at Fort Gordon, Georgia, on July 18, 1968.[34]

Fortunately, the weather conditions that day were a recreation of what would be typically found in Vietnam: temperatures in the mid-nineties and high humidity. Army personnel laid out mines, spider holes, and a simulated punji pit as a test for the civilian-trained German shepherds. Six dogs were to be used, and the atmosphere between the civilian company and the government observers could only be described as tense. Dour-faced officers from the USALWL and Fort Gordon arrived as observers to watch civilian professors and longhaired college students work the dogs. Representatives from Fort Gordon openly disdained the proceedings since they had an ongoing tracker and scout dog program—a true military program, one that did not include slide rule–toting professors or, as one captain stated, "longhaired freaks."

Tensions eased as the day wore on. The dogs smoothly located tunnels and detected hidden army personnel. The highlight of the test came when a German shepherd alerted to a punji pit and promptly sat within two feet of it. A colonel from Fort Gordon wanted to check to see if the pit was improperly camouflaged. The colonel casually mentioned that some of the simulated mines and pits prepared for the demonstration yielded visual clues for the dogs. After crawling around on all fours with eyes to the ground, he promptly stood erect and announced to everyone that this was a false alert and no pit was present. The officer then walked around the dog—and fell into the hole.[35] Fortunately for the colonel, no punji stakes were in place.

Based on the initial test results, the USALWL decided to accelerate the training program. Between January and July 1968, it continued to demonstrate the feasibility of mine/tunnel dogs and establish standard training procedures. This led to the activation of the 60th Infantry Platoon at Fort Gordon in August 1968. Because the 60th was a mixed complement of dogs, it was given the formal military designation "(Scout Dog) (Mine/Tunnel Detector Dog)."

Mine and tunnel dogs each had their own specialized training procedures. It soon became apparent that the dogs would alert in situations they were not trained for. Mine dogs sometimes alerted to tunnels and enemy personnel, and the tunnel dogs would occasionally locate booby traps and to a lesser degree (since they detected ground scents) enemy forces. The army considered this an added bonus for those who would ultimately work the dogs.

To expand the mine and tunnel dog program, the Department of Defense granted Behavior Systems, Inc., a $625,000 contract for training the handlers and twenty-eight dogs for the 60th, and an additional twenty-eight dogs for the Marines. The company hired about 150 people to fulfill the requirements of the contract. The final price tag for one fully trained mine/tunnel dog totaled about $10,000.[36]

Individualized training was conducted for mine and tunnel dogs. Mine dogs worked primarily along roads and railroad tracks, looking for mines, booby traps, and trip wires. Working the dog off-leash, the handler used arm and voice commands for instructions and the dog alerted by sitting about two feet from a planted device or trip wire.

Tunnel dogs also worked off-leash, up to 120 feet away, and were also commanded by hand and arm signals. No voice commands were used since a tunnel could easily be occupied by VC who probably would not take kindly to being located. Like their mine dog counterparts, tunnel dogs alerted by sitting about two feet from the trip wire or tunnel entrance. The dogs were trained not to enter the tunnel, only to alert to its presence. Within ten months, the final test took place for both the dogs and the handlers, as they deployed for Vietnam. Here, trip wires would be attached to real explosives. Punji pits would indeed have razor-sharp bamboo stakes capped with feces. Tunnels and rat holes held the VC or booby traps. Mistakes made in-country meant pain, disfiguring wounds, or death.

The 60th arrived at Chu Chi, a hot area of VC activity, on April 22, 1969, in support of the 25th Infantry Division for three months, and of the Americal Division for two and a half months, as a trial. Mine and tunnel dogs worked a variety of missions: search and destroy, clearing roads of mines, and reconnaissance sweeps. Usually the handler followed fifteen to fifty yards in the rear, depending on the action. During this period, three dogs were wounded in action and two dogs died. One tunnel dog collapsed from heatstroke, and a mine dog suffered congestive heart failure. The 60th IPSD as a whole posted a 25 percent casualty rate.[37]

Two mine dog handlers were killed, but not while working their dogs. Three other handlers were wounded, but only one of them was engaged on an actual mine sweep with his dog. The German shepherd in this case successfully alerted to three trip wires and then detected a fourth. The handler, extremely tired and on the verge of heatstroke, approached the wire. Suddenly he fainted and fell on the wire, releasing the pin from a grenade. The explosion and shrapnel instantly killed the handler and seriously wounded his dog.

The M-dogs alerted to 76 trip wires and explosives and to 21 tunnels, punji pits, and spider holes; they also alerted 6 times to enemy personnel. Another 14 alerts were not checked out. The dogs did miss 12 items, several after heavy rains and others that were very old. But the minesweep teams with electronic detectors also failed to uncover several of these mines. The tunnel dogs worked smoothly, locating 108 tunnels, bunkers, spider holes, and punji pits. They also alerted to 34 mines, booby traps, and trip wires; and one tunnel dog alerted to enemy personnel set to ambush the patrol. Captain Woodrow L. Quinn Jr., while in charge of mine/tunnel dog training with the Military Dog Committee at the U. S. Army Infantry Center, had firsthand knowledge about the successes these dogs had in Vietnam. Taken from the perspective of the dog, he wrote:

> Moving along the dirt road out of Trang Bang was easier than fighting through the heavy brush, and Butch was happy as he trotted swiftly around the curve. Stopping he turned and waited, wishing that his handler, the men with mine detectors and the rumbling vehicles would hurry-up. When they finally made the curve, his handler gave the move-out gestures and Butch resumed his pace. Farther along, he suspiciously watched the water buffalo in the rice paddy, remembering what his handler had done to him the time he chased one. He forgot the water buffalo as he detected the

strong scent of a 50-pound mass of TNT buried in the shoulder of the road. Spinning quickly, he ran toward the source, sniffed to make sure and sat. Where was that handler he thought, wondering how much food he would get for this one.[38]

Some mine dogs during this trial period had experimental transmitters attached to their harnesses that emitted an oscillating tone when they moved. The handler could then listen and easily figure out when the dog found a mine or trip wire and remained motionless. The idea was to provide an extra margin of safety by distancing the handler and the minesweep team from the dog, who, everyone quickly realized, was not infallible. On paper the concept looked good, but platoons quickly realized that because of the dense vegetation, a dog could be out of sight when an artifact was discovered. The dog obediently remained motionless and the platoon had a difficult time locating the dog. Fortunately this idea was only performed in practice trials under controlled situations. In the field, it is much too easy to encounter other mines and booby traps while looking for the dog.

During the testing period, several glaring problems surfaced, and upon review they needed to be emphasized. Like their human counterparts, the dogs were susceptible to the heat and humidity. The unit leaders needed to understand that the dogs should not be made to walk a tiring distance before being committed to an active search role. The maximum distance recommended was four miles before work was to commence. Some unit leaders overworked the dogs, disregarding the recommendations of the handlers. In one case a mine dog on a road sweep was forced to cover twenty-one miles of hard surface in only seven hours. The dog, exhausted and bordering on heatstroke, also suffered from painful blisters and cuts to all the pads on his feet.[39] Sometimes treated as four-legged machines by callous or overzealous unit leaders, the dogs naturally sought shade or water when they tired. When they did work, they often refused the food rewards offered by the handlers and settled for the praise and affection heaped upon them.

At the end of the trial period, all patrol leaders were asked to evaluate the mine/tunnel dogs. Approximately 85 percent believed they enhanced security, while 12 percent felt they had no effect, and only 3 percent believed they hindered security and performed poorly. Those who supported the dog operations made comments such as "The dog team allowed us to move along faster" or "The dog will prove to be a great asset in future operations and has the confidence of myself and my men." Those giving fair or poor ratings stated, "Dog was too hot to work" or "Dog was distracted too much." Unfortunately, the study did not explore the reasons behind those negative comments. Was it a poorly performing dog or was too much expected under the circumstances? One handler's observation about unit leaders was that some people just didn't like dogs.

In 1968 the House Appropriations Committee studied the results of mine/tunnel dog use in Vietnam. Based on testimony received and the overwhelming support of the patrol leaders, continuation of the program was assured. In July 1970, the mine/tunnel dog program shifted to Fort Benning, Georgia, as a consolidation move, but also with the stipulation that the dog's effectiveness and training techniques employed be continuously improved. Based on the results of the army's mine/tunnel dogs, the Marines initiated their own evaluation in 1970. In March of that year, fourteen dogs, along with eighteen handlers, arrived in Vietnam to support the 1st Marine Division. They operated with eighteen different unit commanders, all except one of whom endorsed them.[40]

The success of the mine/tunnel dogs in Vietnam is attributed to the Department of Defense. The real credit belongs to Behavior Systems, Inc., and its dedicated employees, who nurtured the program in its infancy. This company developed the initial group and wrote the training manuals for future handlers and dogs. But success does not always breed future contracts, and the Department of Defense dumped BSI in favor of the army for future development.

As the conflict in Vietnam continued, the performance of these dogs began to deteriorate. Many handlers began to deviate from the original training regimen. New handlers arrived, and each one had less experience than the previous one. This led to the "I have a better way to do it" school of thought. The strict training regimen was abandoned as many handlers tried to employ their personal techniques. Consequently some mine/tunnel dog teams worked efficiently, others were so-so, and the remainder had dismal performance records. Occasionally this led to dissatisfaction with the dogs, and it naturally caused a higher casualty rate for both dogs and patrol members. As troops began to withdraw from Vietnam, the mine/tunnel dog teams migrated, forming up with scout dog platoons and often working together.

If the army could have used more scout dogs in Vietnam, the same holds true for their mine/tunnel cousins. In retrospect, once the extent of VC tunnels that honeycombed the III Corps area became known after the war, tunnel dogs were

A tunnel dog locates a VC spider hole in Vinh Long. The dog's responsibility ended there, and armed volunteers, called "tunnel rats," would enter the tunnel complex to locate and kill the enemy. *(National Archives)*

definitely underutilized. One of the army's biggest bases in the war, Cu Chi, was built on top of these tunnel complexes. For weeks the VC filtered out at night, launched mortar attacks, stole food, and in general wreaked havoc, all the time from inside the base security perimeter. Of course the tunnel dogs and handlers had the easier part of the job: locating the underground sanctuaries. Once this was done, special volunteers, called "tunnel rats," had to enter these tunnels and kill or flush out the hidden VC.[41]

HUNTING THE VIET CONG

The experiences of Vietnam dictated a new concept in conducting counterguerrilla warfare. The idea of reestablishing contact with a fleeing enemy by tracking, although a new concept for the modern army, was directly linked to the use of Indian scouts by the U.S. Cavalry more than one hundred years earlier. In the 1850s the horse cavalry gathered valuable intelligence by using Indians and Indian-raised white men as both guides and forward scouts. The information gathered helped to decide future operations.

In Vietnam, the army also needed intelligence on VC operations and troop movements. As much as everyone wanted to engage the enemy, you had to find them first to confront them. The problem faced by Americans in Vietnam became epidemic. For instance, the Viet Cong, after conducting a mortar attack on a firebase or an ambush on friendly troops, disappeared into the dense jungle without a trace. An early example during the conflict took place in October 1964, when the VC launched a mortar attack against Bien Hoa Air Base. A squadron of American B-57 jet bombers had just recently arrived, and the VC easily positioned themselves near the base perimeter without being detected. After a brief attack six aircraft were completely destroyed and another twenty bombers were substantially damaged. Although search parties went out immediately after the raid, not a single VC soldier (and it is estimated that over one hundred participated in the attack) were to be found.

The first response should be strictly judged all-American: track the VC with bloodhounds. World renowned for their superior sense of smell, they were still a poor choice. The dogs barked and thrashed about so much in their quest that any hope of surprising the enemy would be long gone.[42] The

Bloodhounds were first used in Vietnam in 1962 to track down fleeing Vietcong. However, they proved so noisy on patrol that the practice was soon terminated. *(National Archives)*

bloodhound, as typically stereotyped in movies and on film, pursued an unarmed person and just ran him to ground. Of course, these police pursuits took place in friendly territory with no chance of an ambush by the fleeing quarry. In South Vietnam, more than 170,000 Vietcong were spread out across the countryside, and 30,000 of them formed fifty battalions.

The sophomoric attempt by the army to employ bloodhounds showed that it had limited experience with trackers or tracking dogs in a combat situation. But others had, and they turned once again to the British, whose experience with them extended from their operations during World War II. Toward the end of 1943, the British Fourth Army began a new combat tactic, termed "wrecke" patrols, in an effort to find hidden pockets of Japanese soldiers left behind on numerous islands in the Pacific. Small groups of highly trained men traced Japanese soldiers to hidden caves and tunnels as part of their mop-up operations.

The success of these engagements led them to establish the Jungle Warfare School (JWS) in Johore Bahru, Malaysia. The British trackers saw success against insurgents in such diverse locations as Kenya, Cyprus, Malaya, and Borneo. Not only did they locate guerrillas by employing tracker dogs, they teamed trained civilians familiar with the operating territory with crack British troops.

On May 4, 1966, Gen. William Westmoreland and his staff met with a British representative, Robert L. Hughes, who related his country's experiences using tracker dogs in counterinsurgency operations. A week later Westmoreland sent several senior officers to visit the British school in Malaysia. Among the group was Brig. Gen. A. E. Cowan, director of the Joint Research and Test Activity; Col. M. G. Hatch, commanding officer of the Army Concept Team in Vietnam; and Capt. W. G. Campbell from the USARV.[43]

The army quickly pounced on the British tracker team idea but needed to dance around several diplomatic interests. Since Great Britain had signed the 1954 Geneva Convention, which divided Vietnam along the 17th parallel, foreign governments might view British assistance as a violation of this agreement and their professed neutrality. Also, the Jungle Warfare School was located in Malaysia, which was neutral in Vietnam. Training of American personnel there meant the army needed to twist a few arms and still be diplomatically sensitive. In September 1966, a mutual agreement was reached allowing time for the U.S. Army to train fourteen army tracker teams.

At the JWS, the U.S. Army invested money, resources, and men to field its first tracker groups. The British began training the first two American platoons in October 1966. These became the 63rd Infantry Platoon-Combat Tracker (IPCT), Americal Division, and the 65th IPCT, 9th Infantry Division. Each platoon consisted of three teams comprised of five men and a single tracker dog. A team leader managed the dog and handler, two cover men, and a visual tracker.[44]

Based on the experiences of the British, black or yellow Labrador retrievers were favored as tracker dogs, in contrast to the German shepherds that filled the ranks of scout dog platoons. The Labradors were docile, could tolerate heat reasonably well, and favored the dead scent of ground sniffing. Their alerts could often be subtle: wagging the tail, raising the head, twitching an ear, or simply stopping. Often only the handler himself, being intimately knowledgeable about his dog, would detect these alerts. Tracker dogs, like their scouting counterparts, can be trained in a variety of ways, with the exception of how they alert. Dogs retain this unique characteristic for themselves, effectively reversing the tables on their masters. The dog gets to train the handler—"Pay attention or you'll miss my signal"—in this single instance.

By far the biggest difference between tracker and scouting dogs is that of scenting. Scout dogs alert to any unfamiliar odor, mostly in the air but also on the ground, as in the case of trip wires, enemy personnel, and booby traps. Tracker dogs are trained to follow only one scent on the ground. This scent needs to be given to the dog, usually by having him sniff an enemy footprint or a blood trail. This is called the "scent picture" that the dog frames in its mind, and he then follows it amid hundreds of other odors on the trail. But this scent is as unique as a person's fingerprint or a written signature.

A yellow lab and combat tracker team prepare to land. The team will track the VC, allowing a larger force to engage them once found. *(National Archives)*

An intelligent dog, the Labrador would begin an eight-month training period at two years of age and could be expected to see combat action for up to six years. The breed's mild disposition ensured that only brief transitions would be required between handlers. Never trained to attack, they would still defend the handler and team under certain circumstances. Although not trained to alert to booby traps, they often did, and many reports of this friendly interdiction attest to this. The British provided the 63d IPCT with its first three dogs: Bruce (5201), Lucky (13383), and Sambo (5A15). As integral team members they earned immediate respect. Often the difference between life and death for the CT platoon could be determined by their dog, and each one received careful attention.[45]

The main mission for any tracker team is to reestablish contact with retreating or evading enemy troops and to investigate areas of suspected enemy activity. This may come in many forms, but the overall philosophy is to locate but not engage the enemy. Visual tracking meant all operations took

Private First Class Lloyd Pursley and Sergeant Merles take a break from tracking duties in the 101st Airborne (Airmobile) area of operations. *(Carlisle Barracks)*

place during daylight hours. Of course the Labs could scent just as well at night, but it would be stupid to attempt to follow a trail with no supporting visual clues.

The effectiveness of the team to complete a mission is usually dependent on how old the track is. Ideally the CT platoon would deploy within two to three hours of a known enemy presence. A scent trail up to twenty-four hours old could be followed, but according to Sgt. Samuel A. Blile, a team leader with the 65th IPCT, "The likelihood of reestablishing contact with an old track is very slight."

The United States deployed ten tracker teams to Vietnam in 1968 and added a final one late in 1969. These eleven teams were scattered across the country and shared many of the same locations in which scout dog platoons worked. There were also two Australian combat tracker teams located near Vung Tau and Nui Dat to support the Allied effort. Since these platoons were very specialized, they pulled far fewer missions than their scout dog counterparts. Yet their effectiveness and bravery in the field are by no means diminished. Since combat tracker teams are just small advance parties, principally trained to reestablish contact with the enemy, a good measure of their success is the results yielded by the rifle company that follows them at a distance.

The United States began to develop its own Combat Tracking Team Center at the U.S. Army Military Police School at Fort Gordon, Georgia, in November 1967. The following year the school began to train both dogs and handlers. Select male and spayed female Labradors were obtained from the Army Mobility Equipment Command in St. Louis, Missouri. The dogs, obtained for $330 each, began an intensive five-month training cycle and could then be sent overseas with or without a handler.

The weakest part of the combat tracker concept is the possibility that the team will walk into a VC or NVA ambush. For instance, on January 23, 1970, all patrol members from the 75th IPCT were wounded by hand grenades. The trackers had closely followed a trail, but could not determine how far away the enemy was. Unfortunately this happened all too often. To prevent a scenario like this from happening, a number of combat tracker teams began to bring along a scout dog and handler on patrol. The tracker dog stayed on the enemy trail, and the scout dog gave an added margin of safety by airborne scenting for the enemy.

This team effort could have been employed to a much higher degree in Vietnam. As usual, the army never officially coordinated scout and tracker dog handlers, nor was adequate training ever provided, and most training was just OJT in-country. In fact, toward the end of the American involvement, many tracker dog handlers, trained at Fort Gordon, wound up being scout dog handlers after they arrived in Vietnam.[46]

Specialist Fourth Class Terry Muxlow and Mackey, from the 557th IPCT, keep watch on a trail near Phu Loc district headquarters, about twelve miles south of Hue. Visual trackers check for signs of enemy activity and perhaps a scent trail for Mackey to follow. *(Carlisle Barracks)*

With tracker training being given at Fort Gordon and scout dog training being given at Fort Benning, the problem originated well before anyone even got to Vietnam. Combat trackers yielded excellent results in Vietnam. Better coordination within the army during the early training phase and a centralized facility in the United States responsible for all canine training activity would have benefited every handler and supporting infantry unit during the war. The division of training responsibility and the uncoordinated response to the employment of dogs are problems that have not disappeared from the armed services.

THE SUPERDOG PROGRAM

Dogs in Vietnam were proving to be an overwhelming success, although some limitations led the army to correctly believe that a superior dog could be bred. Although German shepherds were the dogs of choice for sentry and scouting work, several other options needed to be explored. As far back as 1947, Brig. Gen. Frederick McCabe recommended that "experimentation be continued with dog units along all lines, especially breeding, improving techniques of training, and extending the scope of usefulness for the dogs."

German shepherds had been used for years but they were not without their problems. The biggest concern is hip dysplasia, which can develop into arthritis within seven or eight years, effectively ending the military usefulness of the dog. Dysplasia also accounted for the high rejection rate for dogs procured by the air force and caused one of the biggest headaches in meeting annual quotas. An idea that appears to have originated with the U.S. Department of Agriculture called for a selective breeding program. Scientists believed they could produce a line of dysplasia-free dogs.[47]

By June 1966, the Army Research Office had begun to discuss certain criteria for this new breed of scout dogs, referred to as "ambush detector dogs." Besides selective breeding, researchers considered spayed animals, in the event the enemy attempted to use sex lures to confuse the dogs. Although a close rapport between the handler and dog was considered important, the concept of one man–one dog was deemed outmoded. Two avenues existed: several handlers for each dog or one handler for several dogs. Consideration was also given for the army once again to adopt its own breeding program.

In March 1967, the Army Combat Development Command announced a detailed project to be orchestrated by the Walter Reed Army Institute of Research (WRAIR). They in turn designated the Veterinary Corps to handle all the day-to-day activities in developing a superior ambush detection dog. Delays set back the program for about a year. Officially called the Biosensor Research Program, it was more commonly referred to as "Superdog." Besides the benefits gained from the research, Fort Benning would begin to acquire dogs from the program in about eleven months. At this point, and for some unknown reason, the army wished to check the behavioral characteristics of several breeds to investigate their suitability for military work. This appeared to be total nonsense since the Superdog program was already under way and behavioral characteristics of most dog breeds were already well known.

Flush with taxpayers' money for the war effort, the army awarded a contract to Dr. R. W. McIntire, who operated the Canine Behavior Laboratory at the University of Maryland. For this contract the army purchased sixty-six AKC-registered Labrador retrievers, German shepherds, Airedales, English pointers, and standard poodles. In the end, of course, the German shepherd reigned supreme. Did anyone seriously believe that infantrymen would plunge into combat with a poodle as a war dog?

The Superdog program also attracted a wide variety of consultants, including William Koehler, an animal trainer for Walt Disney, and L. Wilson Davis, a dog trainer employed by the Baltimore Police Department. Other participants included the Secret Service, the New York and Maryland State Police, and Dr. Wayne H. Riser, a hip dysplasia expert from the University of Pennsylvania. In essence, the effort did not use any extraordinary experiments or science fiction–type genetic engineering. The thrust of the researchers lay in a controlled environment and selective breeding over a period of years. Once started, about 50 adults and 250 German shepherd puppies were on hand at any one time. Eight years and $1.8 million later, 1,996 German shepherd puppies had graduated from the program.

Scientists felt that if the pups were stressed when young they would be able to cope better in a combat environment as they grew older. To accomplish this, researchers began mildly stressing the pups when they were only five days old by placing them in a tilted drum and rotating it ninety times in three minutes. Then the pups were placed in a thirty-degree refrigerator for one minute. Each pup was then massaged and petted for two minutes before being returned to its mother. This procedure continued for ten days. The pups began socializing daily after the age of four weeks, and veterinarians conducted weekly evaluations after the pups were two months old. This continued for another five weeks. At the seven-month mark, the beginning of more formal obedience training commenced and continued for four months. At this time the dogs were shipped out to other military agencies or kept as breeding stock.

As the Biosensor Research project began to wind down, the U.S. Army Combined Arms Combat Development Agency brought forth what it considered a novel idea: the infantry tactical dog. The best part of this new concept would be the name. It called for combining the skills of the scout, tracker, and mine/tunnel dog into one all-purpose animal. Many people know the old adage "Jack of all trades—master of none." The army did not grasp this homespun reality. It believed that combining these skills would be cost-effective, would reduce the number of people involved, and would ultimately shorten the training time. Anyone remotely familiar with dogs and their capabilities believed it couldn't work. The Infantry Tactical Dog Program began on October 1, 1975, and died a quiet death only three months later. Not only was the program ludicrous but, for the United States, the war in Vietnam was over. And as history has shown, it was long past time to dismember the army dog program.

Many other research programs involving dogs in the military also took place. Throughout history, the military has often diverted its attention to experiments that seemed outlandish in the extreme—or just impractical when viewed by an unbiased observer. One example is the army's idea of training dogs to carry nuclear weapons on their backs. Another is the use of dogs as radiation detectors, an idea considered by the army during the 1960s. Two researchers at Purdue University demonstrated that dogs could be surgically altered to detect nuclear radiation. The researchers placed a small plastic scintillator into one eye of a dog. The scintillator emitted a visible light when exposed to radiation. Within three months, the scientists were able to train a dog to locate radiation sources by sight. The researchers proved the concept viable, but the program was nonsensical from the beginning since nuclear radiation could be detected electronically quite easily.[48]

Without a request by the army to develop a specific detector dog, researchers went ahead with their experiments. With the concept proved, they then asked the army if it required such a service. One idea surfaced that these dogs could detect scattered radioactive remnants after an airplane crash. Considering the odds of an airplane crash that spewed forth hot radioactive elements that could not be found, the army declined to continue the research, proving once more that scientists are often superior in inventing devices that have no practical application. Researchers believed this unusual capability the dog offered must have some use, perhaps with civil defense. The army, in the midst of a major war, passed on the nuclear detector dog, as did everyone else. But how many other military projects, still classified for security reasons, employed the use of dogs is not known.[49]

FOUR-FOOTED RADAR

There are over four hundred breeds of dogs in the world, yet just a handful are deemed suitable for military work. Although the senses of all dogs are similar, their physical size, speed, stamina, and disposition are other attributes to be considered.

For these reasons few dogs were suitable for the rigors of military life in the hostile climate of South Vietnam. The German shepherd, several crossbreeds, and the Labrador retriever coped reasonably well in this environment.

Besides training, the unique sensory capabilities dogs possess are the primary reasons for their success in the military. Although much is known, there are still mysteries that linger on how dogs receive their sensory information and then process it. The sensory sensitivity varies according to breed, although all dogs possess the same physiology. Understanding how these senses work and can be interpreted by man is a key ingredient to understanding the usefulness of a dog in combat.

A dog's powerful sense of smell, known as the olfactory ability, is at least forty times better than that of a human, but this varies substantially among breeds. Odors, consisting of molecules, land on membrane tissue within the nose. This odor information is then gathered, processed, and sent to the brain. For a human, this olfactory center is about half a square inch in size, compared to twenty square inches of tissue for an average dog. The membrane is arranged in folds to help filter smells, and this accounts for a dog's long nose. For a German shepherd, over 220,000,000 sensory cells gather and process the odor molecules. A dog's wet nose doesn't indicate a cold but helps to dissolve odor molecules in the air and clear away old smells. Researchers believe that the nose pigment is also involved, but do not understand how or why.

During World War II it was believed that dogs could be trained to scent according to race. This is only partially true. Humans give off a distinctive odor based on the food they have eaten, and this accounts for why many dogs, upon arrival in South Vietnam, seemed to scent on the enemy only. In a short span of time this ability disappeared altogether. This is acceptable, because a properly trained dog will alert to any foreign scent, including lost soldiers and friendly allies.

Dogs can also distinguish between human individuals, as every human has a scent signature that a dog can interpret. This is why a tracker dog, given the scent of one individual to follow, can lead a patrol after a group of three hundred soldiers. If the group splits apart, trying to confuse its pursuers, the dog will continue to track that one special individual scent. Unless the enemy knows who that individual is, efforts to confuse the dog are usually ineffective.

Handlers in Vietnam found several variations within the same breed regarding olfactory ability. Some scout dogs scented on live personnel much more effectively than on trip wires or booby traps. Dogs found to miss wires in training were often called "duds" and would then be worked off-leash to provide a better margin of safety for the handlers.

Another prime trait dogs possess is acute hearing, and certain breeds, such as the German shepherd, have a superior ability to distinguish sounds. Seventeen muscles can focus on sounds, allowing them to register frequencies as high as 35,000 cycles per second (Hz). This compares to an upper frequency limit of 20,000 Hz for humans. Dogs also have an inner ear they can shut off, helping them to filter out general background noise. Along with a broad hearing spectrum comes the ability to distinguish among sounds of different frequencies. A German shepherd can distinguish a slight difference in tone unnoticed by the human ear. The shape of the ears also determines their effectiveness. As the ears perk up, the dog will swivel its head and then focus on the source of the sound. Floppy-eared breeds like the bloodhound do not have this ability.

A dog's eyes are constructed like a human's, but with a few noteworthy differences. The dog has more rods than cones within the eye, the rods being tiny cells that respond to dim light. Their eyes are not as good as a human's in strong light, but their night vision is superior to that of a human. Within the eye there is a membranous area surrounding the retina called the "tapetum." This region reflects light back toward the retina after it has passed through once, effectively giving the dog two chances to capture the same image. Shine a light into a dog's eye at night and you can see the tapetum as a yellow or blue glare. Dogs are not totally color-blind but do

A handler relaxes while his scout dog stays alert and keeps working. *(National Archives)*

have poor color perception, seeing objects in black and white or in shades of gray and orange. Nearsighted compared to humans, canines are more apt to see objects at a distance when they are moving.

Several other attributes associated with dogs help with their military roles. Powerful jaw muscles can exert 360 pounds of pressure, whereas the average human can achieve only 45 to 65 pounds. An aggressive sentry dog can tear apart an unfortunate individual on the receiving end of its sharp teeth. Although not trained for the purpose, scout dogs were used effectively in the interrogation of VC suspects.

HISTORICALLY, a certain mystique is often attached to what is often described as the sixth sense that many canines seem to possess. It is typically pointed to when no other reason can be found for a dog's actions. Studies have shown that canines do

possess some type of extrasensory perception (ESP), or tele-
pathic power, but this is not clearly understood. And in Vietnam, several occurrences took place that seem to reinforce this
concept—although unscientifically, perhaps.

The story of a scout dog named Troubles, from the 25th
IPSD, is an excellent example.[50] Troubles and his handler,
Pfc. William Richardson, were airlifted into the jungle to support a patrol. Richardson was wounded in a firefight and
needed to be medevacked to the nearest hospital—at An Khe,
more than ten miles distant. He was in no condition to state
that Troubles was also on high priority and should be airlifted along with everyone else. The other members of the
patrol left the dog behind as Richardson was dusted off.

Three weeks later, Troubles was found back at the First
Air Cavalry Division Headquarters in An Khe. The dog, tired
and emaciated, would not let anyone get near him. Troubles
then slowly went to the tents comprising the scout dog platoon
and searched until he found Richardson's equipment and cot.
The dog then simply curled up alongside his master's belong-
ings and promptly fell asleep.

If the pair had walked into the jungle, Troubles's return
would be easy to explain: the dog followed his master's scent
home. And if the dog was to follow a scent trail for this distance, it would take only a short time for him to return. But the
pair had been airlifted in, and Richardson left by helicopter, so
no scent trail could possibly have been left behind. Just how
Troubles found his way home, and where he had been for
three weeks, remains a mystery.

More often handlers describe a familiar bonding with
their dogs. According to one handler: "It's almost like my dog
knows how I feel. If I'm stressed, he's anxious and nervous. If
I'm happy, he jumps with joy." This sixth sense is another
form of communication between humans and canines, one not
seen every day or even understood, but relished by a handler
and a dog in tune with each other. While some handlers departed Vietnam without once looking back, others had difficulty accepting the separation from their dogs. Eventually a

dog would accept a new handler—but did he truly ever forget his former master?

THE HOSTILE ENVIRONMENT

In the Republic of Vietnam many threats to a dog's life came from direct attacks from the enemy or from a host of devices designed to kill and maim. In combat, handlers expected to be fired upon by the enemy in a deadly burst of automatic gunfire or from an incoming mortar round. Booby traps and mines posed a constant threat for a patrol. For military dogs, few injuries and deaths actually occurred because of enemy actions. Less than 3 percent of all the dogs in Vietnam died of direct hostile action, and less than 7 percent were wounded in action (WIA).[51] These figures tell only part of the story and do not represent dogs wounded more than once. For instance, Mitzi (X007), a scout dog from the 49th IPSD, was WIA five times! Accidents accounted for about 20 percent of the injuries, while illnesses peculiar to the region caused most of the canine deaths. The U.S. military also created many problems, causing the dogs not only distress but death.

One would expect the basic military dog food ration to be the most nutritious and tastiest meal a canine could eat. The truth is, for too long military dog food was neither. It was so bad that many dogs refused to eat it—assuming it was even available. Although the Veterinary Corps provided exemplary service in Vietnam, it alone can be held directly responsible for the poor quality of dog food. This is not to say that the Veterinary Corps *caused* the problem—that can be attributed to an indifferent military higher echelon with its own set of priorities. But the buck has to stop somewhere, and the corps did have the power, if exercised properly, to make a difference.

Reports can trace the trouble with military dog food back to 1959. A Veterinary Corps officer, after visiting the manufacturer at the time, recommended that a better product be obtained. The officer submitted his inspection report, but no action took place by either the army or the manufacturer under contract. In Vietnam during 1966, thousands of pounds

Sergeant Samuel Warner and Lux huddle together as a nearby VC mortar round explodes. Neither one was hurt during the engagement. *(National Archives)*

of dog food were found to contain insects and weevils or was rancid and moldy. These problems were caused by both the manufacturer and the army's practice of keeping the food stored for too long a period of time. The average civilian dog back in the States received a more nutritious and palatable meal than a working military dog.

It took the deaths of eight air force sentry dogs from contaminated dog food to force the military establishment to correct this deficiency.[52] The U.S. Army Testing Laboratory, located in Natick, Massachusetts, revised the specifications for dry dog food and tried alternatives similar to the semimoist brands found in the civilian marketplace at the time. A commercial brand called Prime was mixed with horsemeat and low-moisture pellets and packed in five-gallon containers. This provided a more palatable meal and helped to diminish the bloat often seen in dogs who ate cereal-based food only.

This was still not the answer, especially since the availability of horsemeat began to diminish late in the 1960s and the army was finding it increasing difficult to purchase it. Long gone was the Quartermaster Remount Station at Fort Robinson, Nebraska, where horsemeat had been in abundance during World War II. People in many European countries began supplementing their protein with horsemeat, causing a worldwide shortage and escalating prices. But the modified meal, when available, did help to alleviate the gastrointestinal problems many dogs experienced.

The air force, together with Hill's Packing Company, developed a dog food called the Military Stress Diet (MSD). It did not appear in Vietnam until 1971. By this time the drawdown was in full swing and the dogs in-country were on the decline, but the army did adopt the food for its dogs' use. No divine intervention appeared with this meal, since MSD contained little fiber and a lot of fat. The high fat content meant many loose stools and more work for handlers and vet techs to both keep tartar from accumulating on the dogs' teeth and keep the floors of the kennels sanitary. It did surpass anything previously available during the war. It was high in calories and laced with heartworm and hookworm preventatives, which did give it an additional advantage. One would think that after working with dogs for over thirty years, the military could develop a better food.

The horrors of war faced by infantrymen in Vietnam led a few handlers to "disable" their dogs. This problem did not occur with any great frequency, and it involved only a few handlers who were either terrified of being out on patrol or simply did not wish to be in that position. Some would do anything to prevent pulling that duty. According to army policy, if scout dogs went on sick call, the handlers were required to accompany them. So to keep from going into the field, handlers would smash a paw on their dogs with a hammer or run over a dog's foot with a jeep. No one was ever caught doing it, but the veterinarians who treated the dogs knew what was going on. For the vets it was similar to an abused child being taken to the hospital. A doctor, examining the trauma and perhaps its frequency, could rule out accidents as a cause. The problem disappeared when it was determined that if a dog had a certain number of sick days, the handler would be transferred to a rifle company. Here you walked point, but without the benefit of a dog. Once the word passed around about the new policy, canine injuries decreased dramatically, if not altogether.[53]

Just the day-to-day work of a dog involved numerous dangers. Many broke their legs or dislocated their shoulders after jumping from a vehicle or a helicopter that had not yet landed. Often their dewclaws would take the brunt of damage when entering or exiting a military vehicle.

Sentry dogs working at night walked over rocks, coarse grass, and marshes, inducing a variety of foot injuries. Mine/tunnel dogs suffered damage to their pads when forced to walk for long periods on hot, hard surfaces. Boots to fit the dogs had been developed and could easily be made from common materials. But few were distributed and most handlers never realized they existed. Generally dogs do not like to wear shoes, and those who received them promptly ripped them off. Had they been trained early in their careers to wear them, the problem might not have arisen.

Climatic conditions in Vietnam also took their toll on both men and dogs. South Vietnam is subtropical, and it is very common to have temperatures in excess of one hundred degrees Fahrenheit and oppressive humidity. Glowing reports issued in both the military and civilian press detailed how well German shepherds acclimatized to the heat and humidity. Actually, once they lost their inside coat of fine fur they adapted much better, but upon arriving in-country heat posed a constant threat.

Sentry dogs were least affected by the tropical heat; they worked at night and trained during the early morning or late in the afternoon. Scout, mine/tunnel, and tracker dogs had no choice but to go out into the field during the day. Also, since the scout dogs had been trained in the warm climate of Georgia, army personnel felt comfortable dispatching them to their assigned sites almost immediately. Several died of heatstroke before the 936th Veterinary Detachment provided a staging area to acclimatize the dogs before they began going to work. In 1969 alone, 109 dogs died of heatstroke. Some dogs did better than others, but those who recovered from heat exhaustion were prone to relapses quite easily.

But General Thomas had absolutely no jurisdiction over air force flights. Air force regulations specifically stated that dogs needed to be either muzzled or put in a crate. Often an injured dog could not be placed in a crate, and no muzzle was available. Many of these flights were short hops, and they often carried high-ranking personnel. But the air force was not concerned with the safety of these individuals, only their comfort. A scout dog defecating in the hot, enclosed confines of an airplane diminished the esteem of the commanding pilot. Under those circumstances the presumed aura that surrounded many pilots disappeared. This problem went well beyond regulations and displayed the intense interservice rivalry that occurred during the war. In 1969, 2nd Lt. Mark P. Zirngible, CO of the 57th IPSD, summarized the problems with the air force in a monthly scout dog operations report:

> The Air Force is interfering with the transport of scout dogs on passenger flights again. Contrary to existing regulations, they have repeatedly refused in a belligerent, rude and condescending manner to transport my personnel and dogs. When presented with

the regulation itself, they have defied my personnel to try and board their aircraft. This unbecoming conduct extends from the most junior airman to crewchiefs to aircraft commanders. Some of these individuals–to include Lieutenant Colonels–have acted in an extremely reprehensible manner without regard for my personnel, my dogs or their mission in defiance of Air Force regulations, which were quoted to them. I would like to make it clear that I am not censuring the entire U.S. Air Force. However, due to a few strategically placed individuals, my personnel and dogs are subjected to unnecessary hardship, frustration, delay, embarrassment and harassment.

During June 1967, a disease appeared in many dogs that became an epidemic before anyone realized it. Dogs developed a fever for several days or weeks and then apparently recovered. The dog would appear okay for the next two to four months and then suddenly start bleeding from the nose. Quickly the dog lost its appetite and weight and developed sores and weakness in its hind legs. Death came swiftly in only a few short days. Within several months, eighty-nine dogs died in fifteen different platoons from this mysterious ailment. At first the disease was called idiopathic hemorrhagic syndrome (IHS), but later it became officially termed tropical canine pancytopenia (TCP).

The Veterinary Corps launched an investigation into the cause and to find a cure. By 1969 the epidemic had spread to both ARVN and civilian dogs. The disease cut across Vietnam like a scythe. Many platoons were at only 50 percent of their authorized strength at this time. Eventually the problem was traced to ticks imported with the tracker dogs obtained from the British in Malaysia. As dogs rotated through service or sick call and various veterinary detachments, the ticks came along for the ride, alongside scout and sentry dogs in the same kennel areas. It is easy to see how the disease could be spread so fast.

Veterinarians launched a strict tick-control program, including the use of fumigating agents like Sevin and malathion for the dogs and kennel areas. Researchers eventually traced the disease to *Ehrlichia canis*, reported in Algeria as early as 1935. The best treatment available was tetracycline, but that still meant that affected animals could carry the blood disorder to other dogs. Unfortunately there was no centralized disease-reporting system established in Vietnam by the Veterinary Corps. In retrospect, had there been one, TCP would not have gained the foothold it did. The disease sounded the death knell for many dogs and was also the major reason so few dogs were returned from Southeast Asia to the United States.

Surprisingly, the 37th IPSD reported no cases of TCP. The platoon had left Fort Benning and gone in-country with experimental drugs as part of its diet. There were also no cases of heartworm or hookworms in the dogs. Their good fortune ran out with the supplies, since these experimental drugs were not within the normal military supply system. Many of these drugs appeared within a few years on the civilian market and are now staple items at veterinary clinics.

The pattern of care for dogs mirrored that for the troops. The first level of care came from enlisted animal specialists (MOS 91T), referred to as "vet techs" and assigned to each scout dog platoon. Many 91Ts were trained at the Walter Reed Army Institute of Research in Washington, D.C. Their main responsibility was to provide preventive medicine, first aid, and routine treatments. Some went further on their own, trying to perform minor surgery, often under the pressure of a handler or platoon commander who wanted immediate action. Although many provided excellent attention to the dogs, some failed to perform even the simplest of tasks such as dipping the dogs for ticks or cleaning their ears properly.

The vet techs were immediately backed up by graduate veterinarians at dispensaries. In 1966, these dispensaries were situated too far from the immediate tactical areas to provide fast service. Much of their organization was based on sentry dogs at fixed locations—not scout dogs scattered across the countryside and remaining quite mobile. Eventually they adjusted by building new facilities closer to where the action was, providing dispensary service at twenty-two locations in the III and IV Corps areas. Veterinarians also conducted (or at least

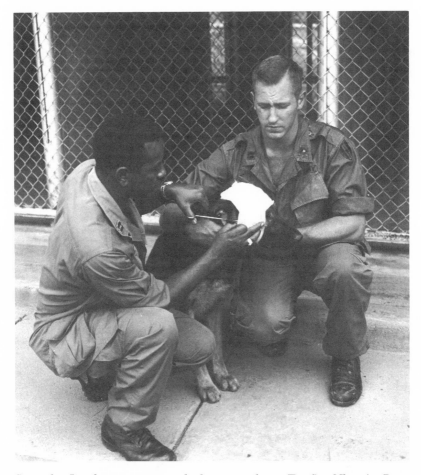

Scout dog Lux has an eye wound administered to at Tan Son Nhut Air Base by members of the 936th Veterinary Detachment. Veterinary care for most dogs in Vietnam was excellent under the prevailing conditions. *(National Archives)*

they were scheduled to provide) monthly field inspections of all the scout dogs.

Veterinarian care for the dogs improved dramatically once America became involved in suppling the ARVN with scouts and sentries. The vets were charged with numerous responsibilities beyond those of caring for the dogs: ARVN food inspection, civic programs involving local livestock, and a host of other projects. Like everyone else, the Veterinary Corps was handcuffed by shifting priorities, primitive laboratory and surgical facilities, infighting, lack of medicine, and the constant stress of what often seemed like an endless war. More than three hundred Veterinary Corps officers served in Vietnam and provided an excellent level of care for the animals in their charge. Their efforts, like those of thousands of other support personnel in South Vietnam, went largely unnoticed; their enemies were diseases, accidents, and injuries created within a environment of war.

EXILE

As the drawdown continued and the United States began in earnest to bail out of the South Vietnam quagmire, it was only natural that many handlers leaving the country wanted to take "their" dogs with them. This was mostly true of the handlers of scout and tracker dogs. Often they spent a year together, and many of the dogs had saved the lives of their handlers or prevented serious injuries. Emotions surged, and handlers were even willing to pay for the expense of bringing the dogs back—this was forbidden under army regulations. A story was written by Sgt. Thomas Mano of the 48th IPSD in 1968 about a special dog and what was expected at war's end. The story appeared as part of the platoon's monthly after-action report summary:

> What has four legs, one eye and can smell a wire you can't see? No, Dum Dum, it's not a cyclops who thinks he's a chair. Give up? Duke is the answer. He's 68 pounds of fur that nobody would like to tangle with, especially the NVA and the VC.
>
> Private First Class James L. Palmer (Scottsdale, Ariz.), handler for the German shepherd, doesn't seem to mind nor do the men in the 196th Infantry Brigade that he works for. "When the men first see that Duke only has one eye, they're skeptical," said Palmer. "But after he performs, they love him."
>
> Duke and PFC Palmer started their relationship when the handler was in Bien Hoa. "I was walking around the kennels when I saw him and we immediately became friends," continued Palmer. "The men there weren't sure Duke could work in the triple-canopy

jungle. I wanted to give him a chance, so they wouldn't put him to sleep." Duke had performed well in the 4th Division, but could he work well in the more thickly vegetated terrain of Military Region I? PFC Palmer had faith and set out to prove it. Four days after they arrived at the 48th Scout Dog Platoon, the team was sent out with Company A, 2nd Battalion, 1st Infantry. The mission turned out to be more of a mutual education than a test.

"We learned a lot about each other that first time out," mused Palmer. "I caught onto his alerts to the point where I could distinguish if he was pointing at a frog or a water buffalo."

After seven days of rest, the team was on the move again. This time to aid infantrymen in finding booby-traps. The first explosive Duke found was a mortar round. "It made me feel good that he could find something underground," reflected Palmer. "He's not trained to find anything buried; that's a mine dog's job."

Duke's spectacular "nosejob" was followed by an assignment to rid the 1st Battalion, 46th Infantry of some snipers. The infantrymen were being held down on a hill and Duke's job was to help them off, quickly! Duke's first find came as soon as he stepped off the hill. The men shot up the bushes in the direction of Duke's alert and found a blood trail.

But this was only a start. During the mission Duke broke up four ambushes with his sensitive nose. "We knew the men [VC] were there because the plastic they were sitting on was still warm," said Palmer. One outstanding trait Duke exhibited was the distance from the enemy at which he alerted. He was catching the scent from 30 to 50 meters. "I was really proud of him," recalled Palmer. "When I went through training, the instructors told us not to expect more than 25 meter alerts in triple-canopy jungle because of the wind deflection off the trees and vines."

Duke has now proven himself in the 196th Inf. Bde. He is respected by the "friendlies" as well as the enemy. He'll never be in want of a job. "When he leaves Vietnam, Duke will probably be put in public service," mused Palmer. "They might even make him a seeing-eye dog."[54]

Duke never left Vietnam. Mano and Palmer, along with many handlers in-country, were never told that their dogs were to be left behind, especially during the early part of the war. Lives of men hung in the balance when working these dogs in the field. How could the army possibly tell the handlers, before they went out on patrols, that the dogs would never go home? Some handlers were so happy to be leaving Vietnam that they just packed their bags without so much as a good-bye to their dogs. This was to be expected. Others maintained strong emotional ties with their dogs upon leaving, and many handlers wrote their congressman, for all it was worth, often trying to have the dogs returned to CONUS.

Usually the dogs themselves whined and remained melancholy for days once their masters left. Some handlers schemed to take their dogs with them, devising elaborate plans to smuggle them back home. But most of this was just talk that usually took place off-duty and grew in scope with the number of beers consumed. Most American dogs were condemned to permanent exile and eventual death in a foreign land.

Few civilians understood that the military considered all dogs as equipment. For the army, the decision to leave the dogs in Vietnam was both logical and practical. It was also cost-effective and did not present any logistical problem. Based on how military command conducted itself during the Vietnam War, the decision about the fate of these war dogs was just another bad link in a long chain of mistakes. Of course they were not pets, but for the men who labored with the dogs in the jungles of Vietnam they were respected as living, thinking creatures—unlike a rifle, a canteen, or a jeep.

History also went against this decision to leave the dogs behind. During World War II thousands of dogs were demilitarized and returned, either to their original owners or to the handlers who had fought alongside them. During both world wars there existed no banning of mascots as long as they did not carry an infectious disease. If there had been such a ban, dogs like Stubby would just be faded memories of European battles for those who knew him, and the name Rin Tin Tin would never have been heard of.[55]

It was during 1970 that Americans, fed up with the war, the military, and the politicians, learned that "man's best friend" had been left behind. This enraged at least the dog-loving segment of an already disillusioned American public, and a swift response by a sympathizing press followed. Several politicians quickly moved to file bills in Congress to address the problem. On September 22, 1970, Rep. John E. Moss, a Democrat from California, entered a bill (H.R. 19421) that would establish retraining or retirement in humane shelters for canine veterans. Representative Rarick later introduced H.R. 19750. Moss cited that most dogs were killed when they had outlived their usefulness and that they had reduced casualties by 65 percent in combat areas. These bills never made it to the floor of the House for a vote and died in committee. This public outcry led the army to adopt its own appeasement policy regarding the K-9s. Enhanced by its own spin doctors, the military would come out looking good one more time. Make the right moves, show some emotion, and the American public will fall for it and, in time, simply forget anything ever occurred.

First the Army Adjutant General's Office asked the Medical Command for a dog-return policy that would present no risk to civilian dogs within the Unites States. Naturally, everything in life carries risks, so the Medical Command said, "If you want zero risk, you'll have to settle for zero dogs."[56] In December 1970, the army, knowing it had to bring a few dogs back to continue the charade, instructed the Veterinary Corps to return only "healthy" dogs to the United States, after meeting the requirements of all the overseas commands.

The Corps knew that most, if not all, of the dogs carried some type of infectious disease. It was therefore decided to exclude those dogs that had TCP, red tongue, and melioidosis, since these were still being studied and were not yet under control. After reviewing the dogs in-country, about 200 were considered for possible return. These were then quarantined at Long Binh, where physicals were done and various treatments rendered. On May 3, 1971, two C-5A transports arrived to pick up the returnees, who now numbered 120. Fifteen scout dogs were left in Okinawa to be retrained as sentries, and 51 others were sent to Lackland AFB. Another 20 dogs went to Fort Benning, and the balance were transported to Fort Gordon.

The army had a surplus dog population in Vietnam at this time, so two hundred dogs were immediately given to the ARVN. But the ARVN already had more dogs than it could handle, and it appears that its acceptance of more was predicated only by the fact that the offer included a large supply of dog food. Tony Montoya, a handler with the 981st MP, was one of the men assigned to deliver dogs to the ARVN on the other side of the air base at Bien Hoa. Montoya recalled:

> Slowly the dogs were weeded out. Most were transferred to the ARVN. I hated to see that. It was really strange. We drove the dogs over to the ARVN side of the base at Bien Hoa, along with a whole truck of horse meat. When we got there, to hand the dogs over, none of the ARVN wanted to come close to the dogs. We had to take the dogs off the trucks ourselves and take them to their stake down area. The Vietnamese were so small. The dogs were bigger than they were and the ARVN were pretty scared. Eventually, one of the ARVN officers took control of the situation and the dogs. We drove back to our side of the base wondering what would become of those dogs.[57]

At this point the army really didn't care, and the home front was pacified and under the impression that more dogs would be returning. Although mass euthanasia was considered, it was undesirable since there was always a possibility that the information would leak to the public. Although it remains unconfirmed, at least one Marine platoon in I Corps reportedly euthanized its dogs rather than see them turned over to the South Vietnamese.[58]

More dogs were turned over to ARVN, and now they possessed a canine force in excess of seven hundred animals. The ARVN were not interested in the trackers, since most of the Labrador retrievers were black and as such were considered bad luck—a superstition obviously never embraced by the American combat tracker teams that employed them. Corps personnel finally convinced ARVN to accept the trackers, but

Marine Corporal Isaiah Martin comforts his dog. Martin's dog was wounded by a VC sniper in the Que Son Mountains. The Vietcong hated the dogs and handlers during the war and went so far as to place a bounty upon them. *(National Archives)*

their final disposition once handed over is open to specula-tion.[59] The general belief is that the dogs became another source of walking protein for ARVN troops. During the period of June 1970 to December 1972, 371 dogs were euthanized as being noneffective, and another 148 died of various causes.[60]

Some handlers expected the scout dogs to be demilita-rized and offered to them as personal pets. This was never to happen, since army policy forbade the release of dogs to pri-vate citizens or organizations. It was doubtful, policy said, that the dogs could be retrained, and as such the army could not guarantee public safety 100 percent. In addition, there was al-ways a chance that the TCP epidemic could be introduced to the civilian dog population. A few years later it was found that TCP had been prevalent in the United States for years.

Before the drawdown and the implementation of the dog return policy, there were several dogs who did come home. Nemo, the wounded sentry dog from Tan Son Nhut, is one ex-ample. Also, in June 1967, the platoon commander of the 40th IPSD received an unusual order to send one of his scout dogs home for the first time in history. Turk, in-country for two years, received immediate leave to return home and report to Walter Reed Army Hospital.

His former handler, SFC Richard L. Castle, wounded while in Vietnam, lay near death. Castle's wife and doctors felt the morale boost might help to bring him out of a coma and help pull him through. The doctors enlisted the aid of Senator Richard Byrd of Virginia, who had easy access to President Johnson. On presidential orders, Turk boarded an air force jet for the United States. Unfortunately, Castle died while his dog was en route. Turk spent several days at Fort Benning before being returned overseas.[61]

Seven months later he was still working patrols, but at the age of six he was now two years older than the average scout dog. Castle's widow asked for Turk to be returned and said that she would take over the care and feeding of the animal. Army officials said that, *unfortunately*, scout dogs posed a threat to society—and promptly denied the request. This return pol-icy for dogs was in marked contrast to the effort made during

World War II. This can be attributed to three major factors. First, civilians during the Vietnam War were not directly involved, as they had been in the Dogs for Defense program during World War II. Second, the military continued to treat war dogs as surplus equipment. Finally, there was the continuing myth that dogs working within the armed forces could not be demilitarized.

Of the thousands of dogs demilitarized and returned to civilians at the end of World War II, only a handful needed to be destroyed because of their temperament. The concern that military dogs would carry infectious diseases from Southeast Asia might have been a valid one—but could have been easily circumvented by placing the dogs in quarantine once they were returned to the United States. Granted, more important issues faced the United States, particularly questions about missing personnel and the possibility of their continued imprisonment by the North Vietnamese. The disposition of dogs during the American withdrawal was only a small consideration compared to the misery suffered by thousands of people—based on the lessons the country learned from the war, could Americans at the time have expected anything else?

7.

LESSONS LEARNED

THE VIETNAM EXPERIENCE

A casual scholar of the Vietnam War (and all previous conflicts) may find the use of military dogs insignificant or even trite. If compared to the thousands of bombs dropped, large-scale engagements with the latest armor and fighting technology available, and the thousands of men killed and wounded, the response would be yes. Still, the bombing of North Vietnam—or any action, anywhere—meant nothing to the men who patrolled a jungle trail, encountered a trip wire, or walked into a VC ambush. For every combat soldier in Vietnam, the war extended only as far as the eye could see.

For dog handlers, whether they came home in one piece, wounded, or not at all was often decided by the dog they worked with in the field. More than nine thousand dog handlers served during the Vietnam War, and few, if any, would engage in combat again without a dog by their side. The effectiveness of the dogs in Vietnam, as in other wars, will always be subjective and open to debate. Estimates vary, but some accounts state that dogs may have been responsible for the saving of at least ten thousand lives in Vietnam.[1]

If you look at the performance of sentry dogs, their accomplishments cannot be based on the number of engagements with the enemy. A more revealing statistic is the amount of time there was no enemy activity present when the dogs and their handlers worked a perimeter patrol at an air base. The number of possible sapper attacks against an air base or ammunition depot that were preempted or broken up is a fig-

Specialist Fifth Class Steven Schanner and Vic, of the 57th IPSD, cross a rice paddy as part of a search-and-destroy mission. Vic would be used when the patrol entered a thickly vegetated area with limited visibility and where VC booby traps might be rigged. *(National Archives)*

ure that can never be truly estimated. Sentry dogs, just by their presence at night, robbed the cloak of darkness, a powerful ally for the Vietcong.

Scout, tracker, and mine/tunnel dogs, placed in an offensive posture, create some revealing statistics by their presence in Vietnam. Based on compilations of monthly after-action reports during the war, army scout and mine/tunnel dog teams conducted over 84,000 missions.[2] They were directly responsible for more than 4,000 enemy killed and over 1,000 captured. By locating caches of supplies, the teams recovered more than 1,000,000 pounds of rice and corn, located over 3,000 mortars, and exposed at least 2,000 tunnels and bunkers.

MONTHLY REPORT OF SCOUT DOG OPERATIONS		RCS: AVHGC-7	DATE 30 Apr 69

THRU: Commanding Officer 198th Inf Bde ATTN: S-3 APO SF 96219	TO: Commanding General HQ USARV ATTN: AVHGC-CS APO 96375	FROM: Commanding Officer 57th Inf Plt (Sct Dog) 198th Inf Bde APO SF 96219

1. MONTH April	2. SDT AVAL 18	3. SDT OP 14	4. AUTH STR PERS 27-1 DOG 28	5. ACTUAL STR: PERS 27-1 DOG 19

6. HANDLER KIA___ WIA___ HOSP___ LIM DY___ TNG___ NO DOG 3 REPL RQR___   7. DOG KIA___ WIA___ SICK 4 BAD___ TNG___ NO HANDLER___ REPL RQR___

8. MISSIONS

SEARCH 36	AMBUSH 70	RECON 18	OUTPOST 1	PERI PTL 27
ROAD CLEARING 15		OTHER CA - 4 Rat Patrol - 8		TOTAL 179

9. SCOUT DOG TEAM SUPPORT DAYS   179

10. SCOUT DOG ALERTS:

   a. Warning of enemy ambush___, occupied base camp___, occupied bunker___, cave 1, sniper___, tunnel___, other___. Spider Hole - 1

   b. Warning of enemy booby traps 1, caches___, mines___, unoccupied base camp___, unoccupied bunker 5, unoccupied cave___, unoccupied tunnel 5, other___.

   c. Warning of enemy movement toward friendly ambush___, friendly outpost___, other___. Attempted penetration of NDP - 2

11. DIRECT RESULT OF SCOUT DOG TEAM ALERT: EN KIA 5   PW___   WPNS___ Detainees - 5 . SUPPLIES Documents; Foodstuffs - 1000lbs .

12. REMARKS OF PLAT COMMANDER:
   PFC Thomas P Mulroney and Scout Dog Ringo, OK62, tripped an M-26 hand grenade attached to a trip wire while engaged in a night movement. Neither dog nor man was injured. Possible reason for dog missing the trip wire was the presence of persistent CS in the locality. Increasing use of American manufactured grenades in VC booby traps is noted. Chicom grenades (previously the dominant form of VC booby trap explosives) are becoming more infrequent than the more reliable, but longer fuzed American grenades.

                CONT'D

13. REMARKS OF REVIEWING OFFICER:

14. NAME AND GRADE PLATOON COMMANDER: MARK P ZIHNGIEL, 2LT, IN, CMDG	15. SIGNATURE:
16. NAME AND GRADE OF REVIEWING OFFICER: THOMAS J AMBROSE, LTC, IN, S-3	17. SIGNATURE:

USARV Form 382 Revised 24 Oct 68 PREVIOUS EDITIONS OBSOLETE

A typical after-action report, in this case from the commanding officer of the 57th IPSD. All scout dog and tracker platoons made out these reports monthly. Toward the end of American involvement in Vietnam, many COs didn't bother to file them. Marine War Dog Platoons were never required to make such detailed reports and listed their activities in a general narrative of activities for a given month.

Although the effect may be short-term, by denying the enemy the weapons of war, food, and medical supplies you have neutralized or weakened his offensive capability. One phrase often heard during the conflict was "Keep the VC moving." And in a guerrilla action, this kept the enemy off balance, making his day-to-day life extremely difficult. When the time finally did come for the enemy to fight, he would be at a disadvantage.

The VC also regarded American dogs as a major problem. They could run, but with a well-trained dog scouting them there was no place to hide. To boost morale and whittle down the American teams, the VC even went so far as to post bounties on the handlers and their dogs—a compliment and testament to their effectiveness in the bush. Although the dogs were not trained for it, or even authorized to do it, it was not uncommon for a scout dog to be present during the interrogation of a VC suspect. Vietnamese people, in general, were always intimidated by a big German shepherd, and answers usually spewed forth before a question could even be asked.[3]

During the phased withdrawal of American troops from Vietnam the United States began to dismantle its military dog program at home. The combat trackers began to withdraw from Vietnam in July 1969 with the disbandment of 65th IPCT, followed by three more platoons the following year. Five more platoons left in 1971, leaving only the 62d and 63d in-country. At this time the school at Fort Gordon also closed. The last tracker team, the 62d, finally left the country in August 1972. Over half of the scout dog platoons were gone by the end of 1970, and ten more left the following year. So many teams were broken up that two provisional (temporary) platoons (the 4th and 34th War Dog Detachments) were formed to keep some sense of order. This left the 48th IPSD, which departed in March 1972, followed by the 34th IPSD, which hung in until August. The Marines, the first to enter the war, withdrew their remaining war dog platoons in June 1971.

Few missions were carried out in 1972 by scout and combat tracker teams. As one handler pointed out, "At this stage of

Specialist Fourth Class Bobby J. Railey and Von (514A), from the 48th IPSD, going out to join D Company 3/21 Infantry on a search-and-destroy mission. By 1970, the American withdrawal was well under way. The 48th IPSD would be among the last scout dog platoons to leave Vietnam. *(Bobby Railey)*

the game, it was the hell with the ARVN and every man for himself. You just wanted to get home alive. The last man out shut the light off." Patrols were cut back to almost nil by March, and no one wanted to be the last man out.

By June 1972, about 130 dogs remained under the control of the United States, none of them approved for the return home. In the fall of that year, the veterinary hospital at Long Binh closed, as there were only eighteen sentry dogs left in-country. Once these were turned over to the ARVN, the final chapter of the American military working dogs and their handlers in South Vietnam came to a close.

Three years later, following military tradition as history has it recorded, the army discontinued its scout dog school at Fort Benning. This is no surprise, as the military working dog program ebbs and flows with the close of one conflict or the start of a new one. What is disturbing is that the lessons learned are not always carried to the next generation and the experiences of the past are often lost, only sometimes redis-covered, and all too often ignored.

CHANGING TIMES

The military closed its book on scout, mine/tunnel, and tracker dogs with the end of Vietnam. Patrol dogs would al-ways be in demand and a staple commodity for both the air force and the army. Beginning in 1971, the air force "discov-ered" that dogs could be used to detect narcotics and explo-sives. After Tet in 1968, drug use in-country skyrocketed, and many American troops returning from Vietnam brought home narcotics stashed in their baggage. The first dogs trained were employed for the detection of marijuana on incoming flights returning from South Vietnam. Success was immediately real-ized and the program was expanded to include hashish, co-caine, and heroin. Even with the drugs sealed in plastic bags wrapped in tape, it seemed that nothing could stop the olfac-tory abilities of dogs.

The success of the explosive sniffer dogs trained by the British in Northern Ireland prompted the air force to adopt a similar program in 1971. During this time, the airlines seemed to be at the mercy of hijackings and bomb threats, a good reason to adopt a more aggressive program for the detection of explosives. Often the dogs would be certified for both pa-trol and explosive detection, and besides the military, other federal agencies like the Federal Aviation Administration, Border Patrol, and Customs became involved. By this time terminology had changed somewhat and the military began to refer to its dogs simply as military working dogs (MWD) along with their specialty (patrol, patrol/explosive, or pa-trol/narcotic).[4]

One agency that took a keen interest in the narcotics MWD program offered by the air force was the U.S. Customs Service. Customs immediately began to beef up its interdiction of narcotics entering the country by screening aircraft, cargo, mail, baggage, ships, and vehicles at international airports, sea-

At Cannon Air Force Base, New Mexico, an airman and a narcotics-detection dog inspect a pallet of luggage returning from exercise Team Spirit '85. *(Official U.S. Air Force Photo)*

ports, and border-crossing points around the country. Unlike the military, Customs officials use a wide variety of dogs such as golden retrievers, spaniels, German shepherds, and mixed breeds. Many of these dogs are acquired from animal shelters and through rescue leagues, their lineage always secondary to their olfactory ability. Tests are made to determine sociability, temperament, retrieval capability, and, of course, trainability to detect contraband. These tests are quite stringent and about 98 percent of the dogs wash out.[5]

A good example of one Customs working dog is Tommy, who stayed on duty for nine years in New York. Tommy is credited with 175 seizures in his career, the largest one being 165 pounds of heroin.[6] Tommy and the other dogs in Customs keep working until they can no longer successfully perform their jobs. Unlike what happened in the military, these dogs usually become household pets for the handlers who worked them or are adopted by a family.

The air force began testing smaller breeds for detector

Air Force Sergeant David J. Filchak works Turbo, a narcotics detector dog, at Caswell AFB, Texas. The air force found smaller breeds extremely efficient for the detection of narcotics and explosives. *(Official U.S. Air Force Photo)*

tasks in 1976 and soon employed a number of these dogs. The bulk of the work stayed with the larger patrol dogs, cross-trained for explosives or narcotics. Although German shepherds still dominate the ranks of military dogs, the air force has also begun to induct the Belgian Malinois breed. This breed offers many of the same characteristics as the German shepherd but without the high incidence of hip dysplasia and genetic defects that have plagued the latter over the past several decades.

The United States invasion of Grenada on October 18, 1983, did not involve any dogs. In 1989, when George Bush decided to oust Panamanian dictator Manuel Noriega in Operation Just Cause, a few patrol and sniffer dogs were included in the action. Little consideration was given during these operations to the advantages of MWD teams.

Two years later, during Operation Desert Storm, eighty dog teams participated, representing each branch of the armed

At Camp Bullis, Texas, Sgt. Lloyd Butterfield and his dog, Brutus, from the 3700th Security Police Squadron, locate "aggressors" during exercise Ripe Warrior in July 1983. *(Official U.S. Air Force Photo)*

services. These dogs provided explosives and narcotics detection as well as the standard security duties. This would be the largest engagement since Vietnam that dogs had the opportunity to participate in. The dogs handled the heat adequately, but needed special eye ointments because of the blowing sand. Veterinary support was excellent, and not a single dog was lost during the entire operation. It was also the first combat operation for the Belgian Malinois breed.

One outstanding dog was Carlo, an explosives-sniffing Belgian Malinois handled by Air Force S.Sgt. Christopher Batta in Kuwait. During their sixty-day tour together, Carlo alerted to 167 caches of explosives, some rigged to explode on contact. One booby trap consisted of a pack of cluster bombs hidden beneath a case of American MRE (Meals-Ready-to-Eat) containers.

Sergeant Batta earned a Bronze Star on October 10, 1991, for his efforts and also learned through the *Stars and Stripes* about the regulation banning awards to animals. After the conclusion of the ceremony, Batta removed his medal and placed it on his dog, saying, "Carlo worked harder than me. He was always in front of me."

These dogs were never used under actual combat circumstances, but far away from the actual fighting and frequently in Kuwait after the Iraqi withdrawal. In Operation Uphold Democracy, which took place in 1994 in Haiti, military working dogs came a lot closer to the action. Explosives-detecting dogs were brought in to sweep the Haitian Parliament Building and several other government facilities, including President Jean-Bertrand Aristide's home. The U.S. Military Police checked these locations for any possible booby traps prior to their being turned over to the legitimate government officials.

During one incident at Port-au-Prince, armed Haitians (called "attachés") launched a grenade attack that killed seven civilians and wounded at least fifty others. Staff Sergeant Brian Twohy and Sonja, a three-year-old Belgian Malinois, were quickly deployed to the immediate vicinity. The MWD team, part of the 10th Mountain Military Police K-9 section from Fort Drum, soon rounded up two Haitians in a nearby building. Seldom are MWD teams brought into such a potentially dangerous situation as this one. Their success may spur the military once again to adopt a more prominent role for them in the future.

Dogs are not anachronisms on the modern battlefield, as can be seen by their use in other countries. The Russian military still trains canines for mine detection and to locate wounded soldiers in the field. Gas masks with built-in radio receivers have been designed, and the deplorable program of teaching the dogs to carry out suicide attacks against tanks continues. The Soviet empire has crumbled, and the military is divided among several commands, but the potential of the dog in modern warfare is still a reality for them.

Although the Russian armies remain dormant, the same cannot be said for the Israeli army, which can be considered one of the most active and technologically advanced of any in the world. Dogs continue to play an active role, especially in the occupied territories and Lebanon. It was here that news of Israeli suicide dogs appeared in 1989 in a military deployment reminiscent of the demolition wolves program, abandoned by the United States during World War II.

As had been done in the past, dogs were trained to follow the enemy into guerrilla-held bunkers and caves. Everyday technology combined with this antiquated maneuver to produce the desired result. It was relatively easy for a soldier to push a switch when the dog was in position and remotely explode the device rather than rely on a crude timing device. Protests emanated worldwide over such tactics, yet the Israeli army remained adamant–the saving of human life takes precedent over virtually every consideration.

This faulty reasoning is evoked whenever a shroud needs to be placed over a military objective. The use of dogs for this type of military operation is not only unwarranted but totally unnecessary. In these cases, technology can easily replace the war dog. The treatment of dogs in this manner is a reflection of today's society and ultimately reflects on how we treat other people. War may be hell–but not one created for dogs.

This brings up the question of quality of life for military

working dogs under the employ of the United States. Many dogs are acquired from European "vendors," but civilians can still sell or donate their dogs to the Department of Defense. The final disposition of the dogs is clearly stated in the U.S. Air Force Fact Sheet titled "Military Working Dogs," which reads in part:

> Once a dog is accepted for military duty and trained, it cannot be returned to a civilian environment. The dogs could not fully adjust to the sudden change from a highly structured, disciplined life to the quieter civilian environment. In addition, they could not tolerate the loss of constant companionship, exercise, and attention that had become their way of life. When they become too senile for continued duty or incurably ill, directives strictly specify humane disposition procedures much like those practiced by civilian veterinary doctors.[7]

Either the Lackland AFB Public Affairs Office has not accurately recounted history or it chooses to dismiss and ignore the facts. Fortunately, humans who were drafted or enlisted into the military often fare much better than their canine counterparts. Soldiers are memorialized and revered; sometimes so is even the machinery of war that helps them accomplish their tasks. Dogs (and it should also be noted that there are other military animals—horses, mules, pigeons, and dolphins) remain unrecognized for their contributions to military actions. Every other country that used dogs in warfare has recognized their participation, and one wonders why the United States is the only country that does not memorialize its canines. The angst faced by the military in this respect has led other individuals, all civilians, to press forward with their own tributes.

On a return visit to Guam in 1989, Dr. William Putney, who commanded the 2nd Marine War Dog Platoon during World War II, was astounded to find the K-9 cemetery at Dededo overgrown by jungle foliage and the headstones vandalized. Once his eyes set sight on the condition of the cemetery, he vowed to do something about it. Fighting the bureaucracy every step of the way, Putney sought to have the

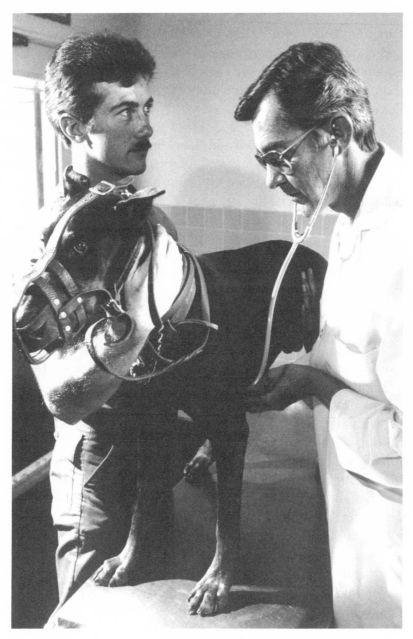

Lieutenant Colonel Lee Townsend examines a Doberman pinscher with the assistance of a veterinarian technician at Lackland AFB. Working military dogs receive the best of care but are never returned to civilian life; that practice was discontinued shortly after World War II. *(Official U.S. Air Force Photo)*

cemetery moved to the War in the Pacific National Historic Park and Museum at Assan, where it would be well protected and cared for. After two years of waiting, permission was not granted for some unknown reason. Fortunately, the U.S. Navy stepped forward at that time and offered a suitable location at its base on Orote Point.

Putney also enlisted the help of the Doberman Pinscher Club of America, and with additional financial support a monument was erected that featured a bronze Doberman pinscher on a granite base inscribed with the names of the war dogs killed on Guam. The life-size bronze statue of a sitting Doberman, sculpted by Susan Bahary Wilner, is titled *Forever Faithful*. Fifty years later, the cemetery was once again rededicated as former Marine handlers placed wreaths in front of each headstone during a memorial service marking the liberation of Guam.

Other tributes, closer to home, also honor war dogs and other military animals. The only other memorial, besides the 1922 statue at Hartsdale Canine Cemetery, that is dedicated exclusively to war dogs, is located in Lincoln, Nebraska. Once again, this tribute was nurtured by one man, Gordon Greene, a Korean War veteran. Greene never handled dogs while serving with the Marines, but at the age of ten, in 1943, he donated his dog, Buster, to the U.S. Army. After hearing nothing at all for more than a year, his family received a telegram stating that Buster had been killed in action.

Greene never forgot about Buster, and an opportunity finally came in 1993 to honor his memory and the memories of all military dogs. At this time the Lincoln Parks Commission set aside land to serve as a war memorial. World War II, Korea, and Vietnam memorials had been planned, and Greene pitched his K-9 monument idea to the parks commission. The city would pay for half of the cost if he could come up with the balance of the money. Greene, with generous help from World War II's CBI detachment handlers and several others, raised funds quickly for the project.

The black granite memorial was dedicated on June 4, 1994. It is unique in several aspects compared to the other memorials at the park. While all the other memorials face inward toward each other, the K-9 stone faces outward, a symbolic gesture to the perimeter and outposts dogs usually worked. It also memorializes individual dogs who served by displaying donor bricks purchased and laid in front of the commemorative stone with the dog's name, brand number, and the war he served in inscribed upon them.

Since World War II, individuals and groups have sporadically petitioned the government for a national memorial, and these requests have fallen on deaf ears. Neither is there a K-9 museum dedicated to the accomplishments of military dogs and the scores of civilian agencies and police departments that have benefited from them over these many years. And as the accomplishments of these dogs continue, they should not go unnoticed.

Our use of dogs is only limited by our own creativity, and a thin line separates exploitation and reasonable employment. Customs officials have placed such a value on their detecting canines that about four hundred dog teams are maintained across the United States, with a specialized training center at Front Royal, Virginia.[8] In 1987, the air force delivered dogs to the Afghan rebels. Fire departments use dogs to locate accelerants in arson cases, and thousands of police departments rely on canines every day. After an earthquake devastates a city, search dogs are called in to look for survivors. Their diverse capabilities mean that dogs can locate lost children, hunt for fugitives, lead the blind, or signal a deaf person. Even the president of the United States is not beyond the need of canine protection, with over one hundred explosives-detecting missions conducted on his behalf in 1994. Every single day of every week of every year, dogs in both military and civilian sectors continue to work for the benefit of humankind.

Continued technological advances will not eliminate the conscription of canines into the military. Their impressive record of service demonstrates an intimacy and bonding with humans that remains an unbroken chain throughout recorded history. If we continue to choose to employ them on our behalf, then we should restudy and explore our relationship with them. If we choose to believe that we are superior to them in every respect, consider that dogs do not create war and are devoid of the racism and hatred that often precipitate such conflicts. Intelligence is indeed all a matter of perspective. The chasm between humans and dogs may be a wide expanse or a threadlike space formed by our association with them—bridging the gap ultimately will be determined by how our debt of gratitude is repaid to them.

EPILOGUE

MORE THAN TWO DECADES HAVE PASSED SINCE AMERICANS abandoned South Vietnam. Long gone are the dogs that served alongside their masters in combat—but they are not just distant memories or faded photographs in an album collecting dust. These dogs may be proving instrumental for the health of many veterans today, who were once exposed to the defoliant Agent Orange. Agent Orange is a carcinogenic chemical that was sprayed over three million acres of South Vietnam, about 10 percent of the country, and mostly in II Corps, where the majority of dogs were to be found.

Dr. Howard Hayes of the National Cancer Institute published an article in the June 20, 1990, institute journal and stated in part:

> During the Vietnam war, the U.S. military working dogs served with their companion dog handlers in close proximity, sharing common exposures to war-related activity, many zoonotic infectious agents, chemical pesticides, phenoxy herbicides, and extensive use of therapeutic drugs. To gain insight in the effects of the Vietnam experience, we investigated the occurrence of neoplasms in military working dogs based on standard necropsy examination by the Armed Forces Institute of Pathology. We observed that these dogs experienced significant elevated risks for testicular seminoma and independently, testicular dysfunction.
>
> U.S. military working dogs proved to be sentinels for the presence of zoonotic infectious agents in their military dog handlers in southeast Asia.

Twice the number of dogs in Vietnam had testicular cancer compared to dogs stationed stateside. Ironically, this twofold increase in testicular cancer is also seen in Vietnam veterans. Perhaps this is not so surprising, since a dog's genital tract is very similar to that of man. Canine seminoma is almost identical to its human counterpart, except with dogs it is usually benign.

For Dr. Hayes the picture is quite clear that there is a direct medical link between the men and dogs that served in Vietnam. Yet in January 1994, testicular cancer was removed from the government's list of Agent Orange effects. Continued research by Dr. Hayes and the National Cancer Institute may prove otherwise. Part of this research involves locating former handlers and studying their medical histories compared with their dogs' necropsy results. This same methodology is being used for the dogs that served during Operation Desert Storm. Many Persian Gulf veterans have contracted strange illnesses linked to their time in Kuwait, Saudi Arabia, and Iraq. The air force is taking one step toward solving the dilemma by monitoring the health of the military working dogs employed throughout the Persian Gulf area. Once again, another link is forged between humans and animals. There is little doubt that this often overlooked medical bonding between man and dogs will also be a military consideration in the future.

Human nature, taken at face value, will ensure that at some time future battles and conflicts will arise because of military, political, or socioeconomic reasons. No doubt the United States will be drawn into and engage in some future "low-intensity conflict." There may be a call for infantrymen to walk patrols where there is a risk of ambush or the presence of booby traps. An idea will surface that *perhaps* dogs could be employed for the early detection of the enemy. Someone will dust off an old army FM 20-20 manual on scout dogs or locate some retired handlers to gain from their experience, and start from scratch. Dogs destined to serve their masters will challenge Death once more and enter into combat again.

Should the military need any combat-experienced handlers, those who served in Vietnam would be rather easy to find. Many of them are members of the Vietnam Dog Handlers Association, a nonprofit organization formed in 1993.

During the crisp, clear morning of November 11, 1994, about one hundred of them gathered for memorial services at the Vietnam Veterans' Memorial in Washington, D.C., as part of their first reunion.

Shortly before the ceremonies commenced, a man holding a German shepherd by a leash approached the stark black marble memorial. A uniformed National Park Service employee came forward and stopped the pair. "Sorry, sir, dogs are not allowed in the vicinity of the memorial," he said. The man looked up and in a clear voice stated, "I'm a former Vietnam dog handler and *we* are part of the service to be conducted here today." The ranger, with a quizzical expression on his face, just nodded and passed the man and dog through. For the first time since its dedication on November 13, 1982, a dog was allowed to participate in a ceremony at the memorial that most people refer to as simply "The Wall."

The Veterans' Day observance honored many men and women whose names are inscribed along the length of The Wall's black face. A special dedication was made during the ceremony to the dog handlers who served during the war. There onstage for everyone to see was veteran hander Mike Quinliven and his dog, Brandy, representing all the handlers who served during the war. For the hundred or so veteran handlers who were in attendance, it was a special day that marked the ultimate sacrifice their fellow handlers made for their country. At the end of the ceremony Bruce Fleming, Mike Cagle, and Paul Morgan, accompanied by his dog, Cody–all representing the Vietnam Dog Handlers Association–carried a memorial wreath along the pathway in front of The Wall. Thousands of people watched as the wreath was laid in a tribute to their fallen comrades.

A national memorial has yet to be established for the dogs that were called to duty. The dogs that served in combat are only recognized by those who accompanied them and few others–perhaps a memorial is not required after all. The reasons humans engage others in battle are varied and will be debated for as long as we choose to conduct war. For dogs to follow men into battle, there is only one reason: they have no choice.

An unknown author offered an explanation in a piece titled "The Creation of Man's Best Friend":

> God summoned a beast from the field, and He said,
>
> "Behold man is created in My image. Therefore adore him. You shall protect him in the wilderness, shepherd his flocks, watch over his children, accompany him wherever he may go—even into civilization. You shall be his companion, his ally, and his slave.
>
> "To do these things, I endow you with the instincts uncommon to other beasts: Faithfulness, Devotion, and Understanding, surpassing those of man himself. Lest it impair your courage, you shall never foresee your death. Lest it impair your loyalty, you shall be blind to the faults of man. Lest it impair your understanding, you are denied the power of words. Speak to your master only with your mind and through your honest eyes.
>
> "Walk by his side; sleep in his doorway; ward off his enemies; carry his burden; share his afflictions; love and comfort him. And in return for this, man will fulfill your needs and wants—which shall be only food, shelter, and affection.
>
> "So be silent and be a friend of man. Guide him through the perils along the way to this land I have promised him. This shall be your destiny and your immortality."
>
> The dog heard and was content.

ENDNOTES

PREFACE

1. Colonel James C. Pennington, QMC, letter to Commander in Chief, United States Army, Europe, June 24, 1958. Jesse S. Mendez collection.

2. "Dogs of War Obey Cry of the Battlefield," *The European,* July 1–4, 1993, p. 16. The Russians teach the dogs that food could be found beneath a tank, a conditioned response with predictable results. The explosives, about twenty-six pounds, would be carried in two canvas pouches wired to a detonator attached to a lever mounted on the dog's back. As he crawls under the tank, the chassis strikes the lever and pushes it backward, detonating the explosive charge. Russia is the only country known to have employed antitank dogs.

3. Elizabeth A. Lawrence, "Weapons of War," *Animal Voice Magazine* 6 (January–February–March 1993), p. 32.

4. The military can be real quirky at times, as witnessed by Dr. Louis F. Fiesler, the father of napalm, who developed a one-ounce incendiary device. In what was called Operation X-ray, army technicians surgically attached the devices to the wings of bats. The idea was that the bats would be dropped by bombers over Japan and start thousands of fires. The first trial run burned down a hangar and destroyed a staff car in Carlsbad, California. The army dropped the idea but the navy ran with it. Navy personnel decided to put the bats "asleep" by flying up to a high altitude, where the cold air would put them into hibernation. After being dropped, they would awaken at the warmer lower altitude. All went well during the first test as the sleeping bats descended through the atmosphere–but they never woke up and met their fate when they returned to earth at an extreme velocity.

1: ORIGINS OF THE MODERN MILITARY WORKING DOG

1. Estelle Ross, *The Book of Noble Dogs* (New York: Century Co., 1922), p. 258.

2. Henry P. Davis, *The New Dog Encyclopedia* (Harrisburg: Stackpole Books, 1970), p. 176.

3. Albert Payson Terhune, *A Book of Famous Dogs* (Garden City, N.Y.: Doubleday, Doran and Company, Inc., 1937), p. 241.

4. The first statutory reference to dogs appears in the Boston Public Library in the records of the Province of the Massachusetts Bay in an act passed by His Excellency the Governor, Council and Representatives in General Court assembled, on November 21, 1706–7, which is indexed in the Province Laws under the caption "Frontiers." The preamble states:

Whereas upon tryal lately made of rangeing and scouring the woods on the frontiers, with hounds and other dogs used to hunting, it has proved of great service to discourge and keep off the Indians; for encouragement, therefore to raise and train up a great number of dogs, to be so improved,–

Be it enacted by such authority aforesaid

Sect. I. That such person and persons, living in any of the frontiers within this province, who shall take, keep and raise up any whelp of the breed of the hounds, and have them at all times in readiness to attend the hunt serjeant, or others improved in that service, when they shall come to such town, and require the same, shall be allowed and paid out of the publick treasury the sum of five shillings per annum, in consideration of their care and charge, for the raising and keeping of every such dog; a certificate thereof from year to year to be transmitted to the commissary-general, under the hands of the commission military officers, and the town clerk of such town; provided

Sect. II. This act shall continue in force for the space of three years next coming, if the war with the Indians lasts so long, and not afterwards.

5. Fairfax Downey, *Dogs for Defense* (New York: McDonald, 1955), p. 2.

6. Ibid.

7. Ibid.

8. The Civil War Library and Museum, letter to Mary E. Thurston, July 21, 1992.

9. The actual weight of these dogs may be slightly exaggerated, but their ferocity is not in doubt. Both Confederate and Union armies tried to acquire the largest dogs possible for sentry duty.

2: THE WORLD WAR I EXPERIENCE

1. Ellwood Hendrick, "Merciful Dogs of War," *The Red Cross Magazine* (February 1917), p. 73.

2. Ibid.

3. Irene M. Givenson, "Man's Loyal Friend, the Dog, in Time of War," *The Red Cross Courier* (February 16, 1925), p. 18.

4. Terhune, *A Book of Famous Dogs,* pp. 228–36.

5. Givenson, "Man's Loyal Friend," p. 17.

6. Walter A. Dyer, "Wanted: More Red Cross Dogs for America," *The Red Cross Magazine* (November 1917), p. 540.

7. The recommendation came from G5, General Headquarters, American Expeditionary Forces, but was dropped by G3.

8. Dyer, "Wanted: More Red Cross Dogs for America," p. 540.

9. A descendant of Rin Tin Tin would later show up at Cat Island during World War II as part of the Quartermaster Corps operation.

10. In literature Stubby has been described as a pit bull, bulldog, Boston bulldog, and probably a few others. Chances are he was blessed with a little something from several breeds.

11. According to one account, Conroy's personal papers and a detailed history of Stubby's adventures was left with the Red Cross Museum in Washington, D.C. When asked their whereabouts, museum personnel were at a loss. Conroy's papers could possibly be stored away somewhere in the vast collection of the Smithsonian Institution.

12. Richardson authored several books on war dog training, including *War, Police, and Watch Dogs* (London: William Blackwood, 1910) and *British War Dogs: Their Training and Psychology* (London: Skeffington and Son, Ltd., 1920). By far he was the most instrumental figure in the training of war dogs during the early part of this century and a benchmark for measuring future endeavors.

13. It is estimated that eight million horses and an unknown number of messenger pigeons were also killed during the war.

14. Avery M. Cochran, "Canine Cartridge Carrier," *Infantry Journal* 47 (July–August 1947), pp. 355–57.

15. Cerberus, "War Dogs," *Infantry Journal* 47 (January–February, 1940), p. 68. It should be mentioned that Cerberus is a mythical dog with three heads that guarded the entrance of the infernal regions. Military dogs did not wear identification tags but were tattooed with a unique number.

3: STARTING FROM SCRATCH

1. During the war, Byrd served as the chief of staff of Naval Operations, evaluating Pacific islands as operating sites.

2. United States Army, *FM 25-6 Dog Transportation* (Washington, D.C.: War Department, United States Government, 1941).

3. Downey, *Dogs for Defense,* p. 16.

4. As cited by Downey in *Dogs for Defense.* The organization was incorporated in New York on January 23, 1942. In its original filing the purpose of the organization is stated as:

> To inspire, encourage and develop the use of dogs for duties and services in connection with defense work and the armed forces of the United States; to disseminate informative material in the form of pamphlets, publications and press releases and otherwise assist in the training and uses of dogs in civilian defense and with the armed forces of the United States: to maintain, conduct and supervise training camps, demonstrations and instructions in the training of dogs as guards, messengers, carriers and sentries and other uses in connection with defense work; to solicit financial and other aid and support the utilization of dogs for defense as a non-profit making movement devoted entirely to the public defense benefit and assistance in connection with civilian and military forces engaged in the national defense of the United States.

5. Ibid., p. 18.

6. Mascots even served on submarines. Called "sea dogs," they were typically small mixed breeds. Crews made collars with combat submarine insignia and service or coats displaying the sub's war record.

7. Technically, a corps consisted of two or more divisions of troops. For most people, "K-9 Corps" is synonymous with any program involving military dogs. For the purposes of this book, "K-9 Corps" or "K-9s" will be used liberally as the prose dictates.

8. The Preston brand system consists of a single letter and two or three digits. The tattoos were seven-sixteenths of an inch high and were usually located inside the skin fold of the left flank. Sometimes this was not always the case and the tattoo might appear inside the ear.

9. Airedale, Alaskan malamute, Belgian sheepdog, Bouviers des Flandres, boxer, briard, bullmastiff, Chesapeake Bay retriever, collie, curly-coated retriever, Dalmatian, Doberman pinscher, English springer spaniel, Eskimo, flat-coated retriever, German shepherd, German short-haired pointer, giant schnauzer, Great Dane, Great Pyrenees, Irish setter, Irish water spaniel, Labrador retriever, Newfoundland, Norwegian elkhound, pointer, rottweiler, Saint Bernard, Samoyed, Siberian husky, standard poodle, wirehaired pointing griffon.

10. Known as Operation Pastorius, the plan was hatched by the German intelligence division (*Abwehr*).

11. Clayton G. Going, *Dogs at War* (New York: The Macmillan Co., 1944), p. 132.

12. U. S. Coast Guard Headquarters, *The Coast Guard at War—Beach Patrol,* vol. XVII (Washington, D. C.: Historical Section, 1946), p. 9.

13. Coast Guard instructors were ranked as Chief Specialist D or First, Second, or Third class and wore the D insignia, which stood for "domestic animals." Instructors for both dog training and horsemanship peaked at about 675 during 1943.

14. Depending on what account you read, Dipsy-Doodle retrieved anywhere from seven to thirty-six bodies from the ocean.

15. Eleanor C. Bishop, *Prints in the Sand—The U.S. Coast Guard Beach Patrol During World War II* (Missoula: Pictorial Histories Publishing Company, 1989), p. 76.

16. Memorandum for record, Training Dogs for Assault, War Department General Staff, July 16, 1942. OPD was not convinced of the practicality or desirability of Pandre's proposal. In lieu of "recent developments," the memo stated the efforts of other countries in connection with dogs. OPD thought something worthwhile might develop. Also, the OPD, knowing the nature of the program, kept the QMC uninformed of its activities. National Archives and Records Administration (NARA) RG407 includes three reels of microfilm (3032, 3033, 3034) consisting of 4,117 pages of war dog platoon letters, memoranda, and histories.

17. Colonel A. R. Nichols, letter to Maj. J. R. Kimmell, Army Ground Forces, Army War College, Washington, D. C., September 13, 1942, NARA RG407. Nichols must have been impressed by Pandre and recommended that Front Royal handlers be replaced and relieved immediately.

18. Ibid. It appears that Nichols originally wanted criminal prisoners as "live bait" and someone else suggested the employment of aliens.

19. Memo, Maj. J. R. Kimmell to Commanding General, Army Air Forces, Washington, D.C., October 24, 1942. Subject: Movement of Japanese-American Detachment from Camp McCoy, Wisconsin, to New Orleans, Louisiana, NARA RG407.

20. Memo, Colonel Ridgely Gaither to Chief of Staff, Army Ground Forces, [date censored]. Subject: Inspection of Cat Island Training Project, January 12–13, 1943; NARA RG407.

21. Ibid.

22. Attachment, "War Dogs in the U.S. Marine Corps, World War II," *Hawaii Marine News,* November 5, 1980.

23. All forty-two dogs were supplied by the army. Thereafter, the Marines procured all its own dogs.

24. Dr. William Putney, letter to author, May 14, 1994.

25. *Hawaii Marine News,* November 5, 1980, p. 5. In declining an invitation, the Corps officially stated: "Participation by the Marine Corps in the Doberman Pinscher show might be interpreted by dog fanciers as an endorsement by the Marine Corps of that particular breed of dog."

26. Downey, *Dogs for Defense,* p. 55.

27. The meat components of the type C ration were meat and vegetable hash, meat and vegetable stew, and meat and beans. The Veterinary Corps found C rations to be satisfactory *supplements.*

28. David Armstrong Jr., letter to author, September 13, 1993. The number of dogs at Rimini as officially reported by the army did not include those purchased from contract breeders. The figure "268" that appears for the total of sled and pack dogs in World War II appears to be the number sent to Fort Robinson when Rimini was closed.

29. The Veterinary Corps had a difficult time establishing a preventive medicine program until an outbreak of canine distemper wiped out most of the dogs.

30. *United States Army Veterinary Service in World War II* (Washington, D.C.: Office of the Surgeon General, Department of the Army, 1961), p. 621.

31. Vaughan's experiences would certainly fit a book and are not done justice here. Among his other accomplishments are the demonstration sled dogs Winter Olympics of 1932, personally rescuing twenty-four aircrew in Greenland, entered twelve Iditarod races, presidential parades of 1977 and 1981, and he gave Pope John Paul II a dog sled ride in 1982. In 1990 Vaughan was inducted into the Musher Hall of Fame. If that wasn't enough, in 1993, at the age of eighty-eight, he returned to the mountain named after him in Antarctica during the Byrd expeditions.

32. C. B. Colby, "Men, Dogs, and Machines–Save Flyers Who Crash in the Arctic," *Popular Science* 147 (November 1945), p. 208.

33. Norman Vaughan, letter to author, June 27, 1994.

34. Headquarters, 1380th Army Air Force, letter to Commanding General, North Atlantic Division, April 18, 1945, "Special North Atlantic Division Dogteam Rescue Unit to European Theatre Operation," history files, Maxwell Air Force Base, Alabama.

4: READY FOR COMBAT

1. Whenever possible a war dog's brand number will accompany the dog's name when first mentioned.

2. Downey, *Dogs for Defense,* p. 69.

3. "Sorry About That Chips," *Army Digest* 23 (February 1968), p. 35.

4. Going, *Dogs at War,* p. 35.

5. There were also some newspaper reports at the time that Chips

also received the Distinguished Service Cross, although the War Department denied it. No medal was ever designed for courageous dogs, but they could be cited in general and unit papers. It should be noted that the British had a heroism award especially for dogs and it was bestowed on six of them during the war.

6. Erna Risch and Chester L. Kieffer, *The Quartermaster Corps: Organization, Supply, and Services,* vol. II (Washington, D.C.: Office of the Chief of Military History, Department of the Army 1958), p. 24.

7. The dogs were Dick, Duke, Husky, Lad, Lady, Ranger, Rocky, and Teddy. Five were killed while on duty and three were destroyed after being found infected with typhus.

8. Lieutenant Robert Johnson, letter to General Headquarters, Southwest Pacific Area, December 6, 1943. Subject: Report on experience of trailing dogs in New Guinea. NARA RG407.

9. *United States Army Veterinary Service in World War II,* pp. 621, 622.

10. United States Chemical Service, Report No. 744. Subject: "Dog Gas Mask E12R8 Engineering Tests" [n.d.]. Chemical Corps Museum.

11. During the wearing and chamber tests, each dog weighed about forty pounds and was of the collie, shepherd, or Airedale type.

12. The model E.12.R8 was considered obsolete in 1968. The army did not replace the model, and there is currently no canine dog mask in inventory.

13. *United States Army Veterinary Service in World War II,* p. 619.

14. Colonel William A. Borden, Office of the Chief of Staff, Washington, D.C., letter to Maj. Gen. S. G. Henry, Director, New Developments Division, War Department Special Staff, November 18, 1943. NARA RG407.

15. Memorandum for General Henry. Subject: Bunker dogs for use in jungle operation, November 27, 1943. NARA RG407.

16. Memorandum to Assistant Chief of Staff, G-4. Subject: Demolition "Wolves," May 7, 1945, Fort Belvoir, Virginia.

17. Colonel Lee A. Denson Jr., memo to Operations Division, War Department General Staff. Subject: Assault Dogs, September 10, 1943. NARA RG407.

18. Memo: Technical Intelligence, HRPE Report No. 1126, January 31, 1945. NARA RG407. Captain Harold S. White, veterinary officer for the 228th, stated: "War dogs are useful only as sentries in rear area–at dumps, or P/W stockades, for example, far behind the front lines. Under fire they are absolutely worthless as sentries, messengers or mine detectors, because they become neurotic very quickly, and shell fire can drive them crazy with fear."

19. Even Colonel Daniels thought the best approach for M-dogs was alerting to soil turned over by humans.

20. Going, *Dogs at War,* p. 96.

21. Ibid., p. 103.

22. Ibid., p. 79.

23. The Office of Strategic Services (OSS) was the precursor of the Central Intelligence Agency (CIA).

24. Lieutenant Colonel Edwin Shaw, report to Chief of Staff, War Department, Washington, D.C., September 5, 1944. Subject: Report on War Dogs. NARA RG407.

25. Richard J. Zika, *War Dogs,* unpublished manuscript [n.d.].

26. Historical Report, 33rd Quartermaster War Dog Platoon, February 1945. NARA RG407.

27. First Lieutenant Archer Ackers, letter to Adjutant General, Washington, D.C., February 5, 1945. NARA RG407.

28. Progress Report, 37th QM War Dog Platoon, February 28, 1945. NARA RG407.

29. Ibid.

30. Ibid., March 31, 1945. NARA RG407.

31. William Kummerer, telephone conversation with author, August 8, 1994.

32. First Lieutenant Bruce D. Walker, letter to Commanding Officer, War Dog Reception and Training Center, San Carlos, California, June 12, 1944.

33. Report No. 164, USAFFE Board, Southwest Pacific Area (War Dogs), September 12, 1944.

34. Karl Rannells, "War Dogs on Morotai Island," *Military Review* 25 (July 1945).

35. Report, Sixth Army, war dogs [n.d.]. NARA RG407.

36. General A. H. Noble, letter to Commandant Marine Corps [n.d.]. NARA RG407.

37. Dr. William Putney, letter to author, May 20, 1994.

38. First Lieutenant William T. Taylor Jr., CO 2nd War Dog Platoon, letter to Commandant Marine Corps [n.d.]. USMC Museum.

39. Second Lieutenant Grant H. Morgan, USMCR, letter to Commanding General, III Amphibious Force, November 17, 1944. NARA RG407.

40. Sled dogs routinely wear boots with no problems. Had scout and sentry dogs been acclimated early in their training, they would have been less likely to tear them off.

41. First Lieutenant James S. Head, letter to Commanding General, Sixth Army, July 18, 1945. NARA RG407.

42. Most of the war dog action consisted of mopping up and sentry duty. Because of the conditions on the island, it probably was not necessary to have dogs at all during this operation.

43. First Lieutenant Wiley S. Isom, letter to Colonel Frank Carr, Chief of Remount, Washington, D.C., April 27, 1945. NARA RG407.

44. Ibid.

45. Colonel George Parker, GSC, Legislative and Liaison Division, letter to Senator Morse, April 25, 1945.

46. Press release, Dogs for Defense, San Francisco office, October 21, 1944. Jesse S. Mendez collection.

47. *United States Army Veterinary Service in World War II,* p. 637.

48. Press release, Dogs for Defense, October 21, 1944.

49. Dr. William Putney, telephone interview with author, September 13, 1994.

50. Brigadier General Edward F. Witsell, Acting Adjutant General, letter to Harry Miller, Executive Secretary, Gaines Dog Research Center, December 1, 1944. NARA RG407.

51. Army officials admitted in 1970 that two dogs were awarded Bronze Star medals in South Vietnam. "Griffin M. Canine" and "Smokey M. Griffin" were cited in General Order No. 10620. The order was revoked when it was learned that the awards were for dogs.

5: POSTWAR AND KOREA

1. Risch and Kieffer, *The Quartermaster Corps: Organization, Supply, and Services,* p. 38.

2. "War Dogs," *Military Review* 33 (July 1953), p. 57.

3. Military History Detachment, The 26th Infantry Scout Dog Platoon Project No. MHD-5, February 21, 1952, to October 30, 1952. Headquarters Military History Department.

4. Ibid.

5. Ibid.

6. Risch and Kieffer, *The Quartermaster Corps: Organization, Supply, and Services,* p. 55.

7. The army soon changed the designation from Scout Dog Platoon to Infantry Platoon Scout Dog. Same meaning, just more words.

8. Risch and Kieffer, *The Quartermaster Corps: Organization, Supply, and Services,* p. 59.

9. Military History Detachment, The 26th Infantry Scout Dog Platoon. Carlisle Barracks.

10. Robert Kollar, telephone interview with author, August 9, 1993.

11. York was also one of the oldest working dogs at twelve years of age. This is rather unusual, as military dogs typically do not work beyond eight years of age.

12. Allen K. McIntosh and L. Westbrook Coke, *A Review of the Military Dog Program* (Washington, D.C.: Combat Operations Research Group, June 1968).

13. "Army to Oust GI Dogs Unless Howls Prevent It," *The Evening*

Star, February 19, 1957, p. 2. In the article the army estimated that it cost $8,000 to train a dog. This seems extremely high.

6: THE VIETNAM SAGA

1. William H. H. Clark, *The History of the United States Army Veterinary Corps in Vietnam 1962–1973,* Ringgold, GA.: Author, 1991, p.7.
2. Ibid., p. 13.
3. "Gets Medal for Going to Dogs," *The Pentagram News,* March 12, 1964, p. 8.
4. Clark, *The History of the United States Army Veterinary Corps in Vietnam 1962–1973,* p. 14.
5. Jesse S. Mendez, interview with author, Columbus, Georgia, February 22, 1994. Mendez returned for a third tour, at Bien Hoa, in 1965. In 1966 he became chief instructor at Fort Benning and trained scout dog platoons until June 1969.
6. Lieutenant Colonel Roger P. Fox, *Air Base Defense in the Republic of Vietnam 1961–1973,* Washington, D.C.: Office of Air Force History, 1979, p. 100.
7. The timing of Top Dog 145 seems to be more than coincidence.
8. John Risse, "Pleiku Air Base–1965," *Dogman* 1 (November–December 1994), p. 1; and telephone conversation with author, February 1, 1995. Risse also stated it was at the discretion of the handler to release his dog during a VC penetration. He did this one night on a sapper attack and an unexpected event took place: the dog began to snap at and try to grab the tracer rounds fired by the VC. No one had ever thought to include this as part of the sentry dog instruction course.
9. Fire support bases (firebases) were temporary artillery bases to support ground operations, usually search-and-destroy missions, within their effective gun range.
10. Some historical books about the Vietnam War state that the VC would wash with American soap so that scout and sentry dogs could not detect them. This is a myth–dogs, properly trained, alerted to any foreign scent.
11. Marsh's sentry post was on the inside perimeter. The VC, who numbered perhaps up to three hundred, would have had to skirt the outer perimeter, manned by sentry dog teams, and then cross a minefield. For those reasons, the VC probably obtained fake identification and were able to filter in throughout the day.
12. At this time, a sentry dog handler was armed with a .38-caliber pistol and a M-16A1 rifle.
13. Some rumors exist that the air force tried to keep Nemo's body for display. Supposedly it was freeze-dried and then thawed out for a taxidermist and promptly fell apart before it could be properly preserved.

14. There are over two thousand species of reptiles in Vietnam.

15. Fox, *Air Base Defense in the Republic of Vietnam 1961–1973,* p. 103.

16. Ibid., p. 104.

17. James Kelley, interview with author, March 12, 1993. Kelley later became a scout dog handler for the 48th IPSD.

18. "Patrol Dogs Rated 'Superior' by Sac," *Air Force Times,* March 26, 1969, p. 4.

19. Booby traps and mines accounted for about 11 percent of the deaths and 17 percent of the casualties during Vietnam. Deaths caused by explosive devices, mines, grenades, booby traps, etc., were 7,429.

20. McIntosh and Coke, *A Review of the Military Dog Program,* p. 28.

21. "War Dogs: Not All Vicious," *Army Times,* October 9, 1968, p. 4.

22. First Lieutenant Robert V. Wilder, letter to Commanding General, III Marine Amphibious Force, April 29, 1966. USMC Museum.

23. First Lieutenant R. S. Neubauer to Maj. J. W. McKinney, Commanding Officer, 26th IPSD, 1st Battalion, 29th Infantry, November 12, 1966. USMC Museum.

24. Ibid.

25. "Combat-Bound Scout Dogs Highly Trained at Benning," *The Bayonet,* August 5, 1966, p. 1.

26. First Lieutenant R. S. Neubauer to Maj. J. W. McKinney, Commanding Officer, 26th IPSD, 1st Battalion, 29th Infantry, November 12, 1966. USMC Museum.

27. "Security Police Dogs," Operation Safeside, chap. 7, 1967, pp. 42–44. Historical files, Maxwell Air Force Base, Alabama.

28. Robert Kollar, interview with author, Lincoln, Rhode Island, August 1, 1993.

29. Robert Himrod, telephone conversation with author, March 2, 1993.

30. Second Lieutenant Richard D. Bruce to Mr. and Mrs. Eugene A. Kuefner [n.d.]. 37th IPSD History, NARA RG472.

31. Officially, according to the army, the 55th IPSD was never deployed overseas. Scout dogs were used in CIA covert activity in Laos, Cambodia, and North Vietnam. In an author's Freedom of Information Act request to the CIA regarding these activities, the agency responded: "Such information—unless, of course, it has been officially acknowledged—would be classified for reasons of national security under Executive Order 12356."

32. In World War II, mines and booby traps accounted for only 2 percent of casualties (see note 19).

33. It should also be mentioned that U.S. Army Limited Warfare Laboratory researchers also conducted numerous animal experiments. Monkeys were exposed to chemical warfare agents, their eyes irradiated, and they were subjected to jolts of 1,200 volts of electricity. Dogs

were shot for training doctors how to operate on wounds. It would be naive to believe that a host of other experiments have not been conducted on dogs.

34. Robert E. Lubow, *The War Animals* (New York: Doubleday, 1977), p. 192.

35. Ibid., p. 193.

36. Ibid., p. 194.

37. Final Report, 60th Infantry Platoon (Scout Dog) (Mine/Tunnel Detector Dog), ACTIV Project ACG-65F, December 1969. Carlisle Barracks.

38. Captain Woodrow L. Quinn Jr., "Dogs in Countermine Warfare," *Infantry* 61 (July–August 1971), p. 16.

39. Ibid.

40. Final Report, 60th Infantry Platoon, p. 8.

41. No justice at all can be given here to those men, often armed with nothing more than a flashlight, knife, and pistol, who entered these underground complexes.

42. Some handlers tried feeding peanut butter to gum up their jaws and keep them from barking.

43. McIntosh and Coke, *A Review of the Military Dog Program*, p. 33.

44. Report, The 1st Air Cavalry Division's 62d Infantry Platoon (Combat Tracker), March 30, 1969. Carlisle Barracks, p. 3.

45. Ibid., p. 8.

46. Bobby Railey, interview with author, Washington, D.C., November 12, 1994.

47. Clark, *The History of the United States Veterinary Corps in Vietnam 1962–1973,* p. 129.

48. McIntosh and Coke, *A Review of the Military Dog Program*, p. 49.

49. Military research activities involving canines and other animals are outside the scope of this book.

50. "The Army's Four-Footed Sentries," *Army Digest* (February 1967) [n.p.].

51. Clark, *The History of the United States Army Veterinary Corps in Vietnam 1962–1973,* p. 207.

52. Fox, *Air Base Defense in the Republic of Vietnam 1961–1973,* p. 103.

53. Clark, *The History of the United States Veterinary Corps in Vietnam 1962–1973,* p. 148.

54. Attached to monthly after-action report narrative, 48th IPSD history files. NARA RG472.

55. During World War I, horses were banned from returning from Europe by the USDA–that is, until General "Blackjack" Pershing came off a ship with his mount at Newport News, Virginia. Rank did have its privileges.

56. Clark, *The History of the United States Veterinary Corps in Vietnam 1962–1973,* p. 150.

57. Tony Montoya, "Handler Brought Dogs Back Home," *DogMan* 1 (September–October 1994), p. 1. Montoya's dog, Patches (M808), made the cut and came home.

58. Unidentified source, interview with author, Vietnam Dog Handlers Association reunion, Washington, D.C., November 11, 1994.

59. The final disposition of all dogs under ARVN control is subject to debate. The ARVN had no tracker platoons, so it is doubtful the retrievers were ever used.

60. Clark, *The History of the United States Army Veterinary Corps in Vietnam 1962–1973,* p. 151.

61. Jesse S. Mendez, telephone conversation with author, December 4, 1993.

7: LESSONS LEARNED

1. Joseph O. White, telephone conversation with author, September 15, 1993.

2. Marines did not use monthly after-action report forms, and their accounts of scout and mine/tunnel dog teams is spotty at best. Army tracker teams probably account for an additional 3,000 missions.

3. Based on army after-action reports and Marine narratives.

4. The first MWD team trained to locate explosives graduated on March 16, 1973. The entire class consisted of civilian handlers from the FAA, Customs, and several police departments. Although the FAA had just started an explosives-detection program, Jesse Mendez had first recommended it in a letter to FAA officials in 1958. Both the military and civilian agencies are hooked on new technology, and the FAA thought it could get by with just metal detectors and X-ray equipment. The simplest and most effective approach is usually cast aside for the bells and whistles sophisticated technology puts forth.

5. Untitled fact sheet (Washington, D.C.: Department of the Treasury, United States Customs, February 1994.

6. Total narcotics credited to Tommy are: 5,181 pounds of marijuana; 6,198 pounds of hashish; 697 pounds of cocaine; and $5,371,400 in currency.

7. "Military Working Dogs" (Lackland AFB: United States Air Force [n.d.]).

8. Between October 1992 and September 1993, Customs canine teams made 5,363 seizures netting narcotics and drugs with a street value of over four billion dollars.

BIBLIOGRAPHY

BOOKS

Bishop, Eleanor C. *Prints in the Sand: The U.S. Coast Guard Beach Patrol During World War II.* Missoula: Pictorial Histories Publishing Co., 1989.

Caldwell, Colonel George L., ed. *United States Army Veterinary Service in World War II.* Washington, D.C.: Office of the Surgeon General, Department of the Army, 1961.

Clark, Colonel William H. H. *The History of the United States Army Veterinary Corps in Vietnam 1962–1973.* Ringgold, Ga: Author, 1991.

Davis, Henry, P. *The New Dog Encyclopedia.* Harrisburg: Stackpole Books, 1970.

Downey, Fairfax. *Dogs for Defense.* New York: McDonald, 1955.

Emert, Phyllis Raybin. *Military Dogs.* Manilato: Crestwood House, 1985.

Fox, Lieutenant Colonel Roger P. *Air Base Defense in the Republic of Vietnam 1961–1973.* Washington, D.C.: Office of Air Force History, 1979.

Going, Clayton G. *Dogs at War.* New York: The Macmillan Company, 1944.

Lubow, Robert E. *The War Animals.* New York: Doubleday and Co., 1977.

Risch, Erna, and Kieffer, Chester L. *The Quartermaster Corps: Organization, Supply, and Services, The Technical Services,* vol. II. Washington, D.C.: Office of the Chief of Military History, Department of the Army, 1958.

Ross, Estelle. *The Book of Noble Dogs.* New York: Century Co., 1922.

Taylor, David. *The Ultimate Dog Book.* New York: Simon and Schuster, 1990.

Terhune, Albert Payson. *A Book of Famous Dogs.* Garden City, N.Y.: Doubleday, Doran and Company, Inc., 1937.

ARTICLES

Albino, Joseph. "Four-Footed Radar in Vietnam." *Popular Mechanics,* September 1967, pp. 76–80, 194, 198.

Berman, Harry B. "Dogs in War." *Coast Artillery Journal* 86 (May–June 1943), pp. 8–11.

Bowen, Staff Sergeant Bob. "Scout Dogs." *Leatherneck* 52 (January 1969), pp. 36–41, 94, 95.

Brimmer, Howard W. "War Dogs." *Field Artillery Journal* 27 (July–August 1940), pp. 8–11.

Cerberus. "War Dogs." *Infantry Journal* 47 (January–February 1940), pp. 67–68.

Cochran, Avery M. "Canine Cartridge Carrier." *Infantry Journal* 47 (July–August 1947), pp. 355–57.

Downey, Fairfax. "Serving the Only God He Knows." *Blue Book Magazine* 85 (September 1947), pp. 28–35.

Dyer, Walter A. "Wanted: More Red Cross Dogs for America." *The Red Cross Magazine* (November 1917), pp. 539–42.

Emery, Harry L. "War Dogs." *Cavalry Journal* 54 (November–December 1945), pp. 52–53.

Fox, Frances M. "The Story of Stubby." *Junior Red Cross News* (November 1929), pp. 54–55.

Frank, Jay. "Corps K9." *Army Life* 24 (November 1942), pp. 6, 7.

Givenwilson, Irene M. "Man's Loyal Friend, the Dog, in Time of War." *Red Cross Courier* 4 (February 1925), pp. 16–18.

Hendrick, Ellwood. "Merciful Dogs of War." *The Red Cross Magazine* (February 1917), pp. 71–75.

Kelch, William J. "Canine Soldiers." *Military Review* 62 (October 1982), pp. 32–41.

Larkin, Lieutenant Colonel Daniel T. "The Combat Tracker." *Military Police Journal* (November 1968), pp. 4–7.

Lawrence, Elizabeth A. "Weapons of War." *Animal Voice Magazine* 6 (January/February/March 1993), p. 32.

Parks, Howard N. "Tactical Employment of the Infantry Scout Dog." Student monograph (1956), pp. 27–28.

Pavia, Audrey. "The Dogs of Desert Storm." *The Kennel Gazette* (June 1991), pp. 66–68, 70.

Rannels, Karl. "War Dogs on Morotai Island." *Military Review* 25 (July 1945), pp. 44–45.

Sackton, Frank J. "Infantry Scout Dogs." *Infantry Journal* 63 (September 1945), p. 53.

Thurston, Mary. "Military Dogs: Are They Simply Equipment?" *Good Dog!* (March–April 1993), pp. 24–28.

Zika, Richard J. "Dog Days in the CBI." *CBIVA Sound-Off* (Winter 1991), pp. 40–42.

Quinn, Captain Woodrow L. Jr., "Army's M-Dogs Detect Enemy Mines." *Military Review* 61 (June 1945), p. 25.

"Combat Trackers." *Infantry* (September–October 1969), p. 32.

"Dogs in Countermine Warfare: Man's Best Friend in Vietnam." *Infantry* (July 1971), pp. 16–18.

"Dogs in the Army." *The Army Information Digest* (January 1949), pp. 31–38.

"Four-Footed Radar." *Infantry* (November–December 1966), pp. 37–40.

"Handling, Feeding and Care of War Dogs." *Military Review* 23 (May 1943), pp. 60–63.

"Is the Army Going to the Dogs?" *Army Digest* (February 1969), pp. 49–53.

"Pigeons: An Experiment in Teaming Pigeons with Dogs." *Signal Corps Tech Info Letter* (January 1944), pp. 45–47.

"Sorry About That Chips." *Army Digest,* February 1968, p. 35.

"Stubby, Dog Hero of War, on Alert." *Red Cross Courier* 6 (February 1927), p. 23.

"The Army's Four-Footed Sentries." *Army Digest* (February 1967), pp. 16–19.

"The Dogs of War in Modern Battle." *Army Ordnance* 9 (September–October 1928), p. 112.

"War Dog Training Center–Hawaiian Dept." *Quartermaster Review* 22 (May–June 1943), pp. 43–44, 138, 139.

"War Dogs." *Infantry Journal* 51 (October 1942), pp. 74–77.

"War Dogs." *Military Review* 33 (July 1953), pp. 57–62.

NEWSPAPER ARTICLES

"Army-Marines Making New Breed." *The Bayonet,* December 10, 1965, p. 34.

"Army Revokes Award of Bronze Stars to Dogs." *New York Times,* November 20, 1970.

"Army to Oust GI Dogs Unless Howls Prevent It." *The Evening Star,* February 19, 1957, p. 2.

Brock, H. I. "The WAAGS." *New York Times Magazine,* September 6, 1942, pp. 12–13.

"Canine Scouts." *Leatherneck News,* July 1967, pp. 22–27.

"Combat-Bound Scout Dogs Highly Trained at Benning." *The Bayonet,* August 5, 1966, pp. 1, 2.

"Corps Canine." *Hawaii Marine News,* November 5, 1980.

"Ft. Belvoir Will Develop System Detector Dogs." *The Pentagram News,* May 29, 1969.

"Life Saving Dogs Are Product of Rigid 12-Week Course Here." *The Bayonet,* May 17, 1968, p. 17.

"Use of Dogs in the War and Proposed Employment in U.S." *Army Navy Register,* May 20, 1916, p. 655.

"War Casualty Dog." *Army Navy Register,* May 6, 1944, p. 3.

"War Dogs: Not All Vicious." *Army Times,* October 9, 1968, p. 4.

"War Dogs Platoon." *Army Navy Register,* June 2, 1945, p. 25.

"War Dogs in the U.S. Marine Corps World War II." *Department of Marine Corps History* [n.d.].

"Wounded G.I.'s in Belgian Snow." *Christian Science Monitor,* March 20, 1945, p. 9.

GOVERNMENT PUBLICATIONS

Combat Tracker and Tracker Dog Training and Employment, Field Manual FM 7–42. Washington, D.C.: Headquarters, Department of the Army, March 1973.

"Detector System–Military Dog." Report, Belvoir: U.S. Army Combat Developments Command, June 2, 1966.

"Fact Sheet on War Dogs." Washington, D.C.: Department of the Army, July 15, 1948.

Final Report, 60th Infantry Platoon (Scout Dog) (Mine/Tunnel Detector Dog) ACTIV Project ACG-65F, December 1969.

Lawrence, George M. Jr. "An Infantry Supporting Weapon Concept Special Study 816–62," USAF University, May 7, 1962, pp. 13–19.

McIntosh, Allen K., and Coke, L. Westbrook. *A Review of the Military Dog Program.* Washington, D.C.: Combat Operations Research Group, June 1968.

Military Dog Training Manual FM 20–20, United States Army, 1973.

News Release No. 277–62, Department of Defense. "Urgent Requirement for Dogs Stressed by Army." February 21, 1962.

News Release No. 39–60, Department of Defense. "Urgent Appeal Issued for Dogs to Guard Nation's Military Sites." January 15, 1960.

"The Sentry Dog in Vietnam." Summary, 18th MP BDE, Long Binh, April 1, 1967. Military Police Regimental Museum, Fort McClellan, Alabama.

"The 26th Infantry Scout Dog Platoon," Project MHD-5, February 1953.

MICROFORM/VIDEO RECORDINGS

Scout Dogs. United States Army, 1968. Videotape.

Use of Dogs in World War II. Record Group 407, reels 3032, 3033, and 3034. National Archives and Records Administration, Suitland, Maryland. Microfilm.

War Dog Cemetery Memorial Dedication. Dr. William Putney, 1994. Videotape.

INDEX

MICHAEL G. LEMISH is the official historian for the Vietnam Dog Handler Association. He writes for numerous popular, association, and trade magazines, including *The Atlantic Flyer* and *The American Legion Magazine*. A member of the National Association for Search and Rescue, Lemish is involved in canine SAR activities. He lives in Westborough, Massachusetts, with his wife, son, and their golden retriever.